Gift of

VIVIAN MILLER

Vancouver,
Washington

1983

PEACE

By the Wonderful People Who Brought You Korea and Viet Nam

AN AUTHORITATIVE INDICTMENT OF
MALEFICENT FEDERAL LEADERSHIP,

AND A SUCCESSFUL FORMULA
FOR CORRECTIVE ACTION

by
Archibald E. Roberts
Lieutenant Colonel, A.U.S., (Ret.)

Foreword by
Hon. John R. Rarick,
Member of Congress

EDUCATOR PUBLICATIONS
Publishers
FULLERTON, CALIFORNIA 92632

COVER PHOTOGRAPH:
GREEK BRONZE DISPLAYED IN THE PUBLIC LOBBY
OF THE UNITED NATIONS ORGANIZATION, NEW
YORK CITY — The house god of the United Nations Organization was originally billed as Zeus, great fornicator and
father of Ares, god of war. This seven-foot pagan deity was
recently renamed Poseidon, god of the sea, by the world
government body.

(Photo courtesy United Nations Organization.)

In memory of my brother,

RICHARD AARON ROBERTS, Major, USAF, Reserve, who served with Gen. Chenault's 75th Fighter Squadron (The Flying Tigers), at Chungking, China, during World War II,

and to the tens-of-thousands of young Americans sacrificed in United Nations wars in Korea and Viet Nam.

THE WAR IN KOREA . . .

A burial service for three American soldiers is held in a United Nations military cemetery near Pusan, South Korea, September, 1950.

*(Courtesy, Director of Public Services,
United Nations, New York City.)*

iv

Library of Congress
Catalogue Card Number
72-93005

**PEACE: By the Wonderful People
Who Brought You Korea and Vietnam**

PEACE

By the Wonderful People
Who Brought You
Korea and Viet Nam

by
Archibald E. Roberts
Lt. Col., AUS, Ret.

Selected legislative testimony and Congressional Record re-print of speeches by the author calling for State investigation of the constitutionality of ratification of the United Nations Treaty by the United States Senate, and other ultra vires acts by agencies of the federal government.

Educator Publications   Fullerton, CA

Other works by Colonel Roberts:

VICTORY DENIED
THE ANATOMY OF A REVOLUTION
THE MARNE DIVISION
SCREAMING EAGLES
RAKKASAN

JOHN R. RARICK
6TH DISTRICT, LOUISIANA

Congress of the United States
House of Representatives
Washington, D.C. 20515

COMMITTEE:
AGRICULTURE

Foreword

by
HON. JOHN R. RARICK, Member of Congress

Most "sane" Americans are afraid to oppose madness in today's climate of political paranoia or are indifferent to the consequences of their failure to act. To be "modern" is to be "tolerant'—but mostly of that which, in normal times, would be recognized as evil.

Even as the U.S. Army, a remnant group of exploited, embittered, rebellious Americans who have been denied victory, is withdrawn from South Viet Nam, a bewildered nation is being conditioned to send its blood and treasure to a new theatre of war, "to defend America against communist aggression" in the Mideast.

The present work, "PEACE: By the Wonderful People Who Brought You Korea and Viet Nam," is an extension of Col. Roberts' previous award winning publication, "Victory Denied."

This significant and well-documented four hundred page study sets out in detail the forthright actions conducted by conscientious citizens at State level to expose the plan to overthrow the Constitution and reduce Americans to the status of economic serfs in the land which once was theirs.

Soldier-author Roberts is an exception to the tradition which forbids our military leaders from becoming politically oriented. Not satisfied merely to reiterate the symptoms of decline which characterize modern American society, he identifies those who have created the American agony to establish a dictatorship of the financial-intellectual "elite" upon the ruins of the American Republic.

The book will serve as a handbook to all men and women who cherish freedom and are searching for a correct procedure for challenging those who have usurped political power.

If the seats of power in America are once again to be occupied by the descendents of the pioneers, the patriots, the builders, and the free men who created this civilization—it will be well to heed the counsel of Colonel Roberts and those who are associated with him.

The central issue, as this volume stresses, is the fundamental law of agency: Actions of an agent are not binding on the principal if those actions are not authorized by the principal, a logical concept called *ultra vires*. Constitutionally, government departments are agents of the States which created them by the first three articles of the Constitution.

Therefore, excesses of the agent, federal government, and its bureaucrats, which have attempted to overthrow the Constitution by de facto actions transferring vast powers of government from the Congress to the United Nations and other private organizations, and by erecting a super-state (in the form of "regional goverance") over the sovereign States of the Union, which must be corrected by the law-makers of the respective State legislatures.

Interlocking subversion in government departments will be halted only when irate citizens demand that those who would overturn the Constitution comply with it.

"PEACE: By the Wonderful People Who Brought You Korea and Vietnam," is a stunning success story against dark powers, and an inspiring promise of new patriotic vigor for Americans who fight for freedom.

To understand the enemies of individual freedom our people must first be able to identify them. Once unmasked and exposed, rhetoric and fancy promises will no longer shield the one worlders from those people who love America and our Constitutional system of limited government.

To such end "PEACE: By the Wonderful People Who Brought You Korea and Vietnam" is must reading and will serve as a ready reference for true American patriots in their fight against the "collectivist" enemies of individual liberty under Constitutional government.

x   PEACE: by the wonderful people who brought you Korea and Viet Nam

Contents

CHAPTER THREE **55**

Invisible Government of Monetary Power

How a secret group of international financiers and industrialists subverted the American republic. Why Infiltration, Subversion, and Rebellion can successfully topple U.S. religious, economic, and social disciplines. What thousands of angry citizens are doing to halt "Revolution U.S.A."
(Congressional Record reprint of an address before members of the Wisconsin Legislature, December 8, 1970. Introductory remarks by Hon. John R. Rarick, M.C.)

CHAPTER FOUR **75**

The Most Secret Science

A succinct examination of the world banking cartel who manipulate money, news media, the national economy, and foreign policy to transform the U.S. republic into a member state of a world socialist government. How the President implemented U.N. "regional governance" directives thus eliminating elective State office and disfranchising voters. Information on the effort to force legislative review of the national crisis.
(Congressional Record reprint of legislative testimony before Wisconsin House of Representatives committee, March 30, 1971. Commentary by the Hon. John R. Rarick, M.C.)

Regionalism: The Quiet Revolution

Transformation of the United States Republic to a dictatorship of the "financial elite," the New World Order fashioned
for Americans by the Council on Foreign Relations, reached
political reality in 1972 under the administration of President Richard M. Nixon.

CHAPTER SIX 267

Integration Syndrome

An historical example of the superiority of United Nations "law" over constitutional authority. The cause for mounting crisis over forced integration.

(A Congressional Record reprint, November, 1969 issue, of an article disseminated by the Committee to Restore the Constitution. Commentary by Hon. John R. Rarick, M.C.)

CHAPTER SEVEN 279

To Support and Defend This Constitution

The constitutional authority and precedent for State legislative review of the actions of federal agents with regard to the United Nations.

(Congressional Record reprint of an address before the student body, Frank Phillips (Texas) College, November 6, 1967. Entered by Hon. John R. Rarick, M.C.)

The United Nations: Threat to Sovereignty?

A study and commentary by the Alabama Legislative Commission to Preserve the Peace, prepared in consonance with a directive by the 1966 Regular Session, Alabama Legislature.

(Inserted in the Congressional Record by Representative John R. Rarick, M.C., September 13, 1967.)

The Campaign To Restore The Constitution

The U.N. Charter

Introduction

The campaign to inspire investigation of United Nations Treaty agreements by the respective State Legislatures is grounded on the charge that the United Nations is an apparatus for covertly dismantling the Constitution of the United States.

The fact of usurped governmental power is demonstrated by the record of hundreds of UN-enforcing "treaties" which were surreptitiously "ratified" by as few as two or three Senators convening in secret during the months immediately following passage of the United Nations Treaty.

Contemporary history reveals that the unconscionable policy of "Perpetual War for Perpetual Peace," the spector of "Revolution U.S.A.," America's economic crisis, and our disintegrating society, all derive from deliberate voiding of the Consititution as the "law of the land."

With little public notice the United States Senate, in a monumental breach of public trust, declared in 1954 that the United Nations Charter is ". . . the supreme law of the land and the judges in every State shall be bound thereby."

A treaty, however, cannot authorize what the Constitution forbids. No federal agency has the power or the authority to modify the Constitution. Only the States, which won their independence as sovereign nations as a result of the Treaty of Peace that closed the Revolutionary War, can be the source of power in the federal government which the States created.

State legislatures are aiding and abetting subversion of the Constitution by failing to clarify the law, and by refusing to enforce the provisions of the Constitution within the borders of the State.

The delinquency of the State creates a presumption which law enforcement officers cannot overturn. Inaction of the State legislators is tacit approval of the unauthorized attempt by federal agencies to exercise power beyond the authority granted by the Constitution.

Corrective process cannot be found in the courts. The Supreme Court cannot declare a statute of Congress "unconstitutional." The Court can exercise only the judicial power conferred upon it by the Constitution. It can no more "unmake" a legislative act than it can make one. To strike down a legislative act requires legislative power. No court has such power.

The ordinary citizen also lacks the capacity to overturn breaches of the Constitution.

The State, however, acting at its highest soverign authority, can repudiate illegitimate acts by its agents in Washington. Through its legislative apparatus the State can legally clarify the question of attempted usurpation of governmental powers.

PEACE illustrates by example the beginning of such a campaign in the United States.

Legal authorities for this effort to restore the United States Constitution as the "law of the land" are explained in, "To Support and Defend This Constitution," page 279, and in the book *VICTORY DENIED*.

Procedures which concerned and indignant citizens are following to achieve this goal are set out in detail in the succeeding works.

The Alabama State Legislature, first of the States to complete an official investigation of the United Nations Treaty, published its findings in, "United Nations: Threat to Sovereignty?," prepared by the Alabama Legislative Commission to Preserve the Peace, which appears as ANNEX "A" of this book.

The reader of *PEACE* will discover that three primary issues are presented for consideration:

1. The crusade to restore the Constitution is a struggle for survival.

2. The solution to national crisis rests with the individual citizen acting through his State legislature to expose and neutralize the madmen who seek to dismantle the Constitution and erect a totalitarian state upon the ruins of the American civilization.

3. The struggle now joined will require participation by every responsible American if the centers of power in this nation are to be restored to the descendents of the pioneers, the engineers, and the warriors who gave their blood and treasure to establish and defend it.

In summary, the common denominator for survival in a society under attack by an entrenched enemy is the conscientious action of the individual citizen.

Archibald E. Roberts, Lt. Col., AUS, ret.
Fort Collins, Colorado — July 4, 1972

TESTIMONY of Archibald E. Roberts, Lt. Col., AUS, Ret., Director, Committee to Restore the Constituion, Inc., on behalf of the WISCONSIN LEGISLATIVE & RESEARCH COMMITTEE, Inc., in support of Senate Resoltuion S-26, introduced by Senator Gordon W. Roseleip, before the Wisconsin Veterans & Government Affairs Committee, on Thursday, 18 March, 1971.

Analysis by the Legislative Reference Bureau

This joint resolution establishes a special joint committee, comprised of 4 senators and 4 representatives to the assembly, to study the constitutionality of the actions of federal agencies with regard to the United Nations, the effect of these actions on the State and possible measures which could be taken by this State to punish unconstitutional actions. The committee shall report its findings to the legislature within 6 months after adoption of the resolution (See Exhibit A). *

CHAPTER ONE

Viet Nam: Another United Nations War

Mr. Chairman, I am Archibald E. Roberts, Lt. Col., AUS, ret., Director, *Committee to Restore the Constitution*, a Colorado corporation. In consonance with your invitations, and on behalf of the *Wisconsin Legislative & Research Committee*, I wish to testify in support of Senate Resolution S-26.

---

* *Exhibits at end of article.*

During the next thirty minutes I will attempt to prove the following charges against the United Nations Organization:

1. *That the Viet-Nam War is a United Nations War.*
2. *That the United Nations is a subversive Organization.*
3. *That vital powers of government held in trust for the American people have been illegally transferred to the United Nations Organization in violation of the prohibitions of the Constitution.*
4. *That the United Nations Charter was foisted upon the American people to serve those who seek to overthrow the Constitution and coerce American citizens into a socialist world government.*

During the course of my indictment of the United Nations it will be well to keep in mind the following military axiom:

Wars — under whatever name — which do not reduce the political power of an officially named "enemy" of the American people, and which do not increase the political power of the United States, must in the end reduce the political power of the United States and thus *serve the secret objectives of a concealed enemy.*

Let us begin by calling on the testimony of Lyndon B. Johnson, then president of the United States: Mr. Johnson told the American people on 13 July 1965, that their soldier-sons are dying in Viet Nam because of United States commitment to the Southeast Asia Treaty Organization.

During a White House news conference on this date President Johnson stated:

"I think that it is well for us to remember that three presidents have made the pledge for this nation, that the Senate has ratified the SEATO Treaty by a vote of 82 to 1, pledging the United States to come to the aid of any nation upon their request who are parties to that Treaty . . ."

President Johnson then went on to say, "We expect to keep that commitment. Our *national honor* is at stake." Four years later, nearly to the day, President Richard M. Nixon was to use the same words in describing our commitment to the SEATO Treaty.

On Monday, 29 July, 1969, in Bangkok, Thailand, headquarters for the Southeast Asia Treaty Organization, Mr. Nixon reiterated his pledge to the SEATO Treaty in these words:

"We are determined," Nixon testified on world-wide television, "to honor our commitment to the Southeast Asia Treaty."

Mr. Chairman, neither Mr. Nixon nor his predecessors have, of course, admitted that the Southeast Asia Treaty, a treaty which our sons "honor" in blood and agony, was framed under the provisions of articles 52 and 53, United Nations Charter.

As we shall see, however, SEATO is a "regional arrangement" formed to deal with matters relating to the maintenance of international peace and security "consistent with the Purposes and Principles of the United Nations."

This strange war has clearly failed to reduce the political power of the "communist enemy." Instead, the war has increased the political power of the United Nations and thus serves the objectives of a concealed enemy.

Our first exhibit is, "The Story of SEATO," a booklet published by the Southeast Asia Treaty Organization.

On page five of "The Story of SEATO," we find the following declaration:

"The members of SEATO have chosen a collective defense system, under the authority of the Charter of the United Nations."

SEATO, in this statement of purpose, asserts that it is an agency — an extension — of the United Nations Organization.

Let us now join this information to exhibit number two; the SEATO Treaty (See Exhibit B).

"The Parties," says Article I of SEATO, "undertake, as set forth in the Charter of the United Nations, to settle any international dispute in which they may be involved by peaceful means . . . and to refrain in their international relations from the threat or use of force in any manner inconsistent with the purposes of the United Nations."

Mounting American casualties in this "no-win" war provide stark evidence that the military "force" used in Viet Nam is applied in a manner consistent with the "purposes of the United Nations."

United States Ambassador to Viet Nam, Ellsworth Bunker, made this point crystal clear in his personal testimony on MEET THE PRESS, 19 November, 1967.

"It seems to me that what we are doing (in Viet Nam) is to make credible our commitments under the United Nations and under SEATO Treaty to resist aggression . . . We have made a commitment."

Unfortunately, Ambassador Bunker failed to identify the U.N. agency which is charged with conducting the Viet Nam war "under the United Nations." The information to fill this important omission can be found under Article IV, SEATO Treaty. I quote:

"Measures" . . . the word "measures" means "military action" . . . "Measures taken under this paragraph shall be immediately reported to the Security Council of the United Nations."

Gentlemen, the chain of command could not be more specific than that: The Security Council is the war-waging arm of the United Nations.

However, let us pin point the U.N. articles which make "credible our commitment under the United Nations and under SEATO," as Mr. Bunker so lucidly explained on MEET THE PRESS.

For this purpose I now introduce the United Nations Charter.

As predicted in "The Story of SEATO" the authority for construction of the UN-SEATO "collective defense system" is revealed in Chapter VIII, "Regional Arrangements." A comparison of U.N. and SEATO articles also shows that the quotations made previously from the SEATO Treaty are, in fact, faithful duplication of the provision of articles 52 and 54, United Nations Charter.

"Nothing in the present Charter," says Article 52, "precludes the existence of regional arrangements . . . provided that such arrangements or agencies are consistent with the Purposes and Principles of the United Nations."

It is immediately apparent that Article I of SEATO exactly reproduces the authority of Article 52, United Nations Charter.

Article IV of SEATO similarly reflects the provisions of Article 54, United Nations Charter.

"The Security Council," commands Article 54, "shall at all times be kept fully informed of activities undertaken or in contemplation under regional arrangements . . ."

This means, of course, that U.S. military operations "undertaken or in contemplation" in Viet Nam are first submitted to the U.N. Security Council for approval.

The evidence permits but one conclusion. The strategy of *"Perpetual War for Perpetual Peace"* . . . a strategy which sends Americans into battle "with neither promise nor hope of Victory" . . . is United Nations strategy.

U.N. war-making powers, and the usurpation of congressional authority which permits it, was dramatically illustrated by James Reston in his column of 13 July 1967, entitled "Isolation Echoes by U.S. Move In Congo."

"The administration's position," Reston testified, "is that it is committed under the Charter of the United Nations, under various treaties, and under the Truman Doctrine, to do whatever it can to maintain peace anywhere in the world."

You now realize, of course, that the real objective of "no-win" wars is NOT "international peace and security" as U.N. supporters are led to believe. The true "Purpose and Principle" of U.N. military adventures is to manipulate the United States armed forces under Security Council control; to force all of the nations into line and to deliver them up to a one world government.

For proof, I invite your attention to Chapter V, U.N. Charter, headed, "The Security Council — Functions and Powers."

Article 24:
"In order to ensure prompt and effective action by the United Nations, its Members confer on the Security Council *primary responsibility* for the maintenance of international peace and security . . ."
and, Article 25:
"The Members of the United Nations agree to accept and carry out the decisions of the Security Council . . ."

In simple language, these two U.N. articles transform the power of self defense, held in trust by the Congress, to a blanket authority to send Americans into battle anywhere in the world at the direction of the U.N. Security Council.

The Constitution is, of course, very specific about the powers of keeping peace and waging war.[1] Nowhere does the Constitution authorize the transfer of these powers to an international agency.

Mr. Chairman, I have established the fact that Senate ratification of the United Nations Charter on 28 July 1945, is in violation of the Constitution of the United States. Being illegal it must be put down.

Perhaps the members of this Committee have wondered

---

1   Section 8, Article 1, Constitution of the United States.

why the war in Korea and the war in Viet Nam saw the outpouring of vast resources of U.S. men and material into a land war in Asia without a formal declaration of war by the United States Congress. Well, Article 39 of the United Nations Charter explains why . . . . and, more importantly, how the U.N. Security Council can, at any time, force the entire ›pulation of this nation into a military posture without the nsent of an impotent Congress.

"The Security Council," Article 39 directs, "shall determine the existence of any threat to the peace, breach of the peace, or act of aggression and shall . . . decide what measures shall be taken in accordance with Articles 41 and 42, to maintain or restore international peace and security."

Articles 41 and 42 spell out the full authority and extent of U.N. military action and authorize the use of "air, sea, and land forces as may be necessary" to maintain or restore "international peace and security."

Additionally, the military muscle needed to enforce Security Council edicts is provided by usurped sovereign powers as spelled out in Articles 43 and 46. These U.N. laws order the transfer of "armed forces, assistance, and facilities" from Member nations to the U.N. Security Council for use as the Security Council may determine in its application of armed forces anywhere in the world.

To give legal coloration to this breach of public trust, the Congress of the United States, on 26 September, 1961, ratified Public Law 87-297, "The Arms Control and Disarmament Act."[2] This unbelievable legislation purports to "legalize" the transfer of the United States military establishment, and American citizens in uniform, to a United Nations one world army.

Gentlemen, your sons now serving in Viet Nam are, by U.N. Charter definition, *members of a United Nations world*

---

2 Public Law 87-297, 87th Congress, H.R. 9118, September 26, 1961, "To Establish a United States Arms Control and Disarmament Agency" (See **Victory Denied** by Arch E. Roberts).

army and take their orders from the United Nations Security Council "consistent with the Purposes and Principles" of the United Nations Organization.

As final proof in my case against the United Nations I read from Joint House Resolution Number 1145, "Gulf of Tonkin Resolution," which was often quoted as Congress's approval to commit Americans to the Viet Nam war (See Exhibit C).

"This resolution," states Section 3, "shall expire when the President shall determine that the peace and security of the area is reasonably assured by international conditions created by the action of the United Nations."

Mr. Chairman, I respectfully submit that my case against the United Nations is now legally established.

a. I have demonstrated that the Viet Nam war is being conducted to serve the "purposes and principles" of the United Nations Charter. The "no-win" war in Viet Nam is, therefore, a United Nations war.

b. I have demonstrated that the articles of the United Nations Charter amend, by *deceit* and *subterfuge,* the Constitution of the United States in a manner not sanctioned by Article V of the Constitution. The United Nations is, therefore, a *subversive* organization and is a *threat* to the freedoms of person and property guaranteed to the people by the Constitution.

c. I have demonstrated that the *authority* to commit Americans to battle anywhere in the world has been *surreptitiously* transferred from the Congress of the United States to the Security Council of the United Nations. Vital powers of government held in trust for the American people have, therefore, been *illegally usurped* by the United Nations Organization in *violation* of the prohibitions of the Constitution.

d. I have demonstrated that the real but *concealed*
    objective of the United Nations Organization is to
    place the military power of the United States at the
    disposal of the United Nations Security Council; to
    force all of the nations into line and to deliver them
    up to a ONE WORLD GOVERNMENT. The United
    Nations was, therefore, foisted upon the American
    people to serve those who seek to overthrow the
    Constitution and coerce American citizens into a
    socialist government.

In this brief indictment of the United Nations I have also
revealed that, as the political power of the United States is
dissipated in 'no-win" military adventures, the political
power of the United Nations, and those who promote its
Purposes and Principles, is *increased*.

The War in Viet Nam thus serves the *secret objectives* of a
concealed enemy.

Mr. Chairman, it is the clear and urgent duty of all
Wisconsin officeholders to outlaw the United Nations Organization within the borders of the State of Wisconsin in consonance with their oath to "defend and preserve this
Constitution."

I therefore respectfully submit the following proposed
state statute for your consideration and adoption (See
Exhibit D).

Exhibit A

1971

STATE OF WISCONSIN
1971 SENATE JOINT RESOLUTION 26

March 2, 1971 – Introduced by Senator ROSELEIP. Referred to Committee on Governmental and Veterans Affairs.

Analysis by the Legislative Reference Bureau

This joint resolution establishes a special joint committee, comprised of 4 senators and 4 representatives to the assembly, to study the constitutionality of the actions of federal agencies with regard to the United Nations the effect of these actions on the state and possible measures which could be taken by this state to punish unconstitutional actions. The committee shall report its findings to the legislature within 6 months after adoption of the resolution.

Whereas, the state of Wisconsin, at the time of its admission into the Union of the States as attested by its ratification of the agreement known as the Constitution of the United States, assumed all obligations to the people of Wisconsin, and to the people of the several states that were parties to the same agreement, to insure that all provisions of the Constitution of the United States shall be respected and enforced within the boundaries and under the jurisdiction of the state of Wisconsin; and

Whereas, 3 federal agencies of government were created by Article I, Article II and Article III of that compact; and

Whereas, it appears, under what has been asserted to be a legal use of these limited and enumerated delegated powers, that the federal executive and legislative branches have negotiated with foreign governments and entered into agreements which may constitute a *surrender* to foreign governments of certain rights and liberties assured to the people under the Constitution of the United States, and which may surrender certain powers of government which this Constitution guarantees to preserve to our people; and

Whereas, as a result of some of these agreements, Wisconsin men have been drafted into the armed forces and sent to foreign countries to fight and die in a series of undeclared "No-Win" wars; and

Whereas, engaging in war without a Declaration of War by Congress constitutes a *violation* of Article I, Section 8, of the U.S. Constitution; now, therefore, be it

Resolved by the senate, the assembly concurring, That the legislature hereby establishes a special joint committee consisting of 4 senators and 4 representatives to the assembly, appointed as are members of standing committees, to investigate the question of whether the agreement which is represented to be entered into by federal agencies, acting as representatives of these United States with regard to the so-called United Nations Organization and treaties made under this organization, be within the power and authority granted to said agencies under the Constitution of the United States; and, be it further

Resolved, that the committee be further authorized and directed to investigate the question of whether these agreements affect the state of Wisconsin, or relate to the relinquishment of any of the laws or rights affecting the state of Wisconsin or its people, and whether there is any change proposed to be made which would deprive the state of Wisconsin or its people of rights and privileges or would involve any change in any of the provisions of the agreement known as the Constitution of the United States without the consent of the government of the people of this state or of the several states; and, be it futher

Resolved, That the committee inquire into what measures may be taken by this state to enforce the Constitution of the

United States and to *punish* any infractions thereof that may appear to be sanctioned by any unlawful use of purported authority by an agency not sanctioned by the Constitution of the United States; and, be it further

Resolved, That the committee report its findings to the legislature not later than 6 months following adoption of this resolution.

(End)

Exhibit B

South-East Asia Collective Defense Treaty (Manila Pact)

The Parties to this Treaty,

Recognizing the sovereign equality of all the Parties,

Reiterating their faith in the purposes and principles set forth in the Charter of the United Nations and their desire to live in peace with all peoples and all governments,

Reaffirming that, in accordance with the Charter of the United Nations, they uphold the principle of equal rights and self-determination of peoples, and declaring that they will earnestly strive by every peaceful means to promote self-government and to secure the independence of all countries whose peoples desire it and are able to undertake its responsibilities

Desiring to strengthen the fabric of peace and freedom and to uphold the principles of democracy, individual liberty and the rule of law, and to promote the economic well-being and development of all peoples in the Treaty Area,

Intending to declare publicly and formally their sense of unity, so that any potential aggressor will appreciate that the Parties stand together in the area, and,

Desiring further to co-ordinate their efforts for collective defense for the preservation of peace and security,

Therefore agree as follows:

ARTICLE I

The Parties undertake, as set forth in the Charter of the United Nations, to settle any international dispute in which they may be involved by peaceful means in such a manner that international peace and security and justice are not endangered, and to refrain in their international relations from the threat or use of force in any manner inconsistent with the purposes of the United Nations.

ARTICLE II

In order more effectively to achieve the objectives of this Treaty the Parties, separately and jointly, by means of continuous and effective self-help and mutual aid will maintain and develop their individual and collective capacity to resist armed attack and to prevent and counter subversive activities directed from without against their territorial integrity and political stability.

ARTICLE III

The Parties undertake to strengthen their free institutions and to co-operate with one another in the further development of economic measures, including technical assistance, designed both to promote economic progress and social wellbeing and to further the individual and collective efforts of governments toward these ends.

ARTICLE IV

1. Each Party recognizes that aggression by means of armed attack in the Treaty Area against any of the parties or against any State or territory which the Parties by unanimous agreement may hereafter designate would endanger its own peace and safety, and agrees that it will in that event act to meet the common danger in accordance with its constitutional processes. Measures taken under this paragraph shall be immediately reported to the Security Council of the United Nations.

2. If, in the opinion of any of the Parties, the inviolability or the integrity of the territory or the sovereignty or political independence of any Party in the Treaty Area or of any other State or territory to which the provisions of paragraph 1 of this Article from time to time apply is threatened in any way other than by armed attack or is affected or

threatened by any fact or situation which might endanger the peace of the area, the Parties shall consult immediately in order to agree on the measures which should be taken for the common defense.

3. It is understood that no action on the territory of any State designated by unanimous agreement under paragraph 1 of this Article or on any territory so designated shall be taken except at the invitation or with the consent of the government concerned.

ARTICLE V

The Parties hereby establish a Council, on which each of them shall be represented, to consider matters concerning the implementation of this Treaty. The Council shall provide for consultation with regard to military and any other planning as the situation obtaining in the Treaty Area may from time to time require. The Council shall be so organized as to be able to meet at any time.

ARTICLE VI

This Treaty does not affect and shall not be interpreted as affecting in any way the rights and obligations of any of the Parties under the Charter of the United Nations or the responsibility of the United Nations for the maintenance of international peace and security. Each Party declares that none of the international engagements not in force between it and any other of the Parties or any third party is in conflict with the provisions of this Treaty, and undertakes not to enter into any international engagement in conflict with this Treaty.

ARTICLE VII

Any other State in a position to further the objectives of the Treaty and to contribute to the security of the area may, by unanimous agreement of the Parties, be invited to accede to this Treaty. Any State so invited may become a Party to the Treaty by depositing its instrument of accession with the

Government of the Republic of the Philippines. The Government of the Republic of the Philippines shall inform each of the Parties of the deposit of each such instrument of accession.

ARTICLE VIII

As used in this Treaty, the "Treaty Area" is the general area of South-East Asia, including also the entire territories of the Asian Parties and the general area of the South-West Pacific not including the Pacific area north of 21 degrees 30 minutes north latitude. The Parties may, by unanimous agreement, amend this Article to include within the Treaty Area the territory of any State acceding to this Treaty in accordance with Article VII or otherwise to change the Treaty Area.

ARTICLE IX

1. This Treaty shall be deposited in the archives of the Government of the Republic of the Philippines. Duly certified copies thereof shall be transmitted by that Government to the other signatories.

2. The Treaty shall be ratified and its provisions carried out by the Parties in accordance with their respective constitutional processes. The instruments of ratification shall be deposited as soon as possible with the Government of the Republic of the Philippines, which shall notify all of the other signatories of such deposit.

3. The Treaty shall enter into force between the States which have ratified it as soon as the instruments of ratification of a majority of the signatories shall have been deposited, and shall come into effect with respect to each other State on the date of the deposit of its instrument of ratification.

ARTICLE X

This Treaty shall remain in force indefinitely, but any Party may cease to be a Party one year after its notice of denunciation has been given to the Government of the

Republic of the Philippines which shall inform the Governments of the other Parties of the deposit of each notice of denunciation.

ARTICLE XI

The English text of this Treaty is binding on the Parties, but when the Parties have agreed to the French text thereof and have so notified the Government of the Republic of the Philippines, the French text shall be equally authentic and binding on the Parties.

Understanding of the United States of America

The United States of America in executing the present Treaty does so with the understanding that its recognition of the effect of aggression and armed attack and its agreement with reference thereto in Article IV, paragraph 1, apply only to Communist aggression but affirms that in the event of other aggression or armed attack it will consult under the provisons of Article IV, paragraph 2.

In witness whereof the undersigned Plenipotentiaries have signed this Treaty.

Done at Manila, this eighth day of September, 1954.

Protocol to the South-East Asia Collective Defense Treaty

Designation of states and territory as to which provisions of Article IV and Article III are to be applicable:

The Parties to the South-East Asia Collective Defense Treaty unanimously designate for the purposes of Article IV of the Treaty the States of Cambodia and Laos and the free territory under the jurisdiction of the State of Vietnam.

The Parties further agree that the above mentioned states and territory shall be eligible in respect of the economic measures contemplated by Article III.

This Protocol shall enter into force simultaneously with the coming into force of the Treaty.

In witness whereof, the undersigned Plenipotentiaries have signed this Protocol to the South-East Asia Collective Defense Treaty.

Done at Manila, this eighth day of September, 1954.

The Pacific Charter

The delegates of Australia, France, New Zealand, Pakistan, the Republic of the Philippines, the Kingdom of Thailand, the United Kingdom of Great Britain and Northern Ireland, the United States of America:

Desiring to establish a firm basis for common action to maintain peace and security in South-East Asia and the South-West Pacific;

Convinced that common action to this end in order to be worthy and effective, must be inspired by the highest principles of justice and liberty;

Do hereby proclaim:

First, in accordance with the provisions of the United Nations Charter, they uphold the principle of equal rights and self-determination of peoples and they will earnestly strive by every peaceful means to promote self-government and to secure the independence of all countries whose peoples desire it and are able to undertake its responsibilities;

Second, they are each prepared to continue taking effective practical measures to ensure conditions favourable to the orderly achievement of the foregoing purposes in accordance with their constitutional procedures;

Third, they will continue to co-operate in the economic, social and cultural fields in order to promote higher living standards, economic progress and social well-being in this region;

Fourth, as declared in the South-East Asia Collective Defense Treaty, they are determined to prevent or counter by appropriate means any attempt in the Treaty Area to subvert their freedom or to destroy their sovereignty or territorial integrity.

Proclaimed at Manila, this eighth day of September, 1954.

Exhibit C

DATE: August 7, 1964
(page 18471 in bound volume)

1964   17885

Congressional Record—Senate

So the joint [Gulf of Tonkin] resolution (H.J. Res. 1145) was passed as follows:

Whereas naval units of the Communist regime in Vietnam, in violation of the principles of the Charter of the United Nations and of international law, have deliberately and repeatedly attacked United States naval vessels lawfully present in international waters, and have thereby created a serious threat to international peace; and

Whereas these attacks are part of a *deliberate* and *systematic campaign* of aggression that the Communist regime in North Vietnam has been waging against its neighbors and the nations joined with them in the collective defense of their freedom; and

Whereas the United States is assisting the peoples of southeast Asia to *protect their freedom* and has no territorial, military or political ambitions in that area, but desires only that these peoples should be left in peace to work out their own destinies in their own way: Now, therefore, be it

RESOLVED BY THE SENATE AND HOUSE OF REPRESENTATIVES OF THE UNITED STATES OF AMERICA IN CONGRESS ASSEMBLED, That the Congress approves and supports the determination of the President, as Commander in Chief, to take all necessary measures to repel any armed attack against the forces of the United States and to prevent further aggression.

Sec. 2. The United States regards as vital to its national

interest and to world peace the maintenance of international peace and security in southeast Asia. Consonant with the Constitution of the United States and the Charter of the United Nations and in accordance with its obligations under the Southeast Asia Collective Defense Treaty, the United States is, therefore, prepared, as the President determines, to take all necessary steps, including the use of armed force, to assist any member or protocol state of the Southeast Asia Collective Defense Treaty requesting assistance in defense of its freedom.

Sec. 3.   This resolution shall expire when the President shall determine that the peace and security of the area is reasonably assured by international conditions created by action of the United Nations or otherwise, except that it may be terminated earlier by concurrent resolution of the Congress.

The preamble was agreed to.

Mr. FULBRIGHT. Mr. President, I ask unanimous consent that Senate Joint Resolution 189 be indefinitely postponed.

The PRESIDING OFFICER. Without objection, it is so ordered.

Exhibit D

A Bill to Provide for Enforcement of the Constitution of the United States With Regard to the So-Called United Nations Organization

WHEREAS, by agreement with her sister States, the State of Wisconsin is duty-bound to enforce the Constitution of the United States within her borders; and

WHEREAS, as the Legislature of this State has inquired into the question of whether certain purported agreements made by certain Federal agencies created by the Constitution of the United States, were within the authority granted by the Constitution of the United States, and

WHEREAS, authority for said purported acts was not granted under the terms of the Constitution of the United States; and

WHEREAS, said agreements purported to abridge rights and liberties of this State and her People, without lawful authority:

BE IT ENACTED BY THE GENERAL ASSEMBLY OF THE STATE OF WISCONSIN, in conformity with the duty of the State of Wisconsin to her People and to her sister States, and in further conformity with the oath of office taken by the governmental officials thereof, that:

1. Those purported treaties and agreements relating to the United Nations Organization, now sometimes referred to as the United Nations, are beyond the authority granted to the agencies purporting to make these treaties and agreements and are therefore, null, void, and of no effect within the jurisdiction of this State, and any attempt to enforce the

provisions of any of said treaties or agreements within this State is unlawful.

2.   Any person who shall commit an act of violation of the provisions of this statute shall be guilty of a *felony* and, upon conviction thereof, shall be fined not less than $2,000.00 nor more than $100,000.00, or confined in the State Penitentiary not less than three years nor more than twenty years, or both.

3.   Any State officeholder, or any Member of the United States Congress from the State of Wisconsin, who shall attempt to violate the provisions of this Act, shall, by that attempt, automatically *vacate* his office, and any citizen of this State may bring quo warranto proceedings, in the county in which said offender last resided or was last known to be, to force the abandonment of any pretext of filling said office by the person so disqualified.

4.   Any person aggrieved by a State officeholder or by any other person acting in violation of the within Statute shall retain his private action against the offender and all of his aiders, advisors, and abettors, jointly and severally, and shall recover triple costs, besides double damages, which no jury, or Court sitting without a jury, shall assess at less than $2,500.00.

5.   Any person convicted of any criminal offense under the provisions of this Statute shall be *incapable of receiving pardon*, and shall be incapable of receiving *parole or suspension* of sentence of confinement.

6.   Any person being a defendant in a civil action brought under the provison of this Statute, who shall have had judgment rendered against him which has become final by the expiration of time for appeal or by final determination of an Appellate Court, shall be denied all exemptions from execution under said judgment.

7. Each representative of this State in the House of Representatives of the United States and in the Senate of the United States, before his election to office may be certified, shall be sworn in the County of his residence in this State, by Oath or Affirmation, to be bound to support the Constitution of the United States, and for breach of this Oath shall be punished as provided by any or all of the provisions of paragraph 2 through 6 above.

Exhibit E

THE MILWAUKEE JOURNAL, Friday, March 19, 1971

U.N. Debated in Legislature, Witness Says It's Subversive

Journal Madison Bureau

Madison Wis.—Anti-Communists crowded a Capitol hearing room Thursday to support a resolution that would have the Wisconsin Legislature investigate the United Nations.

They were accused by Rep. Herbert Grover (D-Shawano) of acting paranoid.

Sen. Gordon W. Roseleip (R-Darlington), chairman of the committee before which the proposal was heard, had to rap his gavel for order several times during the two hour hearing. Roseleip, who supports the study, even had to gavel to stop applause for himself during the Governmental and Veterans Affairs Committee hearing.

The committee took no position on the measure.

Special Committee

The resolution calls for creation of a special legislative committee to investigate the constitutionality of United States relationships with the UN — referred to in the resolution as "the so-called United Nations Organization." The committee, of four state senators and four representaives, would report to the Legislature within six months.

Roseleip sponsored the resolution. An identical resolution is pending in the Assembly.

A former aide to Maj. Gen. Edwin A. Walker was the main witness of those favoring the study. Walker was an Army officer accused 10 years ago of indoctrinating his troops with John Birch Society views. Walker later resigned from the Army.

UN Called Subversive

The aide, Retired Lt. Col. Arch E. Roberts, branded the UN as a subversive organization that had illegally usurped powers of the American people. The UN Charter "amended by subterfuge the United States Constitution," he declared.

He attacked the "no-win war in Vietnam," the Southeast Asia Treaty Organization, the Council on Foreign Relations and other groups.

The Vietnam conflict, Roberts declared, was "a stage managed war to conceal its real objective." The real objective, he said, is to create an industrial complex in the Mekong delta, in line with objectives of international bankers.

Roberts, of Fort Collins, Colo., is director of the right wing Committee to Restore the Constitution. He came to Wisconsin to testify on behalf of the Wisconsin Legislative and Research Committee, Roberts said. The committee is a conservative citizens group.

Roberts was interrupted several times by applause from the audience of about 250 – most of them supporters of the resolution. He also was interrupted once by a balky public address system, which Roberts accused a Capitol messenger of turning off.

Far Reaching Paranoia

Grover, who holds a master's degree in international law, drew groans from the audience when he accused Roberts and other proponents of the study of having misrepresented the facts.

"This resolution stems from the far reaching paranoia that grips Lt. Col. Roberts and his followers," Grover said. "He believes that almost everybody except him and his followers is a part of the Communist conspiracy."

If Communists really controlled the UN, Red China would have been admitted to the organization long ago and Nationalist China expelled, Grover said.*

---

* *Publisher's Note: Of course, this has now happened.*

"These people have had their fun. They've displayed their fantasies," Grover said. "Let's not make this Legislature the laughingstock of the state."

60 Sign Support

Among those arguing for the study were Eben Y. Collins, Waukesha president of the Wisconsin Legislative and Research Committee, and Mrs. Theodore F. Meves, 18310 Bennington Dr., Brookfield, state co-ordinator.

More than 60 persons signed slips in support of the bill, but did not speak. Among them were two American Party candidates defeated in last fall's election — John M. Couture, Muskego, who ran for attorney general, and Karl Koehler, Madison, who ran for the Assembly.

Opposing the bill, besides Grover, was William Osborne Hart, Prairie du Sac state chairman of the Socialist Party.

Exhibit F

Wisconsin State Journal, Thursday, May 27, 1971

State Senate Backs Investigation of U.N.

By James D. Selk
Of The State Journal Staff

The State senate Wednesday voted to investigate the constitutionality of United States participation in the United Nations.

The move was heralded by supporters, including Majority Leader Ernest C. Keppler (R-Sheboygan) as "of momentous importance," and derided by opponents, including Minority Leader Fred A. Risser (D-Madison) as a "waste of time."

THE ACTION came on a 24-7 vote after a morning of oratory scheduled to coincide with the State Capitol visit of anti-United Nations activists who crowded Senate galleries and frequently cheered proponents and booed and hissed opponents.

Such demonstrations usually are forbidden in the Senate but there was no attempt made to stop them Wednesday by either party. The anti-United Nations group is led by retired Army Col. Archibald E. Roberts, who is organizing a national effort to sever United States ties with the New York based world organization.

THE RESOLUTION, which authorizes the appointment of an eight-member investigation committee, now goes to the State Assembly where it awaits an uncertain fate.

Sen. Gordon W. Roseleip (R-Darlington), the main author of the resolution, said the investigation is necessary to determine "if the United Nations is used as a stepping stone to take over the greatest country in the world and the greatest flag, Old Glory."

He praised Roberts as an "outstanding patriot." Roseleip's Governmental and Veterans Affairs Committee recommended adoption of the resolution on a 4-1 vote.

Although there was no estimate of the cost of the investigation, Keppler said the Senate Organization Committee would authorize travel expenses.

"IT WOULD be a good investment in the future of America," Keppler said.

Other vocal supporters included Sen. Joseph Lourigan (D-Kenosha), a member of the Governmental and Veterans Affairs Committee.

"They don't even respect God," Lourigan said of the United Nations. "They are a god unto themselves — a Sigmund Freud, if you please."

Detractors included Sen. Kurt Frank (D-Milwaukee), who said the United Nations is of little importance in the affairs of the United States, and Sen. Carl Thompson (D-Stroughton), who said it provides an alternative to international power bloc politics and war.

Sen. Walter J. Chilsen (R-Wausau), who wound up voting for the resolution, said, "The debate on both sides has been so irresponsible that I wish I could vote against both sides," he said.

Here is the roll call vote for adoption:

Republicans for (18) - Bidwell, Busby, Chilsen, Cirilli, Devitt, Heinzen, Hollander, Johnson, Keppler, Knowles, Knutson, Lorge, Lotto, Murphy, Roseleip, Soik, Steinhilber, Swan.

Democrats for (6) — Lipscomb, Lourigan, McKenna, Martin, Parys, Schuele.

Republicans against (0).

Democrats against (7) — Dorman, Frank, Kendziorski, Peloquin, Risser, Thompson, Whittow.

STATEMENT by Archibald E. Roberts, Lt. Col., AUS, ret., to the subcommittee, General Legislation Committee, House of Representatives, State of Florida, in behalf of FLORIDIANS FOR THE CONSTITUTION, in support of House Concurrent Resolution No. 769, introduced by Hon. Donald H. Reed, Jr., Minority Leader, 20 May, 1971.

Inserted in the Congressional Record by Representative John R. Rarick, M.C., June 2, 1971, pp. H4566-H4570.

Legislative Service Bureau Summary

   Establishes special joint committee to investigate the constitutionality of various United Nations agreements entered into by federal agencies; their effect on Florida and its citizens; and the enforcement sanctions against violators of constitutional rights by acts taken without constitutional authority. Joint committee to consist of four senators and four representatives, to report in six months (See Exhibit A).*

CHAPTER TWO

Invisible Power Behind the U.N.

   The SPEAKER pro tempore. Under a previous order of the House the gentleman from Louisiana (Mr. Rarick) is recognized for 10 minutes.

   Mr. RARICK. Mr. Speaker, American patriot Lt. Col. Arch E. Roberts, Army of the United States, retired, contends that the U.N. Charter has superseded the U.S. Constitution and he is hard at work attempting to rectify this situation.

*   *Exhibits at end of article.*

As head of the Committee To Restore the Constitution, suite 990, Savings Building, Oak at Howes, Fort Collins, Colo., Colonel Roberts is waging a campaign to inspire investigation of the United Nations Treaty agreements by the respective State legislatures, basing his endeavor on the charge that the United Nations organization is an apparatus for *covertly dismantling* the U.S. Constitution.

In testimony given on May 5, 1971, to the subcommittee, house general legislation committee of the State of Florida, Roberts explained the origins of the United Nations and stated that the Vietnam war has never served interests of the American people but has been pursued for purely *economic* reasons. He charged that the lives of American soldiers are being expended in Vietnam to purchase *resources* of Southeast Asia for those who conceived the United Nations.

Believing as does Colonel Roberts that the executive and judicial branches are in some matters following the U.N. Charter rather than the U.S. Constitution, I have reintroduced the bill H.R. 360, to repeal the United Nations Participation Act of 1965.

I insert Lieutenant Colonel Roberts' statement entitled "Invisible Power Behind the U.N.," related news clippings to support his testimony, and the text of H.R. 360:

Invisible Power Behind the U.N.

(Statement by Archibald E. Roberts, Lt. Col., AUS (ret.), Director, Committee to Restore the Constitution, Inc.)

Mr. Chairman, members of the subcomittee, House General Legislation Committee, on May 5th, 1971, I addressed your parent committee in support of House Concurrent Resolution No. 769, introduced by Representative Donald H. Reed, Jr., calling for the formation of a special joint committee of the Florida State Legislature to study the relationship of agencies of the federal government with the United Nations Organization.

In consonance with the thrust of my testimony, and in accord with the purposes of this subcommittee appointed to recommend action on HCR 769, I respectfully request that the following remarks and accompanying documents be inserted into the record of your proceedings.

Mr. Chairman, there is a popular and widely promoted *myth* that the United Nations sprang from the minds and hearts of delegates representing fifty peace-loving nations meeting at San Francisco in 1945.

Like most UN-serving propaganda this belief, too, is *false*.

In the next few pages I intend to prove that the United Nations had its birth in 1941 and that it is entirely the product of *private* interests.

I will show that the UN is a creature of an *invisible* power group who operate through agencies of the federal government to covertly *dismantle* the United States Constitution.

I will demonstrate that the United Nations Treaty is exploited by these private interests as an instrument to coerce the States and their people into a *totalitarian* world government.

The United Nations Organization, lineal descendent of the star-crossed League of Nations, was spawned two weeks after Pearl Harbor in the office of Secretary of State Cordull Hull.[1]

In a letter to President Franklin D. Roosevelt dated December 22, 1941, Secretary Hull, at the direction of his *faceless* sponsors recommended the founding of a Presidential Advisory Committee on Post-War Foreign Policy.

The Post-War Foreign Policy Committee was, as we shall see, the Planning Commission for the United Nations Charter.

The purpose of this Committee, said Mr. Hull, would be to prepare for effective participation in the solution of "vast and complicated problems of international relations which

---

1   Post-War Foreign Policy Preparation 1939-45, Department of State Publication # 3580, General Foreign Policy Series 15, Released February, 1950, pages 63-64.

will confront "the United States and the world after "final defeat of the forces of aggression."

"It," (the Committee) Hull said, "will work in the inseparably interrelated fields of general security, limitation of armaments, sound international economic relationships, and other phases of international cooperation, the implementation of which is essential to enduring world peace and to economic progress."

These world government goals, paralleling the objectives of the Foreign Policy Association (an interlocking agency of the *Council on Foreign Relations*) were subsequently embedded in the Charter of the United Nations Organization – a world government constitution.

All research, interdepartmental government agency coordination, and international cooperation concerning this United Nations Planning Commission was set up in the Department of State "or under its leadership."

In addition to himself as chairman, Cordell Hull listed the following members for his United Nations "brain trust":

Mr. Sumner Wells, Under Secretary of State, Vice Chairman, Member, *Council on Foreign Relations*.

Mr. Norman H. Davis, President, *Council on Foreign Relations*.

Mr. Dean Acheson, Assistant Secretary of State, Member *Council on Foreign Relations*.

Mr. Hamilton Fish Armstrong, Editor, "Foreign Affairs," official publication, *Council on Foreign Relations*.

Mr. Adolf A. Berle, Jr., Assistant Secretary of State, Member, *Council on Foreign Relations*.

Mr. Asaiah Bowman, President, John Hopkins University, Member, *Council on Foreign Relations*.

Mr. Benjamin Cohen, General Counsel, National Power Policy Committee, Member, *Council on Foreign Relations*.

Mr. Herbert Feis, Department of State Advisor on International Economic Relations, Member, *Council on Foreign Relations*.

Mr. Green N. Hackworth, Department of State Legal Advisor.

Mr. Harry C. Hopkins, Chief, Department of State Division of Commercial Policy.

Mrs. Anne O'Hare McCormick, Editorial Staff, *The New York Times*.

Dr. Leo Pasvolsky, Special Assistant to the Secretary of State, Chief of the Department's Division of Special Research, Member, *Council on Foreign Relations*.

On or about December 28, the President wrote on Mr. Hull's letter: "I heartily approve. F.D.R."

Mr. Chairman, of the many designers of the United Nations Charter — both Russian and American — the two principal contributors on the American side proved to be Dr. Leo Pasvolsky, Chief, Division of Special Research, Department of State,[2] and his assistant, *Alger Hiss*, Chief of Political Affairs, Department of State.[3]

It is of critical significance to note that Dr. Pasvolsky, although born in Russia of *communist revolutionary* parents, achieved phenomenal success in the United States Department of State. He was inserted into our Government in 1934 and rose by rapid progression to a *key position* which ultimately led to decisions affecting the transfer of United States sovereignty to the United Nations Organization.[4]

Time magazine, in an obituary dated 18 May, 1953, credits Pasvolsky with being the "architect" of the United Nations Charter.

Alger Hiss, co-author of the first draft of the United Nations Charter and later U.N. General Secretary at the San Francisco conference[5] was at the same time a member of the

---

2   **Time** magazine, May 18, 1953, page 99.
3   **Seeds of Treason**, Ralph de Toledano, page 110.
4   Current Biography, 1945, pages 448-449.
5   **Seeds of Treason**, Ralph de Toledano, page 112.

Harold Ware *communist cell* in Washington, D.C., a Soviet espionage agent,[6] and a member of the *Council on Foreign Relations.*[7]

The final draft of the United Nations Charter, completing the work of the Presidential Advisory Committee on Post-War Foreign Policy, was approved by President Harry S. Truman on 26 June, 1945, at the closing session of the San Francisco Conference.

On July 28, the Senate of the United States, following a reading of the Charter by Dr. Pasvolsky in the Senate Chamber, adopted this extraordinary treaty by a vote of 89 to 2.

In the words of the U.S. Senate, the Charter of the United Nations thus "became the supreme law of the land"[8] and the Constitution of the United States of America passed into history.

"I feel from the bottom of my heart," said the Honorable William Langer, a dissenting Senator, "that the adoption of the Charter . . . will mean *perpetuating war.* I feel that it will mean the *enslavement* of millions of people from Poland to India, from Korea to Java, as well as people in many other places on this earth."[9]

Senator Langer's prophesy was to be confirmed in blood and agony in the succeeding years — *with the most terrible consequences for the American people still to unfold.*

Mr. Chairman, the preceding historical vignette has established the following relevant evidence:

1. Every officer of the fourteen-member Presidential Advisory Committee on Post-War Foreign Policy was a member of the *Council on Foreign Relations*, or under the control of the *Council on Foreign Relations.*[10]

---

6   Witness, Whittaker Chambers, pages 535, 542-543.
7   **The Invisible Government**, Dan Smoot, page 5.
8   Review of the United Nations Charter, Senate Document No. 87, January 7, 1954, page 289.
9   **Congressional Record**, July 28, 1945, pages 8188-8189.
10 The Council on Foreign Relations, Harold Pratt House, 58 East 68th Street, New York, N.Y. 10021.

2. All national and international research and coordination for the Committee on Post-War Foreign Policy was set up in the U.S. Department of State "or under its leadership."

3. The end product of the work of the Committee on Post-War Foreign Policy, the United Nations Charter, resulted in the transfer by deceit and subterfuge, of powers of government from the Congress to the United Nations Organization.

Mr. Chairman, this evidence on the origins of the U.N. points to the *real objective* of the "no-win" war in Viet Nam.

Massive brainwashing by national news media has attempted to convince Americans that the unconscionable policy of *"Perpetual War for Perpetual Peace"* somehow defends the United States against "communist aggression." It is clear, however, that this *interminable conflict* has reduced neither the military nor political power of "communism." *In fact, while sending millions of young men to fight on the mainland of Asia, "with neither the promise nor hope of victory," the federal government has contracted extensive trade and cultural agreements with the very nations which kill our sons.*

I submit that the commitment of American blood and treasure to the Indochina theatre has *never* served the interests of the American people. I charge that this strange United Nations war is being pursued for purely *economic* objectives. I declare that lives of America's soldier sons are being expended in Viet Nam to *purchase the resources* of Southeast Asia for those who conceived the United Nations Organization.

The facts can no longer be ignored.

I offer for examination a full page feature from *Chicago Today,* dated March 29, 1971, headed, "Oil fuels up Indochina politics."

"Clues are beginning to pile up that there may be huge quantities of crude oil in the waters of the Far East and Southeast Asia," declared this *Chicago Tribune* publication. "Discoveries by Natomas, Atlantic Richfield, and Union Oil have triggered a frantic exploration race off Indonesia. An optimistic report by a United Nations team about possible oil deposits between Japan and Taiwan is fueling speculation that the entire Far East could contain oil deposits rivaling those of the Middle East."[11]

In another article from *The Oregonian*, dated May 1, 1971, a Portland manufacturing executive stated that, "The United States will form a 'strange, new partnership' with Red China because of a new economic factor — major oil discoveries off the shores of South Vietnam."[12]

Mr. Chairman, under the guise of supporting our military forces in Viet Nam many manufacturing plants have been erected in the Mekong Delta to exploit copper, tin, and other resources of the Far East. Southeast Asia has, in fact, been transformed into a *vast industrial complex* and merged into the world industrial society envisaged by the monetary powers which established the United Nations Organization. *The private profits accruing to these banking and industrial interests are enormous.*

Upon the documented record presented here can be constructed these deductions:

A. The U.S. Department of State and other federal agencies are controlled by an international body, the Council on Foreign Relations.

B. *The Council on Foreign Relations*, its membership comprising about fourteen-hundred leading financiers, industrialists, politicians, media directors, educators, and militarists in America, has as its long-range goal the establishment of a United Nations *world government* which *they* command.

C. *The Council on Foreign Relations*, on July 28, 1945, through its State Department apparatus, foisted upon the

---

11 "Oil fuels up Indochina politics." **Chicago Today**, March 29, 1971 (See Exhibit B).
12 "U.S.-Chinese thaw linked to oil find," **The Oregonian**, May 1, 1971 (See Exhibit C).

American people the United Nations Charter, a world government constitution, in *violation* of the prohibitions of the Constitution of the United States of America.

D. *The Council on Foreign Relations* is the *invisible government* of the United States and its members *covertly, maliciously,* and to their *personal profit,* direct foreign and domestic matters concerning the United States and its citizens.

Mr. Chairman, I have shown the United Nations Organization to be a *subversive* instrument for *global conquest* devised by the *Council on Foreign Relations.* The proper party to now challenge the validity of the ultra vires United Nations Treaty is a party to the constitutional compact, a sovereign State. Through its legislative apparatus the State of Florida can legally clarify the question of attempted usurpation of governmental powers and restore the Constitution as the "supreme law of the land."

The Florida State Legislature, being the reservoir of *true political power, is morally* and *legally obligated* to defend the Constitution and protect the freedoms of person and property guaranteed to the people by the Constitution.

In support of my testimony, and in addition to the evidence noted therein, I present to your subcommittee four hundred seventy-seven pages of documents in loose-leaf folio. The raw information contained in Books One and Two of this World Government File provides substantive proof for the following conclusions:

(a) The United Nations Organization is a product of mutual cooperation between the governments of the Union of Socialist Soviet Republics and the United States of America.

(b) Interlocking world government organization reveals *collusion* between U.S. Government agencies and other public and private agents in a *conspiracy* to overthrow the Constitution of the United States and to erect, by *guile* and *deceit*, a totalitarian, socialist state upon the *ruins* of the American republic.

(c) The global proliferation of international agencies originating in New York City indicate central funding of vast operations from reservoirs of *unlimited* financial power.

(d) The United Nations Treaty has *nothing* to do with world peace. Its purpose and objective is to transfer the U.S. Military establishment, and U.S. sovereignty, to the United Nations Organization so as to *force* all nations into line and to deliver them up to a one world covenant.

(e) The world government covenant, of which the United Nations is a part, is *controlled* and *manipulated* by an international money aristocracy for *private profit.*

Mr. Chairman, I respectfully urge favorable consideration of House Concurrent Resolution No. 769 and the formation of a special legislative committee to examine the relationship of the agencies of federal government with the United Nations Organization.

Respectfully,

Lt. Col., AUS, Archibald E. Roberts, ret.,
Director, Committee to Restore the Constitution.

H.R. 360
A bill to repeal the United Nations
Participation Act of 1945

Be it enacted by the Senate and House of Representatives of the United States of America in Congress assembled. That the United Nations Participation Act of 1945 is hereby repealed.

Exhibit A

HCR 769

By Representative Reed
Prefiled April, 1971

House Concurrent Resolution No. 769
A CONCURRENT RESOLUTION establishing a special joint
committee to study the constitutionality of the federal
government's relation with the United Nations.

DELETED (see Exhibit A, State of Wisconsin, Senate Joint
Resolution 26, Chapter One, page 10.)

Exhibit B

OIL FUELS UP INDOCHINA POLITICS
Huge Deposits Add New Angle
to U.S. War Policy

It has passed the rumor stage. Clues are beginning to pile up that there may be huge quantities of crude oil in the waters of the Far East and Southeast Asia. Discoveries by Natomas, Atlantic Richfield, and Union Oil have triggered a frantic exploration race off Indonesia. An optimistic report by a United Nations team about possible oil deposits between Japan and Taiwan is fueling speculation that the *entire* Far East could contain oil deposits rivaling those of the Middle East.

Some of these deposits would almost certainly lie off South Viet Nam. Nobody yet knows for sure because no drilling has taken place. But preliminary United Nations surveys have given the area good marks. And there are plenty of rumors. One is that a British company has found signs of oil on the prison island of Con Son, east of the southern tip of Viet Nam.

The political implications, of course, are enormous. But if the oil is there, or even probably there, the question of who rules in Saigon takes on more than political significance. Already, United States antiwar groups are beginning to suggest that a desire to ensure friendly governments in the Indochina area could slow down President Nixon's withdrawal from the war. An organization called "Another Mother for Peace" has flooded the Senate Foreign Relations Committee with over 10,000 letters calling for public hearings.

Not surprising, the oil companies are less than anxious to discuss the topic. Walter Levy, a New York-based oil expert and consultant to many of the companies, says flatly: "I don't want to comment. It's become a political issue."

"We haven't made up our minds yet," says a spokesman

for Mobil Oil, asked whether his company would bid for concessions. Another dodges the question: "Texaco is not participating in exploration in Viet Nam."

Queried about his government's plans, Ngo Thanh Tung, an economist at the South Vietnamese embassy in Washington, says: "Several companies have been sending their proposals, but none of them have yet been considered." But oilmen expect Saigon to ask for bids quite soon.

In a conference last year, Chase Manhattan Chairman *David Rockefeller* made a little-noticed speech that created a quiet stir among Asia-watchers. By 1980, Rockefeller said, the oil industry could pour $36 billion of capital investment into the *Asian Pacific.* This kind of money could give the area the boost it needs to enter the industrial age. It could help make up for the loss of U.S. military expenditures by substituting oil wells for military bases.

To give a sense of proportion, the total, free world investment Chase predicts for 1969-1980 is $250 billion. But the Asian Pacific share will almost equal the total slated for Latin America, Africa and the Middle East. "The Asian Pacific," commented *Petroleum Engineer*, a trade journal, "looks like the next big international boom area."

If the oil is there, the boom will undoubtedly follow. The Asia area is the fastest-growing oil market in the world. Japan, which burns 3.4 million barrels a day, is forecast to consume over 10 million a day by 1980. While Southeast Asia consumes relatively little oil, consumption could rise at a brisk pace if industrialization plans catch hold.

"Just think of all those people who are now burning charcoal and using oxcarts," sighs one oilman.

Where is all the oil coming from? Southeast Asia may contain enough offshore crude to fuel that growth. Right now its production doesn't come close. Indonesia, the largest producer, turns out only 900,000 barrels a day. Japan must therefore rely on the Middle East for 85% of its oil, but Japan is uneasy at its dependence on this volatile area.

Compared with Middle East oil, moreover, South Asian

oil will be close to its markets, reducing transportation costs. Drilling and the production costs are reasonable, because the offshore areas of Indonesia and Viet Nam are relatively calm and very shallow.

Perhaps most important, the oil found so far off Indonesia is exceptionally low in sulphur content, less than 1 per cent compared with the 3 per cent-plus content of Middle East crude. This would give it a major cost advantage in Japan, which is imposing strict pollution controls.

Much of the oil could find its way into the rest of the world market, where more oil will be needed within the next 15 years than has been produced in the history of the oil industry. The low sulphur content could make the oil very attractive to the west coast American market, where pollution is a big issue. The uncertainties of Middle East politics, the higher prices being imposed by the organization of Petroleum Exporting Countries and the delay in finding a way to transport crude from the North Slope of Alaska to the 48 states add to the prospects.

A veteran oilman puts it this way: "We don't have the oil in the U.S. to meet our future requirements. Either we are going to have our future committed to those crazy Arabs or we are going to develop Southeast Asia, the West Coast of Africa and the West Coast of Latin America as alternative sources—and hopefully, build the Alaskan pipeline."

In any case, mounting U.S. activity in the area raises huge political questions that must be balanced against the *economic* benefits for Southeast Asia and the U.S.:

Might a discovery lead to pressure for slowing down the pace of U.S. troop withdrawals?

Might oil industry agreements with the present Thieu-Dy regime commit the U.S. even closer to this controversial government?

If the war in Indochina bogs down permanently, won't the oil industry run the risk of being made the scapegoat for whatever goes wrong?

Is a "friendly" regime in Saigon really vital to U.S. access to such oil? After all many Arab countries are rabidly unfriendly to the West but sell their oil there.

What will the effect be on the political and military policies of Japan and China?

Oil seems forever feted to be a *political* mineral.

Exhibit C

U.S.-Chinese Thaw Linked to Oil Find

(By Blaine Schultz)

The United States will form a "strange, new partnership" with Red China because of a new economic factor—major oil discoveries off the shores of South Vietnam, a Portland manufacturing executive said Friday.

Monford A. Orloff, president of Evans Products Co., told a shippers' group at the Portland Hilton Hotel the importance of the oil will speed up "the game of musical chairs" between nations.

But he intimated it would be naive to assume that the honeymoon between the United States and mainland China simply grew out of favorable reception in Peking of an American ping pong team.

At first, most of the oil from the new deposits will be delivered to Japan, he said.

"Then China will take more and more of this extremely valuable asset," Orloff said at the closing luncheon of the three-day National Association of Shippers Advisory Boards.

Purposely side-stepping a talk that would deal with transportation alone, Orloff indicated that the "increasing turmoil and unrest which plagues our country" called for openness and that the *protests* by the younger generation are *understandable*.

In his talk to businessmen, the Portland manufacturer talked about inflation, the controversial topic of Vietnam, and the new American relationship with Red China.

At the end of the talk, almost the entire dining hall of transportation people and shippers stood to applaud. The gathering, for the most part, was "over forty."

Orloff said he could understand how the nation's leaders

would be frustrated by the "rising tide of protest" led by the younger generation against the war.

"Frustrating, yes, but surprising, no," Orloff declared, as he noted that the difficulties arose "because of the insistence of our leaders in applying the panaceas of the Fifties and Sixties to the problems of the Seventies."

By 1966, he said, "we found ourselves engaged in a terrible, costly war, the likes of which were never thoughtfully contemplated and the results of which gave rise to most of the serious problems with which we are confronted today."

He said American involvement in the war "has spawned inflation, civil unrest, unemployment, high interest rates, lower profits, and, possibly, a major shift in the political control of our country."

Voters Age Changing

By 1972, he said, there will be some 42 million voters between the ages of 18 and 30.

The cure of our inflation, he said, has been a "trade-off" of higher unemployment and lessened profits in return for a somewhat lessened rate of inflation.

But the greatest inequity, he said, "the result of which will be felt for the next decade at least, was the decision to fight the war using almost entirely our young people, and particularly, the less advantaged sector of the younger generation."

He said it was the first war fought by the United States in which participation by the citizenry was "limited to those of us who have not reached the age of 26."

In addition, he said, the citizen army was disproportionately drawn from the nonwhite sector and the non-college ranks.

Because of the latent threat of intervention by Red China and the changing attitude of the American people against the war, the conflict cannot be ended by invasion or destruction of the landscape, Orloff said.

"In the not too distant future," he predicted, "our government will announce a time for final withdrawal."

"Macabre Aspects" Cited

And he said there are "macabre aspects" to suggestions that the withdrawal be slowed until the prisoners of war are returned home. He said there are some 1,600 "men missing," but in the meantime, there is a casualty rate of 250 men a week "of whom 50 are killed."

Orloff said he believed that America's limitation of renewed relations with Red China "stems from the fact that the new major oil discoveries off the shores of South Vietnam have introduced a new economic factor which transcends political and social theory and calls for hardheaded realism" in how the oil is to be used.

In the not too distant future, Orloff said, "you will see our relations with Red China improve markedly," and because of the political power of the young voters, he predicted that "the war in Vietnam will quickly and speedily be ended."

Exhibit D

Evans Seeks Permission for China Trade Mission

Olympia (AP) — Gov. Dan Evan's letter to the mainland Chinese travel agency at Hong Kong asking permission to send a Washington trade mission to the Communist nation probably will be followed by direct correspondence with Peking, a state official said Friday.

Daniel B. Ward, director of the State Commerce and Economic Development Department, said the letter, dated April 22, was mailed to Hong Kong on the advice of persons experienced in trade with the Red Chinese.

"We had to decide whether to go through Hong Kong or through Ottawa, where the Chinese have some people," Ward said. "It was decided it was best to make the original overture through Hong Kong."

The letter asks permission for Evans and a 10-man group to visit the Asian nation, a possibility created by President Nixon's announcement earlier this month of relaxed market restrictions in the area.

"This mission would be limited to about 10 people who desire to promote two-way trade between the peoples of mainland China and the United States," Evans wrote.

"I seriously doubt if we'll get a quick answer to the letter," Ward said, "but when we do, it will probably be followed up with direct correspondence with Peking."

In a telephone interview from Vancouver, B.C., Ward said Evans' letter was part of a research effort to try to identify where the potential is, in Chinese trade.

He said there would be no final answers for at least three or four weeks when the State Department is expected to issue a list of items that may be traded legally with China.

"We're hoping our state's products, like agriculture and

Boeing aircraft, are part of the list, and if they're not, you can be sure we'll do everything we can to arbitrate their inclusion," Ward said.

He said State Department officials have told him it's still too early to say what will be on the list.

Exhibit E

Reed's Study of the U.N.
(By David Cook)

The House General Legislation Committee listened to testimony on Rep. Reed's bill to study the relationship between the United Nations charter and the U.S. Constitution Wednesday.

In the end the bill was put in a special subcommittee for further study and probably oblivion. It seems most unlikely at this point that the State Legislature will name a joint committee to see if U.S. affiliation with the U.N. is constitutional.

While the significance of a state probe of alleged violations of the Constitution may not be readily apparent to the public, the proponents of Reed's bill see it as an important step in getting the states to reassert their constitutional powers.

The proponents say Congress isn't about to reverse itself on the United Nations, so it is necessary for the states to demonstrate that Congress, particularly the Senate, has *no constitutional right* to enter into treaties which *subvert* the Constitution.

And it is the contention that ratification of the U.N. Charter, plus other treaties, puts the U.S., its government and military forces, under the control of the United Nations.

They make a good case, because the language of the charter and various treaties is clear. Where the case breaks down, however, is in recognition that the U.S. must be willing to submit to the power of the U.N. and it will not do that:

Except for some idiotic developments during the Korean war and apparently during the Vietnam war, the U.S. has not fallen into the U.N. trap painted so vividly by those people who want us out of it.

Proponents of the Reed bill include members of the Committee to Restore the Constitution, Women for Constitutional Government, Daughters of the American Revolution, and Sons of the American Revolution. About 75 were on hand for the hearing.

Spokesman for the group was Archibald E. Roberts, a retired Army Colonel, who talked for a half hour or so about how the U.S. has subverted the Constitution.

He claimed the Vietnam War is a United Nations war and read appropriate documents to prove it. He declared the U.N. a *subversive* organization.

In addition he said "vital powers of government held in trust for the American people have been *illegally* transferred to the United Nations in violation of the prohibitions of the Constitution."

His claim is that the U.N. Charter was "foisted upon the American people to serve those who seek to overthrow the Constitution and coerce American citizens into a socialist world government."

Col. Roberts' evidence is *impressive*, and he left a great deal of it with the General Legislation Committee. Whether he convinced anyone who wasn't already opinionated on the subject is questionable.

It is doubtful that he convinced committee members that the Florida Legislature could do anything about the situation even if his charges proved 100 per cent correct.

Reed argued the charges should be examined by the Legislature because "we are American citizens." He emphasized that all he asked for was a four-man committee to look into the situation and report back its findings.

Introducing Col. Roberts to the committee was former U.S. Congressman Bruce Alger of Texas, now of Boca Raton, which also is Reed's home town.

Alger also contended the Constitution is subverted by U.S. membership in the U.N. He reported that Florida Congressman Bob Sikes has introduced a resolution calling for a full review of the U.N. charter.

He added, however, that it still is necessary for the states to assert themselves on the issue. He indicated an effort is being made to get other state legislatures to look into it.

"I don't consider myself a nut on this subject," Reed said. "But a lot of people have questions about the real relationship between our government and the U.N."

He said he didn't grasp the full impact of the situation and therefore felt an inquiry should be made so the Legislature could draw some conclusions about it.

The motion to shunt the bill into a subcommittee came from Rep. George Firestone of Miami. He exhibited a notable lack of sympathy with the proceedings.

Reed will be lucky if he ever hears from his bill again.

ADDRESS presented to members of the State Legislature and Directors of the Wisconsin Legislative & Research Committee, Inc., December 8, 1970, to explain the purpose and objective of the Wisconsin campaign to inspire legislative investigation of the United Nations (See Exhibit A).*

Colonel Roberts' speech, entered in the Congressional Record by Representative John R. Rarick, M.C., issue of December 14, 1970, p. E10400, succinctly reveals the covert attack upon the American people and illustrates how interlocking subversion in government departments can be exposed and neutralized.

CHAPTER THREE

Invisible Government of Monetary Power

Mr. RARICK. Mr. Speaker, this week Congress is to consider House Joint Resolution 1146, authorizing a $20 million grant to the U.N.O. for the purpose of expansion of its headquarters in New York City. This grant is in addition to all other assessments against our country by the United Nations and represents 20 percent of the $80 million cost of the expansion. The remaining $60 million is planned to be derived as follows:

Five million dollars from the UNICEF fund, derived by selling Halloween candy and Christmas cards, supposedly to be able to help disadvantaged children.

Twenty million dollars from the city of New York, whose mayor professes that his city is in such financial distress that it is necessary to lay off city employees.

---

* *Exhibits at end of article.*

Twenty-five million dollars from the regular U.N. budget assessed against the 127 member nations.

More and more people are becoming disenchanted at the United Nations and are taking a second look. Most people support the idea of an international body working for world peace so long as its operations do not deny us our national sovereignty. However, more and more people are aware that while the United Nations has not achieved peace it is infringing upon our national sovereignty and as such constitutes a *clear* and *present threat* to the liberties of our individual citizens. Most, upon learning the truth, are *fearful* of what they find and are organizing to extricate the United States from this trap.

Noteworthy, among many such distinguished constitutional Americans, is Lt. Col. Arch E. Roberts, AUS, retired, who on December 8, 1970, addressed a conference with members of the Wisconsin State Legislature at Waukesha, Wis.

I include Colonel Roberts' speech, "Invisible Government of Monetary Power"; his proposed bills for State legislatures, drafted by two nationally recognized constitutional authorities, Mr. T. David Horton, of Battle Mountain, Nev., and the late Mr. John Janney; and several pertinent newsclippings which follow:

[From the *Washington Post*, Sept. 10, 1969]

U.N. Building Plan Funded

UNITED NATIONS.—A $10 million investment by the United Nations Development Program has cleared the way for construction of a major addition to the U.N. headquarters building in New York.

Approval came in a 24-4 vote at a special meeting of the program's governing council on Tuesday. It had been strongly urged by the United States, which has pledged to provide $20 million of the estimated $80 million cost of the new building.

New York City will furnish $20 million for the project in addition to the $12 million value of the land on which the seven-story addition is to be located. The regular U.N. budget will supply $25 million of the cost and the U.N. Children's Fund $5 million.

In recent years the U.N. Secretariat has been increasingly cramped for space, and both the Development Program and UNICEF have had to rent quarters in private buildings. The new seven-story addition will cost more than the 38-story secretariat building, completed in 1951 for a little over $65 million.

Invisible Government of Monetary Power
(Address by Lt. Col. Arch E. Roberts)

It is appallingly clear that America the beautiful has fallen into the hands of political madmen!

Our citizens are *exploited* by coercive domestic policy at home, our sons are *betrayed* in "no-win" military adventures, and our national honor is compromised all over the globe.

This strategy of defeat has led America to the brink of *economic collapse*, has generated *violence* in our schools and *revolution* in our cities, and has resulted in a *shocking decay* of the American morality.

We believe that these symptoms of decline are interrelated, and that they are inspired by a heretofore *invisible government of monetary and political power*.

We therefore recommend a public *investigation* of the men and the system behind "Revolution U.S.A.," and ask the State legislature to enact laws which will neutralize those who secretly promote *nihilistic doctrine* in this nation.

The Committee to Restore the Constitution, and those affiliated with us, are determined to expose a *concealed plan* to transform the United States into a SOVIET America.

Not satisfied to merely unmask the conspiracy, we further propose a practical, attainable solution to this threat to the freedoms of person and property guaranteed to the people by the Constitution.

Let us now sketch the parameters of the problem and outline an approach to its solution.

For the purpose of illustration we refer to the grave situation of revolution in America.

There are few here who would slight the obvious threat to life and property posed by revolutionary violence. It is clear that you and I are exposed to a *rising tide* of *revolt* which, unless reversed, will engulf every institution of freedom in this land.

"Revolution U.S.A." has become a crisis of major, and perhaps fatal, proportions.

Most of us are, however, satisfied to identify the bomber and the police killer as the instigator of revolution. This faulty reasoning fails to consider the fact that revolutions cost money, lots of money.

It must be obvious to the most casual observer that the financing of "Revolution U.S.A.," and the intellectual leadership of it, cannot originate within the ranks of the poor, the student, the black, or the working class, as we have been led to believe.

Instead of directing our fear and anger at the street people (who are, of course, our sons and daughters) we must have the wit and the courage to seek out the concealed base of power for this fratricidal conflict—a civil war which threatens to tear our nation apart. When we do, we will find that today's hostilities had their beginnings at the turn of the century.

In 1905 an ambitious and morally degenerate group of financiers and industrialists fixed upon a long range *plan* which would ultimately deliver *control* of America and the world into their hands.

The basic objective of their plan was to *dismantle* the

Constitution of the United States and erect in its place a *world government covenant* which the Financial/Industrial cartel would command.

To achieve their objective the conspirators adopted an operational procedure of *Infiltration, Subversion,* and *Rebellion* aimed at the religious, economic, and social disciplines of the existing order. By massing their wealth and influence to *secretly* sponsor *nihilistic* doctrine, they felt that they could capture the intellectual leadership of church and college. Domination of pulpit and professorial chair, they reasoned, would lead to *mastery* of the entire spiritual-educational process, the *corruption* of mass-communication media, and the creation of a fractured, rudderless society which would serve their purpose.

Achieving political authority was an obvious prerequisite to success. The cartel therefore, in 1912 forced a major penetration of the United States political structure and elevated Woodrow Wilson to the Presidency.

Quick to capitalize on this advantage the conspirators in the closing days of the 1913 Congress, affected passage of three legislative acts which *emasculated* the Constitution and established a political power base for suceeding operations. These acts were:

a. *the Sixteenth Amendment to the Constitution.*
b. *the Seventeenth Amendment to the Constitution.*
c. *the Federal Reserve Act.*

Of these three legislative actions by Federal Agents, all of which had the effect of *emasculating* the Constitution, the most *ominous* was the creation of a *central bank* in America. *The Federal Reserve Act* surreptitiously granted to the conspirators the authority to manipulate the public credit of the United States for *private profit.*

To appreciate the enormous lien placed upon the American people by such banking manipulation of public credit it must be noted that when the Federal Reserve Banks were set up and began operations on November 15, 1914, their total assets were listed at $143,000,000.00. On December 23,

1949, testimony before the House Banking and Currency Committee showed that the Federal Reserve Banks listed assets in excess of $45,000,000,000.00. The percentage of profits is so *fantastic* that it would take an economist from Rockefeller's University of Chicago to compute it.

Congressman Wright Patman, House Banking and Currency Committee, in a letter dated April 14, 1952, stated:

"The Open Market Committee operations is the most important function of the entire Federal Reserve system. It," he said, "provides either hard money or easy money. It makes conditions good or bad. It determines whether or not we will have a depression in this country or whether or not our country will remain prosperous."

"All central (private) banks," said Eustace Mullins in the book, *The Federal Reserve Conspiracy,* "have the power of issuing currency in their respective countries. Thus, the people do not own their own money in Europe, nor do they own it here. It (Federal Reserve Bank notes) is privately printed for private profit. The people have no sovereignty over their money, and it has developed that they have no sovereignty over other major political issues such as foreign policy."

Upon this irresistible and unchallengeable base of political and monetary power, the conspirators established a brain trust which was to be shaped into an instrumentality for global conquest. The organization was named the Inquiry and was formed around a nucleus of members drawn from the Intercollegiate Society, a socialist-oriented group of American intellectuals.

The Inquiry, in 1914 began recruiting and training an "intellectual elite" who, under the guidance of their hidden sponsors, prepared the Covenant of the League of Nations. The League of Nations was, of course, the long-sought world government envisaged by the Industrial/Financial conspiracy.

When the United States Senate, in 1918, refused to ratify the League of Nations for a world government, the Inquiry was reorganized, and in 1919, named the *Council on Foreign Relations.*

The headquarters of the C.F.R. is at Harold Pratt House, 58 East 68th Street in New York City, which is, of course, the financial center of the world.

Twenty-six years were to elapse before the secret government of monetary power, through its instrument, the Council on Foreign Relations, would reach its long-range goal of world government.

The propaganda climate generated during World War Two provided the opportunity, and on July 28, 1945 a refurbished League of Nations Covenant with a new title — the United Nations Charter — was ratified by a *subverted* United States Senate and the Constitution of the United States *passed into history.* *

On page 287, Senate Document No. 87, Review of the United Nations Charter, released January 7, 1954, we find the official view of the United Nations Treaty held by elected officials in Washington.

"The Charter (of the United Nations) has become 'the supreme Law of the Land'; and the Judges in every State shall be bound thereby, anything in the Constitution or Laws of any State to the contrary notwithstanding."

It is now clear that Federal agents, acting under what they assert to be a legal use of the limited powers enumerated in the Constitution, have negotiated with foreign government and special interests in an attempt to coerce these United States into a United Nations Treaty which, if valid, would *surrender* to these foreign government and private interests the rights and liberties assured to the people under the United States Constitution.

The conclusion is inescapable:

Our elected and appointed agents in judicial, legislative, and executive office now conduct our affairs in consonance with the provisions of the U.N. Charter.

---

* *Deleted information appears in preceding section, "Invisible Power Behind the U.N."*

Americans, of course, have been assured that the constitutional legality for the United Nations Treaty is found in Article VI of our Constitution.

A treaty, however, cannot authorize what the Constitution forbids.

No Federal agent has the power or the authority to modify or to dissolve the Constitutional Compact.

It must be said, too, that the Supreme Court cannot declare a statute of congress "unconstitutional." The Court can exercise only the judicial power conferred upon it by the Constitution. It can no more "unmake" a legislative act that it can make one.

To strike down a legislative act requires legislative power. *No court has such power.*

The ordinary citizen also lacks the power to overturn breaches of the Constitution.

Only a State, acting in its highest sovereign capacity can repudiate unauthorized acts of its agents.

Therefore, the proper party to now challenge the validity of the United Nations Treaty, and other ultra vires acts of the Congress, is a party to the Constitutional Compact, a sovereign State.

The sovereign power of the State, through its legislative apparatus, can legally clarify this question of attempted usurpation of governmental power.

Attempts by Federal agents to exceed the limited powers of the Constitution are void and, in law, are no acts at all.

However, when the State fails to repudiate the unauthorized acts of its agents, a presumption arises that the State has approved. The vitality that is thus given to the purported act of the Agent arises from the power of the State in question. The power does not come from the limited agents who had no power to act.

The reason that the People of each State have been burdened with the acts of Federal agents in their surrender of the powers of government is because the State has not repudiated the attempts of its Agents to act beyond their authority. These acts had the effect of "law," not by reason of any non-existent authority of the Federal agents, but because of the authority that the State gave to those acts by failing to challenge the attempts of its Federal agents to exceed their authority.

The emasculation of our Constitution by the so-called United Nations Treaty agreement, the Federal Reserve Act, and other ultra vires acts, most certainly was not authorized by the parties to the Constitutional Compact. Lacking this authority, it is against the law. Being unlawful, it must be put down.

In this respect, State officeholders have a positive duty to enforce the provisions of the Constitution. It is a continuing obligation and may not be met merely by an empty oath taken upon accepting public office.

The language of Article VI, paragraph 3, United States Constitution, "...shall be bound by Oath or Affirmative to support this Constitution..." imposes a continuing duty upon these officeholders as long as they continue in office.

Therefore, in conformity with these duties and obligations, I propose that the legislators of this State now do what is necessary to defend the Constitution and to protect the rights of the People.

The limits of authority given by the Constitution must be enforced and violations of those limits must be punished.

Events in Washington and in the State disclose a *systematic attack* upon the liberties and freedoms guaranteed to the People under the Constitution. I, therefore, suggest that the legislators of the State appoint a special committee comprising members of the House and Senate, to investigate the legality of the action of Federal agents with regard to certain ultra vires acts which have had the effect of *amending* the Constitution without the *knowledge* or *consent* of the State or its People.

Such State committee must determine whether there is any change made under the United Nations Treaty and other acts which deprive the State or its People of rights and privileges, or would involve any change in the provisions of the Constitution of the United States or of the several States.

And I suggest that this Committee inquire into what measures may be taken by the State to enforce the Constitution of the United States within the borders of the State, and to punish any infraction thereof resulting from unlawful attempts to use authority by any agency of government not sanctioned by the Constitution of the United States.

Those who occupy executive, legislative, and judicial office at the Federal level of government have demonstrated that they are unwilling or unable to defend the freedom, the proper interest, and the security of the People of the United States and of the several States.

The Financial/Industrial cartel remains *invisible* and *unchallenged* in their continuing, long-range *conspiracy* to *overthrow* the Constitution and erect upon the *ruins* of the American civilization a *world government covenant* which they command.

The manipulators of monetary power, controlling the American economy through the Federal Reserve System, have created a deepening depression so as to coerce Americans into accepting life in their "industrialized society," a soviet America.

They use their *vast power* over information media and tax-free funds to inspire and support the promotion of nihilistic doctrine so that resulting *anarchy* will topple our institutions of freedom.

And, they secretly direct a policy of *permissiveness* in America thus creating a fractured, rudderless society which will serve their one world government scheme.

Effective resistance to tyranny by an invisible government must now, therefore, begin at the source of all governmental power — *the American citizen acting through his State legislature.*

To initiate corrective legislative action I respectfully invite your attention to two proposed State statutes included in the packet of background information provided to each person attending the conference:

Exhibit A. A bill to investigate the legality of the actions of Federal agents with regard to the United Nations and to provide means for the enforcement of the Constitution of the United States in relations thereto (deleted, see pages 10 and 42).

Exhibit B. A bill to provide for enforcement of the Constitution of the United States with regard to the so-called United Nations Organization (deleted, see page 22).

If it is your desire to explore this proposal further, I will be happy to answer questions to the best of my ability.

Thank you for your attention.

Exhibit A

(A bill to investigate the legality of the action of Federal agents with regard to the United Nations and to provide means for the enforcement of the Constitution of the United States in relation thereto)

Deleted, see pages 10 and 42.

Exhibit B

(A bill to provide for enforcement of the Constitution of the United States with regard to the so-called United Nations organization)

Deleted, see page 22.

Exhibit C

[From the *New York Times*, Dec. 13, 1969]

Soviet and West Said to Plan Think Tank' on World Issues

A report in the weekly magazine *Science* says that Soviet and Western representatives have been holding secret discussions on the establishment of a large-scale, internationally staffed "think tank" to study the problems of industrialized societies.

The report made public yesterday, said "concrete action to set up the proposed institution might possibly come early next year."

The two principals in the deliberations have been Dzherman M. Gvishiani, a first deputy chief of the Soviet State Committee for Science and Technology, and McGeorge Bundy, president of the Ford Foundation, the magazine said.

The report, under a Paris dateline, was from Dan S. Greenberg, the European correspondent of the magazine. *Science* is published by the American Association for the Advancement of Science.

The magazine said Mr. Gvishiani is the son-in-law of Premier Aleksei N. Kosygin, and is widely regarded as an influential "bridge-builder" to the West. Mr. Bundy became involved in the deliberations in 1966, after leaving his post as President Johnson's special assistant for national security affairs.

Mr. Bundy could not immediately be reached for comment on the report but a Ford Foundation spokesman confirmed that Mr. Bundy and Mr. Gvishiani had met in the Soviet Union during the summer.

The report said others who took part in the discussions included Sir Solly Zuckerman, chief scientific adviser to the British Government; Aureilio Peccei, an executive of Italy's Olivetti Corporation, and also West German and French representatives.

The article quoted a source as having said that the institution would be concerned with developing techniques that might be universally employed in dealing with such common problems as pollution, transportation, housing and education.

Exhibit D

[From the *Rocky Mountain News*, Denver, Colo., Oct. 19, 1969]

Bundy: United States Needs New Constitution

South Hadley, Mass.—McGeorge Bundy, president of the Ford Foundation, suggested Saturday the United States may need a *new* Constitution to meet the crisis in the nation.

Bundy made the suggestion in remarks prepared for delivery at the inauguration of David B. Truman as president of Mount Holyoke College, a private girls' school.

Bundy, who was a special adviser to President John F. Kennedy and Lyndon B. Johnson, said the conflict in the nation over the "American dilemma—the persistent gulf between our ideals of individual dignity and equal opportunity, and the centuries of behavior which has assumed and enforced both the denial of personal worth and the practice of intense discrimination"—is "sharper, more bitter, more violent and even perhaps more dangerous than anything we have known since the Civil War."

He said that to resolve this conflict requires minimum governmental reforms that would include a radical reconstruction of the executive and congressional branches of the federal government and of state and local governments.

"It is not unthinkable that this country may need a new constitution," Bundy said, adding that if he had to vote on that question today he would vote no "because I believe that we very likely could not do better, even now, than our forefathers."

Bundy said that governmental "transformation of the magnitude I am describing will come only when there is a new politics that learns how to engage an effective majority for a level of social and political change that has no precedent in our history.

"I find my own hope in the rising generation," Bundy said, quickly excluding what he called "the apocalyptic fringe which has renounced politics for force and substituted childish shock for dialogue."

Exhibit E

[From the Montrose (Calif.) *Ledger* Nov. 29, 1970]

U.N. Panel Doesn't Want to Hear Objections to World Government

(By Jo Hindman)

Tactics employed by a roving United Nations panel exposes the type of pressure being exerted to promote internationalism instead of Americanism in the U.S.

The President's Commission for the Observance of the 25th Anniversary of the United Nations conducted its first hearing at Atlanta, Ga. Branded by citizens as "farcical," that meeting was followed by others at St. Louis, Des Moines, Rochester, N.Y. with one to go at San Francisco next January, 1971.

The Portland (Ore.) daylong Nov. 18 hearing exposed the commission's methodology of bias. Press releases invited public officials, private citizens and representatives of organizations to testify, but obviously the purpose of the series is to collect feedback from the UN's own propaganda. The slanted findings then are to be used as a base in preparing for the President a report designed to prop the sagging UN.

An observer sent by the UN from San Francisco, the commission's next stop, stated enigmatically that she came to learn "how to avoid the errors" made at the Portland meet.

Welcomed affably by the UN panel at Portland were witnesses who proposed: that Communist China be granted UN membership, which means that anti-Communist Nationalist China would be expelled from the UN to make room for the Communists.* Also requested was repeal of the U.S.-protecting Connally Amendment; ratification of the Genocide Treaty; and mandatory UN membership, to be "not an op-

---

*   *Accomplished.*

tion but an obligation upon every nation," and so forth.

Panel members plucked eagerly at witness proposals that fell in line with the UN agenda at the Stockholm proceedings slated for 1972, such as coastal estuaries "which will be a prominent item of business," also United Nations control of the sea and seabeds.

Stacked Deck

The Portland audience was swelled by numerous rejected witnesses, notably individuals with local reputations for promoting USA Constitutional Government rather than observance of the UN's global rule. One who applied early when an abundance of hearing time was available observed that although she was shut out, due allegedly to lack of time, another witness, pro-UN, claimed to have been summoned by a phone call from the arrangements committee to testify.

Procedure required (1) witness to identify self with request to be heard, (2) written copies of remarks.

Two presentations in the morning session critical of the UN proceeded from witnesses who filed their written briefs after, not prior to oral delivery of their remarks. UN panel members made no attempt to conceal *suspicion* and *hostility* toward those viewpoints which had slipped through the screening set up by the local arrangements committee.

The National United Nations Research Assn.—perhaps given time due to the words "United Nations" in its title— proved astonishingly critical. NUNRA blasted UN's Katanga military war in the Congo, UN's economic war against Rhodesia: cited as dangerous the weighted vote conceded to the Soviets, and the Communist control of UN military operations. NUNRA urged the UN Commission to support a complete review and legislative correction of the United Nations organization.

Recommendations of the second witness (yours truly) who also pierced the UN screening net, called for abrogation of the United Nations Charter and eviction of the UN headquarters from the United States of America.

TESTIMONY before the State Affairs Committee, Wisconsin Legislature, March 30, 1971, in support of 1971 Assembly Joint Resolution A-34:

> *"Establishing a special joint committee to study the constitutionality of the federal government's relations with the United Nations.*

"The Most Secret Science," is a definitive critique on how America was lost, and how it may be restored to the descendants of the pioneers, the engineers, and the warriors who gave their blood and treasure to establish and defend it.

Introductory remarks by Hon. John R. Rarick, M.C., Congressional Record, April 19, 1971, E 3212.

CHAPTER FOUR

The Most Secret Science

Mr. RARICK. Mr. Speaker, "power to the people" is a slogan used not only by radical socialists in their plans to communize America but also by *President Nixon* in his New American Revolution.

In his state of the Union address on January 22, 1971, the President stated:

> So let us put the money where the needs are. And let us put the power to spend it where the people are.
>
> The further away government is from people, the stronger government becomes and the weaker people become. And a nation with a strong government and a weak people is an empty shell.

---

* *Exhibits at end of article*

I reject the idea that government in Washington, D.C. is inevitably more wise, more honest, and more efficient than government at the local or State level . . .

The idea that a bureaucratic elite in Washington knows best what is best for people everywhere and that you cannot trust local government is really a contention that you cannot trust people to govern themselves. This notion is completely foreign to the American experience. Local government is the government closest to the people and it is most responsive to the individual person; it is people's government in a far more intimate way than the government in Washington can ever be.

People came to America because they wanted to determine their own future rather than to live in a country where others determined their future for them.

What this change means is that once again in America we are placing our trust in people.

I have faith in people. I trust the judgment of people. Let us give the people of America a chance, a bigger voice in deciding for themselves those questions that so greatly affect their lives.

Whereas the rhetoric of the President is desirable and encouraging, the words unfortunately are made suspect by *actions*. By consistently asking for more and more tax funds for more and more Federal programs which add to the Federal payroll an increasing number of bureaucrats who increasingly control more and more facets of the daily lives of citizens; by grouping the States into regions with unelected Federal overseers, thereby removing power farther from the people; and by promoting such programs as the Atlantic Union which if effected would remove power still more distant from the people, the Chief Executive is, in effect, fostering power *over* the people rather than "power to the people."

"Power to the people" is a traditionally American concept which is what the Constitution of the United States is all about. When the necessary number of the Original Thirteen Colonies ratified the U.S. Constitution, they established a government in which political power was decentralized. By the constitutional contract they surrendered to the Federal Government only specified powers. Powers not delegated to the Federal Government were reserved to the States and to the people. And rather than to permit such a logical conclusion, the 10th amendment so specified the intent.

Under this concept of government, power was concentrated at the bottom—at the lowest denominator of government—the level closest to the people and most responsive to the desires and wishes of the individual person.

Locally controlled governments and systems of education, a basically religious people who in large measure recognized the Holy Bible as a guide to conduct, and a free enterprise economic system with a minimum of government interference produced the most prosperous and powerful Nation on earth. America abounded in Peace, opportunity, and true progress so long as America adhered to the Holy Bible and the Constitution.

The second decade of the present century saw the beginning of a trend in the direction of removing power from the hands of people at the State and local level and concentrating more and more power over the lives of people in the hands of unelected bureaucrats at the regional and Federal levels, in fact, even the *surrendering* of national powers and prerogatives to *international* bodies.

This trend was given impetus in 1913, with the enactment of the *Federal Reserve Act*, which took away people's control over their money; the 16th amendment to the Constitution calling for the graduated Federal income tax—a plank of the Marxist platform—and in 1919, with the establishment of the Council on Foreign Relations which has been instrumental in promoting world government.

The ratification of the U.N. Charter, a plan for world government, by the U.S. Senate in 1945, transferred "people power" still farther away from the people at the local level. The present emphasis being given to regional government and to an Atlantic Union, both of which have the President's approval, further erodes the Constitution and are obstacles to circumvent "people power."

Thanks to the seeds of knowledge planted during the past 2 or 3 decades by various constitutional groups and individuals, more and more Americans are becoming informed as to who the anti-Americans are and what they are doing to emasculate our Constitution and to destroy our country by trapping us into regional and world government. Action at the local and State levels by informed groups and individuals to salvage and restore the Constitution and, as a consequence, "people power" is a most encouraging sign.

One such organization is the Committee to Restore the Constitution, Inc. which recently presented its case to a Special Joint Committee, Wisconsin State Legislature.

I insert to follow my remarks the testimony entitled *"The Most Secret Science"* before a special joint committee of the Wisconsin State Legislature by Lt. Col. Archibald E. Roberts, A.U.S.—retired, director of the Committee to Restore the Constitution; resolution No. 1 of the Wisconsin Legislative and Research Committee, Inc; 1971 Assembly Joint Resolution 34 of Wisconsin Legislature; statement by the president on Restructuring of Government Service Systems; White House Press Conference of Daniel P. Monynihan, Philip S. Hughes and Ron Ziegler; an enlightening article on regional government by Mary M. Davison; a provocative article entitled "While We Slept, the States Were Being Abolished" by the eminent writer Don Bell; an article entitled "Roberts Wants People Power," and several informative articles by Jo Hindman, expert writer in the field of metro government.

The material follows:

The Most Secret Science
(Testimony by Archibald E. Roberts)

In consonance with the provisions of 1971 Assembly Joint Resolution No. 34, Wisconsin State Legislature, "Establishing a special committee to study the constitutionality of the federal government's relations with the United

Nations," I respectfully invite the members of this Special Legislative Committee to hear my testimony on proofs of a conspiracy to overthrow the Constitution of the United States and erect a socialist state governance over the American people.

Intelligence which I have previously submitted to every member of the Wisconsin State Legislature ("United Nations —Creature of the Invisible Government of Monetary Power," Congressional Record, December 14, 1971) provided evidence to indict an *ambitious* and *morally degenerate* group of *financiers* and *industrialists* who seek to erect an international, non-elected authority upon the *ruins* of the American civilization. This documented study explained how, via interlocking subversion, the *Council on Foreign Relations* (Harold Pratt House, 58 East 68th Street, New York City) captured principal agencies of the Federal Government and created the United Nations Organization as their private instrumentality for global conquest.

In documents subsequently submitted to Wisconsin Legislators, I illustrated the charge that so-called "Revenue Sharing" and "Regional Government" is the final technique for stripping away State sovereignty and eliminating elective office at State and national levels.

During the next few minutes I will show how this same group of international bankers and industrialists, by guile and deceit, gained *control* over the money and credit resources of the United States and thus *captured* the power centers of the American civilization.

First, however, I offer my credentials.

My ancestors, like yours, were mostly farmers, preachers, soldiers and laborers.

They arrived on the North American continent long before there was a United States of America and challenged the wilderness with a confidence borne of an abiding faith in God. My people fought in the Revolutionary War and have served this country in every succeeding conflict to the present day.

Our forebears, yours and mine, raised up mighty cities and established a civilization of free men—the envy of all others. The blood and sweat of our clans fertilized the soil of America. Their achievements constitute our heritage; their culture a legacy for our children and our children's children.

Or so it seemed a few short years ago.

It is now evident that a subtle and perilous change has occured in our America. Within the past two or three generations the civilization of our forefathers has come under sophisticated assault. The structures of freedom erected at such great cost in blood, sweat and treasure, are crumbling. Our God is *blasphemed,* our lineage *reviled*, and our Constitution *dismantled.*

Our destiny has turned to dust.

The descendants of the pioneers, the warriors, and the engineers of this unique order are now economic serfs in an industrialized society ruled by a self-anointed elite. We are *manipulated* by massive propaganda, *betrayed* in international military adventures and *exploited* by a rapacious, insatiable bureaucracy.

The founders of this nation, in the Declaration of Independence, established a   course of action to which every responsible citizen must adhere when government becomes master instead of servant.

"Governments are instituted among Men, deriving their just powers from the consent of the governed . . . whenever any form of Government becomes destructive of (Life, Liberty, and the pursuit of Happiness) it is the right of the People to alter or abolish it. . ."

If we are to survive as a race and as a nation, the People must regain control over the centers of power in America.

Let us begin by reviewing the manner in which they were lost.

The most secret knowledge, a science which outdates history, is the science of control over people, governments and civilizations. The foundation of this ultimate discipline is the *control of wealth.*

Through the control of wealth comes the control of public information and the necessities of life.

Through the control of news media comes *thought control.*

Through the control of basic necessities comes *direct physical control of people.*

The rule is to finance the education of members of the money aristocracy in the professions, business, political science, management, research, public speaking, writing and education. By placing trusted members, well trained and financed, in positions of influence in their communities, and in positions of leadership in nearly all organizations including the religious order and in opposing associations, it is possible to direct local, regional and national policy toward long-range objectives.

The fate reserved for less fortunate citizens, those not born of the money aristocracy, was succinctly stated by Mr. John D. Rockefeller, Sr. In a policy statement published by his General Education Board, forerunner to today's ill-famed Rockefeller Foundation, John Rockefeller heralded the plan to mold an American *peasantry* through control of educational process.

"In our dreams," said Rockefeller, "we have limitless resources and the people yield themselves with perfect docility to our molding hands. The present educational conventions fade from our minds," Rockefeller predicted, "and, unhampered by tradition, we work our own good will upon a grateful and responsive rural folk. . ." (Occasional Letter No. 1, General Education Board, 1904).

A significant portion of the American public is yet to become aware of "The Invisible Government of Monetary Power" although this knowledge is common in Europe. Americans still believe that they are working toward a better way of life. Surreptitiously, however, social customs and forms of administration in the United States are being carefully and gradually modified. The change from one type of culture to another is thus accomplished without arousing serious public challenge.

The stark truth is that America is now passing from a constitutional republic into a totalitarian, world wide government. World dominion is the ages-old dream of the *mattoids* who have mastered the science of control over people.

Their success in the United States is directly related to two central issues:

One — transfer of money control from the people into the hands of an international banking combine, and

Two — creation of a complex and confusing judicial system designed to frustrate justice.

The remainder of this presentation will be concerned with the first principle—money, and those who control it.

In 1913 the money aristocracy effected a major advance toward their long-range goal of world dominion. They duped the United States Congress into adopting the *Federal Reserve Act.* This coup resulted in the transfer of the power to coin and regulate U.S. money from the Congress to their private banking combine, the Federal Reserve System.

Since passage of the Federal Reserve Act, the American destiny and the personal life of every citizen has been controlled by a financial elite whose sick-brained policies have spawned depression, war and revolution.

The existence of an "Invisible Government of Monetary Power" was dramatically confirmed in 1933 by the late Louis T. McFadden, Chairman, Banking and Currency Committee, United States Congress, who said:

"Every effort has been made by the Fed to conceal its powers but the truth is—the Fed has *usurped* the government. It controls *everything* here (in Congress) and it controls *all* our foreign relations. It makes and breaks governments at will."

Representative John R. Rarick, denouncing President Nixon's plan for deficit spending ("Deficit Financing," Congressional Record, February 1, 1971) also revealed the dominant position held by the Federal Reserve System over the American economy.

"He" (President Nixon), said Mr. Rarick, "has asked the independent Federal Reserve System to come up with enough new money to reach a projected increase in the GNP by $88 billion in order to achieve his 'objective of prosperity without inflation.' "

"The Federal Reserve," Congressman Rarick pointed out, "is not an agency of Government. It is a private banking monopoly."

"As I have said many times before," Rarick declared, "the policies of the monarch are always those of his creditors."

Gentlemen, the safety of the State and the peace and security of Wisconsin citizens now urgently require an investigation of the vast powers claimed by the Federal Reserve System.

The first consideration should be a public examination of the authority which the Federal Reserve System says established its legal status as a Government agency. Such authority is quoted in a statement submitted to Congressman Wright Patman, House Banking and Currency Committee, by the Board of Governors, Federal Reserve System and Federal Reserve Banks, dated April 14, 1952.

"The 12 Federal Reserve Banks," said the Federal Reserve Board, "are corporations set up by Federal law to operate for public purposes under Government supervision."

The Board further advised Mr. Patman that, "The Board of Governors was created by Congress and is a part of the Government of the United States. "Its members," they said assuringly, "are appointed by the President, with the advice and consent of the Senate, and it (the Fed) has been held by the Attorney General to be a Government establishment (30 Op. Atty. Gen., 308, 1914)."

Retorting to these impressive claims to "legality" and "public service" Congressman Patman stated:

"There is no free market that can cope with a national

debt of $272 billion (1952), with $85 billion of it to be refunded within one year. "Free market," he said, "means private manipulation of (private) credit."

Private manipulation of PUBLIC credit is, of course, the purpose and objective of the Federal Reserve System. This international banking cartel, as will be shown, manages the credit of the United States for the profit and advantage of its foreign and domestic members. In so doing the Federal Reserve *exploits the entire producing strata of the American society for the gain of a select, non-producing few.*

"The Federal Reserve Board, to my mind," continued Mr. Patman, "is guilty of the grossest kind of misconduct in failing to support the Government of the United States at a time of its greatest economic peril in Government securities."

Congressman Patman then revealed the contradiction in the spurious Federal Reserve claim of "Government agency" status and explained how the Fed generates ILLEGITIMATE profits for its members.

"The Open Market Committee of the Federal Reserve System," he said, "is composed of the 7 members of the Board of Governors and 5 members who are presidents of the Federal Reserve banks and who are selected by private commercial banking interests. The Open Market Committee has the power to obtain, and does obtain, the printed money of the United States—Federal Reserve Notes—(free) from the Bureau of Engraving and Printing, and exchanges these printed notes, which of course are not interest bearing, for United States Government obligations that are interest bearing. After making the exchange," Patman explained, "the interest bearing obligations are retained by the 12 Federal Reserve banks and the interest collected annually on these Government obligations goes into the funds of the 12 Federal Reserve Banks."

Exploding the myth that the Federal Reserve System is an instrumentality of the Federal Government, Mr. Patman declared:

"These funds (interest from Government obligations) are expended by the (Federal Reserve) system without an adequate accounting to the Congress. In fact there has never been an independent audit of either the 12 banks or the Federal Reserve Board that has been filed with the Congress where a Member (of Congress) would have an opportunity to inspect it. "The General Accounting Office," he stated, "does not have jurisdiction over the Federal Reserve. For 40 years (1952) the system, while freely using the money (credit) of the Government, has not made a proper accounting."

Governor W.P.G. Harding of the Federal Reserve Board, in testimony before Congress in 1921, admitted that the Fed is a private banking monopoly.

"The Federal Reserve Bank is an institution owned by the stockholding member banks," he said. "The Government has not a dollar's worth of stock in it."

The Government does, however, give the Federal Reserve System free use of its billions of dollars of credit. This gives the Federal Reserve the characteristic of a central bank; the power to issue currency on the Government's credit.

Americans do not have Federal Government notes or gold certificates as currency. We have Federal Reserve Bank notes, fiat money issued by private banks. Every dollar the Federal Reserve System prints is a dollar in their pocket.

The compatible meshing of the Federal Reserve System with a network of international banking was explained by Mr. W. Randolph Burgess of the New York Federal Reserve Bank in an address before the Academy of Political Science in 1930.

"In its major principles of operation, the Federal Reserve System is no different," he told Congress, "from other banks of issue, such as the Bank of England, the Bank of France, or the Reichsbank."

It is obvious that when control of money is transferred from the People to private banking centers, as is the case in Europe and America, the sovereignty of the People is surrendered, too. Control of wealth confers upon those who control it final decision in the domestic and international affairs of nations. When the financial aristocracy usurp the "coin of the realm," the People are disfranchised and real political authority passes into the hands of an "Invisible Government of Monetary Power."

Our founding fathers knew this principle very well.

"I believe that banking institutions are more dangerous to our liberties than standing armies," said Thomas Jefferson. "Already they have raised up a money aristocracy that has set the government at defiance. The issuing power (of money)," he said, "should be taken from the banks and restored to the people to whom it properly belongs."

Though but dimly perceived today the Declaration of Independence was actually a proclamation that the colonists would not serve a money aristocracy. The American Revolution was a struggle to wrest control of wealth from the Bank of England and to restore the centers of power to the People where it "properly belongs."

The Constitution is specific about the authority of the People, through their elected officials, to control the money, and thus, the affairs of their Government.

"The Congress shall have the power . . . To coin money (and) regulate the value thereof. . ." (Article, 5, Section 8, United States Constitution).

Nowhere does the Constitution authorize or permit the transfer of this vast power to a money aristocracy.

Exposure of the hidden forces which have cheated the people of Wisconsin of their birthright must be of gravest concern to members of this State Legislature, each of whom has sworn to "defend and preserve this Constitution." I propose that we begin the task of identifying the men behind the Federal Reserve conspiracy.

A clue to the origin of the Federal Reserve Act was given by Colonel Ely Garrison, friend and financial adviser to President Theodore Roosevelt and President Woodrow Wilson. In his autobiographical book, *"Roosevelt, Wilson and the Federal Reserve Act,"* Garrison wrote:

"Mr. Paul Warburg is the man who got the Federal Reserve Act together after the Aldrich Plan aroused such nation-wide resentment and opposition. The mastermind of both plans," declared Garrison, "was Alfred Rothschild of London."

In a preface written for a group of Warburg's essays calling for a central bank, Professor E.R.A. Seligman, of the international banking family, and head of the Department of Economics, Columbia University, said:

"The Federal Reserve Act is the work of Mr. Warburg more than any other man in the country."

Paul Moritz Warburg, whom President Wilson subsequently appointed first Chairman of the Federal Reserve Board of Governors, was an immigrant from Germany. His primary allegiance was to his family banking house of M.M. Warburg Company of Hamburg and Amsterdam.

During World War I the M.M. Warburg Company financed Germany's war against the Allied forces. Paul's brother, Max, headed the German Secret Service.

During the war years, Paul Warburg's firm of Kuhn, Loeb Company had five representatives in the United States Treasury Department in charge of Liberty Loans, thus financing America's war effort against the Kaiser.

It is unlikely that considerations of humanitarianism or patriotism inspired such interlocking, international financing of the agony of World War I.

Mr. Eustace Mullins in "The Federal Reserve Conspiracy," noted that, "Woodrow Wilson and (Senator) Carter Glass are given full credit for the (Federal Reserve) act by contemporary historians, but of all the politicians concerned, Wilson had the least to do with the fight over the Act in Congress.

Mr. George Creel, veteran Washington correspondent, wrote in *Harper's Weekly* of June 25, 1915:

"As far as the Democratic Party was concerned, Woodrow Wilson was without influence, save for the patronage he possessed. It was (William Jennings) Bryan who shaped Congress into line on . . . the currency bill. Mr. Bryan later wrote, "That is the one thing in my public career that I regret — my work to secure the enactment of the Federal Reserve Law."

Mullins summed up the effect of this fantastic law in the following words:

"The money and credit resources of the United States were now in the complete control of the banker's alliance between J.P. Morgan's First National Bank group, and Kuhn, Loeb's National City Bank, whose principle loyalties were to the international banking interests then quartered in London, and which moved to New York during the First World War."

Congressman Charles A. Lindbergh of Minnesota, father of the famous flyer, made a prophetic statement on the swindle which had been foisted on the American people. Speaking on the floor of the House on December 23, 1913, the day the Federal Reserve Act became law, Mr. Lindbergh said:

"This Act establishes the most gigantic trust on earth. When the President (Wilson) signs this bill the invisible government of the Monetary Power will be legalized . . . the worst legislative crime of the ages is perpetrated by this banking and currency bill."

The crimes alleged by Congressman Lindbergh were subsequently defined by the Honorable Louis T. McFadden.

In a statement of particulars, here offered in abridged form, Chairman McFadden, on May 23, 1933, brought impeachment charges against members of the Federal Reserve Board and the heads of the 12 member banks (Congressional Record, bound volume, pp. 4055-4058).

"Whereas I charge them jointly and severally with having brought about a repudiation of the national currency of the United States in order that the gold value of said currency might be given to private interests . . . .

"I charge them . . . with having arbitrarily and unlawfully taken over $80,000,000,000.00 (eighty billion dollars) from tne United States Government in the year 1928 . . . .

"I charge them . . . with having arbitrarily and unlawfully raised and lowered the rates on money . . . increased and diminished the volume of currency in circulation for the benefit of private interests . . . .

"I charge them . . . with having brought about the decline in prices on the New York Stock Exchange . . . .

"I charge them . . . with having conspired to concentrate United States Government securities . . . and thus . . . having conspired to transfer to foreigners and international money lenders title to and control of the financial resources of the United States . . . .

"I charge them . . . with having published false and misleading propaganda intended to deceive the American people and to cause the United States to lose its independence . . . .

"I charge them . . . ," Congressman McFadden concluded, "with the crime of having treasonably conspired and acted against the peace and security of the United States, and with having treasonably conspired to destroy the constitutional government of the United States."

Congressman McFadden's shocking indictment of the members of the Federal Reserve System, and those who maneuvered its adoption by the Congress, was moved to the Committee on the Judiciary. It still awaits reporting to the House floor and action to impeach both former and present members of the Board of Governors and Federal Reserve Banks for criminal conspiracy against the People of the United States.

The final decision as to whether or not an "invisible Government of Monetary Power" will continue to control the American destiny and the lives and fortunes of her People must ultimately be made by the citizens of this nation.

To begin the task of exposing and neutralizing the men and the system which seeks to overthrow constitutional government and impose a world governance over our domestic and foreign affairs, I am empowered to present to the law-makers of the State of Wisconsin the following resolution adopted by the Wisconsin Legislative and Research Committee, and subscribed to by constituents who support the Wisconsin campaign to restore the Constitution:

"A resolution declaring that the people of this State should debate the question of whether or not any agency or instrumentality of government which derives its powers from the consent of the governed can voluntarily, by treaty or otherwise, alienate the political sovereignty of a free people."

The resolution calls for an investigation by the Wisconsin State Legislature of the actions of Federal agents who have purported to negotiate with foreign governments and with private interests to transfer vast powers of government, and to surrender rights and liberties assured to the People under the Constitution of the United States, to foreigners and to international money lenders in violation of the prohibitions of the Constitution.

The resolution further requests that the Wisconsin State Legislature promulgate and enact appropriate statutes which will provide for the enforcement of the Constitution of the United States within the boundaries of the State of Wisconsin, to include criminal sanctions for violators, with regard to the United Nations Charter, the Federal Reserve Act, and other ultra vires acts by agents of the Federal Government who have, by these ultra vires acts, attempted to amend the Constitution of the United States in a manner not sanctioned by Article V.

We respectfully demand, if it be God's will, that the elected representatives of the People of Wisconsin act at once to restore America's legacy of Freedom to the descendants of the pioneers, the warriors, and the engineers who gave their blood, sweat and treasure to establish and defend it.

Thank you for your courtesy and attention.

Exhibit A

Resolution No. 1.
Wisconsin Legislative and
Research Committee, Inc.

*(A resolution declaring that the people of this State should debate
the question of whether or not any agency or instrumentality of
government which derives its powers from the consent of the governed
can voluntarily, by treaty or otherwise, alienate the political sovereignty of a free people.)*

Whereas, Federal Agencies, by treaty and other acts,
allege the transfer of vast powers of government from the
Congress of the United States to international agencies in
violation of the prohibitions of the Constitution and without
the knowledge or consent of the State of the People, and

Whereas, a compliant Congress permits the commitment
of America's soldier sons to international military adventures
"with neither promise nor hope of Victory;" and

Whereas, the actions of Federal agents exhibit a contempt
for the limited delegated powers enumerated in the United
States Constitution, which is very explicit about the authority for making war and keeping peace; and

Whereas, American citizens, acting through their State
Legislature, are morally and legally obligated to do what ever
may be necessary to insure that all provisions of the Constitution of the United States shall be respected and enforced,
be it therefore

Resolved that the Wisconsin Legislative and Research
Committee does hereby call for an investigation of the
actions of Federal agents with regard to United Nations
agreements and other ultra vires acts and demands *enforcement* of the Constitution of the United States in relation
thereto.

To implement these objectives, the Wisconsin Legislative and Research Committee submits to the Legislators of the sovereign State of Wisconsin, in accord with the oath to which these officeholders subscribed upon accepting position of public trust ("to support this Constitution") and in consonance with the obligations of the parties to the Constitutional compact ("to insure that all provisions of the Constitution are respected and enforced within the boundaries of the State"), the following proposals and demands:

1.   That the Wisconsin State Legislature investigate the actions of certain Federal agents who have purported to negotiate with foreign governments to coerce the State into agreements which would surrender to foreign governments the rights and liberties assured to the People under the Constitution of the United States, and

Which would surrender the powers of government which this Constitution guarantees to preserve to our People, and

Which would transfer citizens of the State of Wisconsin now serving in the United States military establishment to a United Nations army in the name of "international peace and security."

2.   That the Wisconsin State Legislature promulgate and enact appropriate statutes which will provide for enforcement of the Constitution of the United States with regard to the United Nations Charter and other ultra vires acts within the boundaries of the State of Wisconsin.

3.   That such deliberations, decisions and statutory enactments by the Wisconsin State Legislature shall be disseminated in compliance with Section I, Article IV, and shall respect the provisions of Section 2 and Section 4, Article IV, of the United States Constitution.

Adopted this 25th day of July, 1970, by the Wisconsin Legislative and Research Committee, Inc., Post Office Box 45, Brookfield, Wisconsin 53005.

Exhibit B

1971 Assembly Joint Resolution 34
of the State of Wisconsin

(Deleted, see pages 10 and 42).

Exhibit C

Statement by the President on Restructuring of Government Service Systems

The Reorganization Act which the Congress has passed and which I am signing today gives the President important tools in his effort to make the machinery of government work more effectively. As a part of that same effort, I am announcing today certain structural changes which I am making in the systems through which the government provides important social and economic services.

It was possible for me to take these particular actions without the authority extended under the Reorganization Act. I announce them at this time, however, because they provide specific illustrations of ways in which we can make significant improvement in the quality of government by making it operate more efficiently.

This restructuring expresses my concern that we make much greater progress in our struggle against social problems. The best way to facilitate such progress, I believe, is not by adding massively to the burdens which government already bears but rather by finding better ways to perform the work of the government.

That work is not finished when a law is passed, nor is it accomplished when an agency in Washington is assigned to administer new legislation. These are only preliminary steps; in the end the real work is done by the men who implement the law in the field.

The performance of the men in the field, however, is directly linked to the administrative structures and procedures within which they work. It is here that the government's effectiveness too often is undermined. The organization of federal services has often grown up piecemeal—

creating gaps in some areas, duplications in others, and general inefficiencies across the country. Each agency for example, has its own set of regional offices and regional boundaries; if a director of one operation is to meet with his counterpart in another branch of the government, he often must make an airplane trip to see him. Or consider two federal officials who work together on poverty problems in the same neighborhood, but who work for different Departments and, therefore, find themselves in two different administrative regions, reporting to headquarters in two widely separated cities.

Coordination cannot flouish under conditions such as that. Yet without real coordination, intelligent and efficient government is impossible; money and time are wasted and important goals are compromised.

This is why I said in the campaign last fall that "the need is not to dismantle government but to modernize it." The systematic reforms I announce today are designed to help in that modernization process. I would discuss those reforms under three headings: rationalization, coordination and decentralization. It should be recognized, of course, that the three elements are interdependent. Without one the others would be meaningless.

I. The first concern is to rationalize the way our service delivery systems are organized. I have therefore issued a directive which streamlines the field operations of five agencies by establishing—for the first time—common *regional* boundaries and regional office locations. This instruction affects the Department of Labor, the Department of Health, Education and Welfare, the Department of Housing and Urban Development, the Office of Economic Opportunity, and the Small Business Administration. The activities of these agencies — particularly in serving disadvantaged areas of our society — are closely related. Uniform boundaries and regional office locations will help assure that they are also closely coordinated.

The eight new regions and the locations of the new regional centers are as follows:

Region I (Boston) — Connecticut, Maine, Massachusetts, New Hampshire, Rhode Island, and Vermont.

Region II (New York City) — New York, New Jersey, Puerto Rico, and the Virgin Islands.

Region III (Philadelphia) — Delaware, District of Columbia, Kentucky, Maryland, North Carolina, Pennsylvania, Virginia, and West Virginia.

Region IV (Atlanta) — Alabama, Florida, Georgia, Mississippi, South Carolina, and Tennessee.

Region V (Chicago) — Illinois, Indiana, Minnesota, Michigan, Ohio, and Wisconsin.

Region VI (Dallas-Fort Worth) — Arkansas, Louisiana, New Mexico, Oklahoma, and Texas.

Region VII (Denver) — Colorado, Idaho, Iowa, Kansas, Missouri, Montana, Nebraska, North Dakota, South Dakota, Utah, and Wyoming.

Region VIII (San Francisco) — Alaska, Arizona, California, Guam, Hawaii, Nevada, Oregon, and Washington.

I am asking all other federal agencies to take note of these instructions, and I am requesting that any changes in their field organization structures be made consistent with our ultimate goal: uniform boundaries and field office locations for all social or economic programs requiring interagency or intergovernmental coordination.

My directive also asks that the five Departments and agencies involved provide high-level representation in cities where regional offices do not exist. Such physical relocations as are required will be made over the next eighteen months, with special efforts to minimize disruptions to the programs, the employees, and the communities involved.

II. The second step in this reform process emphasizes coordination. It calls for an expansion of the regional council concept from the four cities where it presently operates (Chicago, New York, Atlanta, and San Francisco) to all eight of the new regional centers. The regional council is a coordinating body on which each of the involved agencies is represented. It offers an excellent means through which the various arms of the federal government can work closely together in defining problems, devising strategies to meet them, eliminating friction and duplications, and evaluating results. Such councils can make it possible for the Federal government to speak consistently and with a single voice in its dealings with states and localities, with private organizations, and with the public.

III. The third phase of this systematic restructuring of domestic programs focuses on decentralization. I am asking the Director of the Bureau of the Budget to join with the heads of nine departments and agencies in a review of existing relationships between centralized authorities and their field operations. Participating in the review will be the Departments of Agriculture; Commerce; Health, Education, and Welfare; Housing and Urban Development; Labor; Transportation; Justice; the Office of Economic Opportunity; and the Small Business Administration.

This review is designed to produce specific recommendations as to how each agency: (1) can eliminate unnecessary steps in the delegation process; (2) can develop organizational forms and administrative practices which will mesh more closely with those of all other Departments; and (3) can give more day-by-day authority to those who are at lower levels in the administrative hierarchy. Decentralized decision-making will make for better and, quicker decisions — it will also increase cooperation and coordination between the Federal government on the one hand and the states and localities on the other. Those Federal employees who deal every day with state and local officials will be given greater decision-making responsibility.

Again, this action is a concrete manifestation of a concern I expressed during the campaign: "Business learned long ago that decentralization was a means to better performance. It's time government learned the same lesson."

Some of the reforms which I am announcing today have been urged for many years — but again and again they have been thwarted. This inertia must be overcome. Old procedures that are inefficient, however comfortable and familiar they may seem, must be exchanged for new systems which do the job as it must be done.

The particular reforms I have discussed here are part of a broad and continuing process of restructuring the basic service systems of government. The reorganization of the Manpower Administration in the Dapartment of Labor — announced on March 13 — is another example of this process. So are the reforms which are being made in the postal system and in the Office of Economic Opportunity.

I have established both the Urban Affairs Council and the Office of Intergovernmental Relations in part so that the government could be better advised on additional improvements in service systems. Further systematic restructuring is on the way. Each reform, I believe, will have a major impact on the quality of American government — an impact which will benefit all of our citizens — in all parts of our country — well beyond the lifetime of this Administration.

The Federal government has been assigned many new responsibilities in the last several decades—many of which it carries and many of which it fumbles. Many of the disappointments and frustrations of the last several years can be blamed on the fact that administrative performance has not kept pace with legislative promise.

This situation must be changed. The actions I announce today are important steps toward achieving such changes. By rationalizing, coordinating, and decentralizing the systems through which government provides important social and economic services, we can begin at last to realize the hopes and dreams of those who created them.

(The White House, March 27, 1969)

Exhibit D

Press Conference of Daniel P. Moynihan, Assistant to the President for Urban Affairs; Philip S. Huges, Deputy Director, Bureau of the Budget and Ron Ziegler, Press Secretary to the President

Mr. Ziegler. You have the statement by the President on restructuring of Government service systems. It is relatively self-explanatory. Dr. Moynihan and Sam Hughes are here to discuss this with you and answer any questions you may have. Their comments are on the record, contrary to yesterday when it was a background basis.

Is Frank Porter here? (Laughter.)

Dr. Moynihan.

Dr. Moynihan. One can say anything one thinks on the record on something about the public administration because it never gets printed anyway. If we had a war to announce, by golly, everyone would be here.

This is about the first major reorganization which the President has put into effect. I think it is a matter of some interest, as Sam Hughes, our distinguished Deputy Director of the Budget will attest, that it has been something Presidents have been trying to put into effect for almost 20 years now.

This is the first time in the history of the American Republic that the regional boundaries of the major domestic programs will be co-terminus.

You see how quickly you lose audiences with things like that? (Laughter.)

The pattern has built up that each department, when departments have been established and agencies have been

established, their regional boundaries have responded to the
sort of peculiarities of subjects or the Congressional arrangements that led to their enactment or just randomness. The
result has been that there has been wide variation in the
regional headquarters.

There are two subjects, if I could point this out. One is
what is the city which has the regional headquarters, and
secondly, which are the States that make up the region. Both
the States have varied and the regional headquarters have
varied. This, as we have gradually found in domestic affairs as
more and more we have had to work one program in relation
to another or we have developed programs such as Model
Cities, which, by definition and by statute presumed the
working between different departments on a common subject, that the regional arrangements simply impeded us very
seriously.

It made it possible to stand in the Fish Room, now in the
Roosevelt Room, and announce enormous events and nothing happened, because there was no structure out there to
make it happen, because if there is a rule in political science,
it is that Government follows its structure.

What the President has done in the face of not a little bit
of presumed difficulty, is to draw common boundaries to
establish common regional headquarter cities for this beginning group of domestic departments with the expectation
that they will be expanded in the future.

It is this, I think, that begins to make not just the
question of coordination of Federal programs a serious issue
and a possible result, but also begins to give some structure to
the subject of decentralization. It can't be decentralized
government unless you have a system of arrangements in the
field to which, with authority, with discretion and responsibility, it can be given.

I think we are creating such a structure. It will be a long
time, perhaps, in becoming a reality, but it is an absolutely
indispensable first move. As I say to you, for 20 years we
have sought this arrangement and now, at length, we have it.

I suppose my final comment would be that there is still quite a bit of detailed working out of the forms in which authority is delegated from different agencies to their regional headquarters. As between different departments, there are quite different levels of regional responsibilities, initiative and so forth, and bringing some responsibility into that is the work of years to come — the year to come in any event.

Q. Can you really put these together in a field where you do have a central office or are we going to have a half dozen or dozen offices to go to? Can one person speak with authority in the regional authority?

Dr. Moynihan. Sam, do you want to join me here at the lectern?

That is the work of the years to come. We have already begun in four cities a Regional Council, begun last August; just getting some sense in itself, not more than announced, really. But the question of how much of a coherent decision-making apparatus we will be able to develop at regional levels remains to be seen.

It becomes a question of how much you want, but it is now possible to find that out, and up until now it has simply been a hypothetical question for professors.

Q. Will these offices all be in one office building?

Dr. Moynihan. Some of these are pretty large offices. There is a Federal Office Building in each of these cities. In some cases they will all be in the same structure and in other cases they will not. Some of these are big places.

If I could just say, in the whole question of public administration, making the Government work, in delivering public services, the biggest single weakness of the American National Government has been its field structure.

Mr. Hughes. I agree.

Dr. Moynihan. And not to attend to that is just not to be serious about this subject. It is perhaps the least exciting subject in Government, and that has been the source of the problem, just not in being able to muster the attention of persons to its absolutely essential nature.

For that reason it was almost the first issue we took up in the Urban Affairs Council out of the experience that if you didn't take it up early and get it done fast, other more glamourous issues would drive it into the next Administration.

Q. Will you save money, too, or is this just for efficiency?

Mr. Hughes. I would regard it as in the interest of efficiency. In your terms it is a management action. It could produce savings. It is not designed to do that. Rather, it is designed to make it easier to manage Federal programs out in the field where services must be delivered, and also to make it easier for the States and cities to deal with the Federal agencies.

Think of the Governor of Colorado, for instance, or the Mayor of Denver, who must deal with Federal regional offices in Denver, San Francisco, Fort Worth-Dallas, or Kansas City. He has an almost impossible kind of a problem, in a physical sense, to span. He is left with correspondence and telephone calls and so on.

So the co-location is the starting point for a whole range of actions which, as Pat said, we hope to evolve over the coming months.

Q. How many Congressmen are losing offices in their cities and how mad are they about it?

Mr. Hughes. On the latter point, I am not really an authority. My impression is that the decibels, at least at this point, are not impossibly high. Part of the difficulty over the years, the major part of the difficulty has been, as Pat said, on the one hand this is not a glamorous kind of action, and on the other hand it has been a kind of controversial action and has taken courage and determination on the part of the agency heads, the Urban Affairs Council and the President to bring it off.

If you are interested, we have a map of the revised organizational structure, and a listing of the State movements that are involved, agency by agency. The picture gets fairly complicated because each agency, and in some instances even bureaus within agencies, have a different field structure, so you have to look at it in fairly fine detail.

Dr. Moynihan. Could I add one point? In those cities which have been regional headquarters for departments and will cease to be, we are leaving behind a high-level department representative responding to the fact that those are important cities and are intended to be sub-regions at the very least.

There will be very little actual movement of people here as compared to that which would take place in the normal course of events.

Q. What do you estimate, about 1,800 people?

Mr. Hughes. Probably less than that net, and we anticipate that the moves would take place, to the extent they are necessary, over a year or a year and a half, so that the personal impact could be minimized.

Dr. Moynihan. These are high-level and particularly high-level people in America tend to move around anyway.

Q. Do you mean you are not closing offices?

Mr. Hughes. I think the situation is this: With eight regions obviously there are major concentrations of population that would not have a regional office in them. On the other hand, to have as many regions as would be implicit in that kind of arrangement creates an impossible kind of administrative structure.

So as we see it the ideal would be to have cities not included as regional headquarters, like Kansas City, St. Louis, Detroit, Pittsburgh, perhaps, as focuses within a particular region, focuses of Federal personnel also, and having significant Federal representation and some authority in their own right.

Q. Can either of you name the cities that are losing regional headquarters?

Dr. Moynihan. There are five times eight.

Mr. Hughes. We can list cities. There are lots of moves back and forth. Because of the change in structure certain agencies move one way and other agencies move another. We can, if you would like, take an agency at a time after this session, if you want to, and discuss the moves individually. We know this but — —

Q. Are there 40 different regional offices now?

Dr. Moynihan. You can have eight regions and five agencies. You don't have 40, but you have a maximum of 40. The areas from which people are moving in and out are much simpler.

Mr. Hughes. I can run through the list. Charlottesville will be affected; Washington, D.C., Austin, Kansas City has been discussed; Birmingham, Baltimore, Nashville. There are a number of moves back and forth involving New York City itself, depending on whether the particular agency had headquarters there or not. New Orleans, Cleveland, Seattle—

Mr. Moynihan. I will give you an example of the kind of thing involved. New York City is no longer a regional headquarters for HUD, but it becomes a regional headquarters for the other agencies. People who were in New York City in a HUD arrangement who will move to New England and HUD—

Mr. Hughes. HUD stays.

Dr. Moynihan. But the New England people go out, HUD's regional headquarters remain in New York, but there will be a transfer of persons who have been in New York working on New England which now goes to Boston. It sounds complex, but it is a simple reorganization.

Q. Will Buffalo, New York be affected by any of these moves?

Mr. Hughes. No so far as I know.

Q. The President said the things you are doing today are not involved in the signing of the Reorganization Act. What are you planning to do with the Reorganization Act to streamline the Government, or what are the plans of using the powers of the act the President has just signed?

Dr. Moynihan. Don't you think we have enough trouble for one day? (Laughter.)

Q. You don't have that in the works?

Dr. Moynihan. Yes. Remember that the reorganization powers have existed for 20 years, and are sort of a standing concomitant of the Presidency and in a normally effective Government reorganization considerations are always going on. It is a more intensive point than in the earlier Administration and President Nixon has spoken with special interest on this. I think you can look forward to proposals, but we have nothing right now.

Mr. Hughes. Lots of things are being looked at.

Q. You pointed out that for 20 years people have been interested in this. Can you identify some of the obstacles that have come up over the years?

Dr. Moynihan. I think Sam put it best. This is the kind of subject that people who are close to Government are very passionate about and people out of Government don't even know about. It always happens. To be associated with the movement of some resources from one part of the Congressional map to another. So there have always been people who by definition will have to be against it.

This combination of a rather low level of local opposition has meant by and large that no President has ever been willing to bite the bullet. Now we have done so.

Mind you, once it takes place, then the new arrangements become sacred and absolutely imbedded in the Constitutional division of the Republic.

Mr. Hughes. I think a factor, also, is the growing obviousness of the need to do this sort of thing, given the structures that the President has set up, the Urban Affairs Council, the interrelationship that this group of agencies and others who are involved in urban problems.

Q. What progress is being made in those cities picked for Regional Councils?

Mr. Hughes. The Regional Councils that have been established are four in number. They were established at the only four cities where the four agencies involved happen to have co-located regional offices.

Interestingly enough, none of those regions coincide. For instance, the New York regional office, those four agencies have only one State in common, New York State. So that they have been experimental in nature thus far. They have proved, in our judgment and I believe in the judgment of the people who have participated in the Councils, to be a very useful and productive experiment in working together in a fashion that is increasingly necessary, but still is somewhat novel in Federal activities, and this particular geographic action that we are talking about here is designed to encourage that kind of cooperation.

The Federal Government has been organized categorically over the years, and agency programs, I think, have tended to construct walls around themselves. We need, by these kinds of measures, to attempt to pierce these walls and put doors in them, and so on, and by the process of co-location and the advantages that are obvious in these four cities, have people being able to meet and discuss common problems, whether it is the Model Cities program or any other of mutual interest.

Those advantages, I think, have appeared in these four locations, and we do plan, hopefully, if the experiment succeeds, to extend it in other areas and to other agencies and programs where there is this same kind of relationship and need.

Dr. Moynihan. We are going to establish Regional Councils in the four regional headquarters. Automatically that is done today.

Q. What is the make-up of these Regional Councils? Who sits on them?

Dr. Moynihan. HEW, HUD, Labor and OEO.

Mr. Hughes. We started with these as a nucleus. We don't regard it as the end of it all, but we do want to keep the Councils more or less homogeneous in terms of their interest and involve those agencies essentially that would be involved in the Urban Affairs Council structure here in Washington.

Q. The figure 1,800 was dropped, and then you seemed not sure of that. How many people are going to be moved out of the cities?

Dr. Moynihan. The problem there is that these moves will be phased over 18 months and an unknown number of those people will leave their jobs for other reasons, find other places they can stay in and so there will be an empty slot moved – join the Army.

Q. Can you give me a count at all?

Mr. Hughes. I would say 1,200 or 1,400 may be confronted with a move at some time in this period. I hate to use the numbers, because they focus attention on a problem that may not exist, given the time interval, given turnover, and given the opportunity to establish what may be called essentially sub-regional offices in some of these cities where the employees might otherwise have to move from.

Q. Are these only high-level people, or are you talking about clerical support, too?

Mr. Hughes. The numbers involve the total range of personnel. Some of them obviously will elect to stay, perhaps, in these agencies or otherwise disassociate from the regional office so they don't have to move. That is part of the problem of estimating the moves.

Q. Do you mean then that there will be 400 who might find jobs in the cities that are now working within Government? Is that your estimate?

Dr. Moynihan. Sure. It is a long-established industrial practice now when you have to make changes in personnel to do them through the normal turn-over as much as you can. These end up to be surprisingly painless affairs if they are given time and advance notice.

Q. I am still not clear on whether any of the current regional offices will completely close in Kansas City.

Dr. Moynihan. Is Kansas City a regional headquarters?

Mr. Hughes. Yes.

Dr. Moynihan. It will no longer be. That is the one that immediately comes to mind.

Q. Some will disappear but reappear as sub-regional offices?

Dr. Moynihan. Yes. They may have to go around and write "sub" on some of the windows.

Q. Is Kansas City—

Mr. Hughes. There is a map which would show the new regional structure and we have a map which shows agency by agency the impact in terms of boundaries.

Q. How about the numbers of jobs?

Mr. Hughes. The jobs we don't have, simply because we don't know what the impact will be over a period of time on these people. We don't know how the sub-regional structure will be involved.

Dr. Moynihan. If we seem to be a little vague on this, it is not that we are vague, it is because this is an immensely complex subject. If you want to know why we are doing it you ought to sit down and spend the day trying to find out what is the present state. We set up a regional council of four major departments in New York City — New York City being the headquarters for each of these departments or agencies — only to find that the only State those four departments had in common was New York itself. It is just not beyond any-body's comprehension, it is just a very complex business.

Q. You have not said exactly whether there will be any regional offices completely closed down. Is the answer no?

Dr. Moynihan. Yes, there will be, in terms of specific departments.

Q. Which ones?

Dr. Moynihan. All over this map. We can spend the after-noon on it and we will give you the data.

Q. Are those the ones you read?

Mr. Hughes. I read the list of cities where there are now regional offices or equivalent which would be affected by this action.

Q. Does that mean they will be closed down?

Mr. Hughes. No. It means that that will no longer be a regional office. There may be — and in my judgment pro-bably will be — personnel remaining there, perhaps the same personnel, but that will not have the label on it, on the door "Regional Office."

Dr. Moynihan. Let's be very clear. There are not going to be any doors locked in this process. There is no major city in the country that doesn't have in it offices of almost all the major departments of Federal Government. The question is: Where we have tried to establish regional systems, we have settled on eight, and the question is: can we transfer to those areas a measure of initiative, a measure of responsibility and authority so that in fact the work of Government in those very areas can go on closer to the areas involved. Most of these regions are, in terms of population, if you broke these eight regions up and put them in the U.N. Gazetteer, they would be the 8th, 9th, 10th, 11th, 12th, 13th and 14th biggest and richest countries in the world.

Finding a structure where you can give real power and authority is difficult. It is not a question of the taking of people out of Kansas City and into St. Louis and so on. There are going to be HUD and HEW, DOT and Labor people in all those places. It is a question of where do you locate the man you call Regional Director and what kind of authority do you give him and do you give to each of your people a sufficiently convergent set of powers and responsibilities so they in fact can sit down and make decisions of their own that have consequences.

Q. Implicit in that, it seems to me, there will have to be a coordination among these agencies in the level of authority granted regional directors.

Dr. Moynihan. That is correct. That is the next phase of our operation.

Q. Is there going to be any single man representing all of those?

Dr. Moynihan. No, we have specifically rejected that idea.

Q. How about in the cities where you are leaving some people behind, is there going to be a single man there?

Dr. Moynihan. No. The curious fact of the American National Goverment is that there is only one "single man" and he is called the President and that is the arrangement we have.

Q. I would like to talk about Kansas City. You are going to move HEW, OEO and Labor. That is 825 people involved. That is $10 million a year in payroll. HEW said it will cost them $800,000 to go to Denver. The Missouri and Kansas delegations, Republicans and Democrats alike, are upset. They don't understand why you are moving three bigger offices to Denver instead of two smaller ones to Kansas City.

Dr. Moynihan. There are numbers that have to do with the headquarters functions. They do not in any sense reflect a necessary net loss to that city of Federal employees or Federal payroll. They just don't. It would be our hope that any actual change to this would be very minimal, indeed.

They are changes in our organizational structure, not in the economic structure of Kansas City.

Mr. Hughes. I think that is a fair statement. The reasons for Denver versus Kansas City — judgments differ on this — but there are reasons of transportation networks, regional practices, regional associations, the suitability of Denver versus Kansas City as the headquarters city for the mountain states and those sorts of things.

We have tried, also to minimize the moves within the total structure.

Dr. Moynihan. Let's be very candid. When you ask what is the difference between Kansas City and Denver, the answer is that a good case can be made for either, but if you are going to have one regional headquarters you have to have one. It has just been the unsatisfactory nature of the decision that has been part of taking 20 years to make it.

Mr. Hughes. One of the problems here is that you can slice 50 States and some territories and so on almost an infinite number of ways and it has been extremely difficult to get any measure of concensus or agreement as to the best arrangement. In evolving an arrangement, you cannot just look at the mountain states or Kansas City or Denver. You have to look at the country and the feasibility of fanning out from Washington, how many regions there ought to be in total and those kinds of questions. That is what we tried to stress.

Q. Can we find out about our specific regions?

Dr. Moynihan. The Bureau of the Budget has it.

Q. Should we call the Bureau?

Dr. Moynihan. Yes.

Mr. Ziegler. We will pass out maps, together with that release, which spell out the area covered in each region. They will give you an indication of what area the various headquarters cover.

The Press. Thank you.

(Office of the White House Press Secretary, March 27, 1969)

Exhibit E

[From the *Woman Constitutionalist* Jan. 9, 1971]

Regional Government: Voices of Prophecy

(By Mary M. Davison)

Many years ago Don Bell (Don Bell Reports and Closer Up) warned of a plan on the part of those who have usurped the Washington government to establish within our borders a Regional Government composed of twelve regions whose capitals would be in the cities occupied by the twelve Federal Reserve Regional banks. It was not a very glamorous story and received little attention.

Several years later David Brinkley, addressing students in an Ohio University, predicted the *abolition* of the States, saying that within the lifetime of most of those students there would be no more sovereign States; something else would replace them. Nobody paid any attention to that either; not even the students. Now some startling facts have come to light.

At a Press Conference held at the White House March 27, 1969, Mr. Daniel P. Moynihan officially revealed the creation of eight regions – eight separate governments within the United States (two others were added later in that year, 1969), leaving two to go to meet the Don Bell prophecy. And strangely enough the capitals of these Regional Governments are located in the cities housing the *Federal Reserve branches*. We will quote some of the discussion of the Moynihan Press Conference which we believe to be indicative of the manner in which the Government is being run; not by Congress, much less by the hand-picked Presidents from the stables of the *Council on Foreign Relations*.

Mr. Moynihan. "One can say anything one thinks on the record about the public administration because it never gets printed anyway. If we had a war to announce, by golly, everyone would be here ... This is about the first major reorganization which the President has put into effect. I think it is a matter of some interest ... that it has been something Presidents have been trying to put into effect for almost 20 years now. This is the first time in the history of the American Republic (??-ed.) that the regional boundaries of the regional domestic programs will be coterminous. You can see how quickly you can lose your audience with things like that. Laughter." (The language was designed "to lose your audience," reporters as well as the rest of us—ed.). The next paragraphs probably explain why the news media failed to report this most momentous incident — the "restructuring" (rebuilding—ed.) of the United States Government without the knowledge or consent of the Congress or the People. This, the job "presidents have been trying to put into effect for nearly 20 years."

Mr. Moynihan. "The pattern has been built up that when each department, when departments have been established and agencies have been established their regional boundaries have responded to the sort of peculiarities (word "peculiarities" scarcely describes them—ed.) of subjects or the Congressional arrangements that led to their enactment or just randomness. The result has been that there has been wide variation in the regional headquarter."

The above is typical of the hokum Congress is subjected to hours on end, when they call in some of the over-educated phonies of State, Defense, Treasury or other departments of "government" to explain such activities as Viet Nam, Interest rates, Prisoners of War or other vital subjects. Congress, for the most part, sits openmouthed listening to this senseless babble, then compliments them on their, "scholarly presentation" and their "erudition" and suggest the need for a pay raise. When the "erudite" ones are out of ear-shot, they —the

Congressmen— ask one another if they knew what in tunket they were talking about.

Our State representatives who have been pleading for "taxsharing" with the Federal "Government" might, if they could muster a little extra concentration, find that they have "tax shared" themselves out of business. The Fed has no intention of sharing anything. They intend to operate all the "services" out of the Regional Governments.

Mr. Moynihan. "If I could just say, in the whole question of public administration, making the Govenrment work, in delivering public services, the biggest single weakness of the American National Government has been its field (State) structure . . . And not to attend to that is just not to be serious about this subject. It is perhaps the least exciting subject in Government and that has been the source of the problem, just not being able to muster the attention of persons to its absolutely essential nature."

Why could they not "muster the attention of persons to its absolutely essential nature?" Have the lines of communication with the One-Worlders broken down or was the necessary publicity too risky? They had taken the State Governments for a ride with a downhill pull and even under the watchful eyes of agencies, the scheme just might come to the attention of some person or group with sufficient interest and influence to prevent the eradication of State Government.

Q. "Will you save money, too, or is this just for efficiency?" **Mr. Hughes.** "I would regard it in the interest of efficiency. In your terms it is a management action. It could produce savings. It is not designed to do that. Rather, it is designed to make it easier to manage Federal programs out in the field (the States—ed.) where services must be delivered and also to make it easier for the States and Cities to deal with the Federal agencies." (which will be handling all the "tax sharing" money—ed.)

Mr. Moynihan. "Remember that the Reorganization powers have existed for 20 years, and are sort of a standing concomitant of the Presidency, and in a normally effective Government reorganization, considerations are always going on. It is a more intensive point than in the earlier Administrations and President Nixon has spoken with special interest in this. I think you can look forward to proposals, but we have nothing right now."

Mr. Hughes. "Lots of things are being looked at." (And somebody with an interest in the nation should be helping them "look"—ed.).

Q. "You pointed out that for 20 years people have been interested in this. Can you identify some of the obstacles that have come up over the years?"

Dr. Moynihan. ". . . This is the kind of subject that people who are close (but not too close—ed.) to Government are very passionate about, and people out of Government don't even know about (it is none of their business—ed.). It always happens. To be associated with the movement of some resources from one part of the Congressional map to another. So there have always been people who by definition will have to be against it (if they ever find out about it— ed.) . . . This combination of a rather low level of public interest and a rather specific level of local opposition has meant, by and large, that no President has been willing to bite the bullet. Now we have done so. Mind you, once it takes place (and it has—the President, by his own admission signed it on March 27, 1969—ed.) then the new arrangements, become sacred and absolutely imbedded in the constitutional division of the republic."

This is something to think about. A Council on Foreign Relations President and a covey of Council on Foreign Relations empire builders, *elected by nobody,* have divided the United States into at least 10 regional governments, at least four of which have already been set and are ready for action:

Region 2—New York City; Region 4—Atlanta; Region 5—Chicago; Region 9—San Francisco. (Press Release by the President May 21, 1969).

While the Congress was turning the Federal Government over to the United Nations and the States were surrendering their powers and the sovereignty of the People to Rockefeller Brothers 1313 agencies, the One World operation in Pratt House, New York, *(CFR—ed.)* was cutting up the United States like an enormous pie.

Each of these regional governments will have all the appurtenances of government. In the beginning, says Mr. Nixon in his May 21, 1969 Press Release, each regional government will be equipped with its own Departments of Labor, Health, Education and Welfare, Housing and Urban Development, Office of Economic Opportunity and the Small Business Administration. These are the very agencies from which the 1313 State legislatures expected to collect a juicy "tax-sharing." We might note in passing that 10 of the Regional Government capitals are located in the cities housing the Federal Reserve branches. At the time of this report (May 1969) Cleveland and St. Louis were excluded. This may now have changed.

A few years ago your editor conducted a one woman campaign against 1313, charging that it was operating in violation of Article 4, Section 3, of the Constitution of the United States, i.e.:

". . . nor any state be formed by the junction of two or more states or parts of states without the consent of the legislatures concerned as well as of the Congress."

Lawyers convinced me that 1313 was not in violation because they had not organized by law but by voluntary agreement. But now we have the United States divided into regions by *law,* for Congress and all the legislatures have passed laws permitting the division of the United States. The laws at both Congressional and State levels are drawn in such language that it might take an Einstein two weeks to decode them, but they are there and if the people of the States permit the continuation of this outrage the prophecy of David Brinkley that the States would be abolished in our lifetime will have proven true.

I have spoken with probably the most knowledgeable man to have served in a State legislature in recent years and he expressed the opinion that no State legislature in the country would have enacted this legislation if they had known what they were doing. He was not in the legislature at the time the legislation was enacted but having received a copy of that particular Bill we feel that he will realize that they did not understand the Bill and that is the reason for its passage. Inasmuch as every State (together with Puerto Rico and the District of Columbia) are covered by the legislation, it is quite likely the Bills were written at a central point and distributed to the States.

It should therefore be a matter of top priority for all persons who desire to live in a sovereign State to acquaint our State representatives, Congressmen and Senators immediately of the realities of the "Reorganization Acts" of States and Nation, insisting that these bills be promptly reviewed and rescinded. Remember that Mr. Moynihan stressed the fact that once it had been adopted—as it became sacred and "absolutely embedded in the Constitutional division of the Republic."

This is not possible under the Constitution which guarantees "to every State in this Union a republican form of government . . ." Get busy — consult your lawyers, particularly those lawyers in your State legislatures. Demand a return to Constitutional Government which has been the prime objective of Women for Constitutional Government from the beginning.

Exhibit F

While We Slept, The States Were Being Abolished

Dear American—"New States may be admitted by the Congress into this Union; but no new State shall be formed or erected within the jurisdiction of any other State; nor any State be formed by the junction of two or more States, or parts of States without the consent of the Legislatures of the States concerned as well as the Congress."—United States Constitution; Article IV, Section 3, Paragraph 1.

President Nixon currently is engaged in the promotion of a plan to consolidate the twelve existing Cabinet-level Departments and reduce them to eight, allegedly to save money, increase efficiency, eliminate duplication of services, streamline the admittedly cumbersome machinery of bureaucracy, etc. And the plan, on first reading, sounds commendable — until one discovers that this is to be one more step in an overall plot to consolidate the fifty States and reduce them to Regional Departments; thus abolishing the States!

Lest we be labeled an alarmist without a cause, permit us to present the facts in more or less chronological order:—

When the Constitution of the United States was ratified by the original Thirteen States, there was established a kind of government different from any ever conceived before; not because it was a Republic, but because the political power was decentralized. The Federal Government was ceded certain specified and enumerated powers; all other powers were reserved to the States and the people.

No such system of government had ever been tried before: the greatest power was confined to the *local level* of government; and this for over 200 years prevented power-grabbers from gaining too much power. In all other countries, power was concentrated at the top; so ours was indeed a unique form of government.

And for this very reason, our system has been attacked, called inefficient, horse-and-buggy government for a nuclear age, etc. And over the years — especially since 1917 — there have been repeated and almost constant attempts to reverse the flow of political power and make ours a centralized government, like other nations of the world, republics or otherwise.

The plans became more or less solidified through the efforts of a network of organizations which came to be called Terrible 1313, and which we exposed as early as February, 1958. The plans called for the establishment of Metro, megalopolitan and regional governments that cross State lines; of gigantic authorities stretching from city to city and denying State authority while appealing to the Central National authority; of the abolishment of States altogether . . .

As early as 1933, Luther Gulick, a Planner, a promoter of Metro, etc., declared: "The American State is finished. I do not predict that the States will go, but affirm that they have gone." And in his blueprints they were gone, replaced by regional districts after the manner of the twelve Federal Reserve Districts into which this Nation already has been divided.

In 1934 a writer (William Kay Wallace, in Our Obsolete Constitution), observed that "the multiplicity of forty-eight states . . . has no valid social or political reason for being preserved."

In September, 1969, Representative _____ of New York, told the U.S. House of Representatives: "I recently discussed with Governor Nelson Rockefeller, of New York, at a public meeting of the Intergovernmental Affairs Subcommittee of the House Government Operations Committee, the need for reorganizing our State governments. One suggestion I made was that the 50

States be abolished and regional governments be substituted for them."

To justify his suggestion, ––––––––– submitted a study made by the Committee for Economic Development, a satellite organization of the powerful Council on Foreign Relations, which has been called our *Secret Government*, and justifiably so called. The CED study concluded that "the failure of state governments to meet their commitments was attributable to geographic handicaps, outmoded structures, inadequate resources, and political weaknesses ..." The study hinted that States should be abolished and new regional boundary lines be drawn, with such regional authorities looking to Washington for guidance.

Now, let's drop back to 1965, and we quote from an article written by Lee Bolman, which appeared in *The Freedom Press*:

"The 'Public Works and Economic Development Act of 1965' became law last August ... This Act, cited as Public Law 89-136, provides the master plan for Dictatorship of the United States ... Close analysis of the Act itself will prove there is 'no way back' if the States and local officials do not withhold cooperation and 'hold-the-line' against Federal Commissioners and their direct dictatorial powers through "federal fund blackjacks."

"This Public Works and Economic Development Act authorizes the setting up of 'regions' throughout the United States ... These 'regions' would eventually wipe out State boundaries. America may remain as a continent but you may end up saying you are from Federal Region No. 9 instead of from California ... We would be asked to give up towns, cities, counties, and States, for Regions, Districts, Areas, and Centers. But this is not merely a transfer of labels; the new boundaries will be very mobile and overlapping, changing at the whim or pleasure of the Secretary of Commerce and his staff, who have the final decision (if the President agrees) ...

"By law, the United States is to be broken up into 'Regions,' and each 'Region' must have a comprehensive master plan. No one can disregard this plan which will include something for every square inch of American land and the compliance of every person in it." (End of quotation.)

Now, let's note how President Nixon chose to invoke and utilize the power contained in the above mentioned Public Law 89-136. We call you attention to an article appearing in the Washington, D.C., *Evening Star* of March 27, 1969, which we reprint. We call your attention to the President's apology for having waited from 1965 to 1969 to put the changes into ·effect: "fumblings, disappointments and frustrations" are blamed. Here is the article, in full:

Exhibit G

Nixon Coordinates City Aid

(By Garnett D. Horner)

President Nixon today directed five government departments and agencies dealing with urban and poverty programs to establish common regional boundaries and regional office locations in eight cities for their field operations.

He also ordered expansion of regional councils to the eight headquarters to coordinate the work of the agencies involved. In a third directive, he asked nine departments and agencies to move toward greater decentralization of their operations to give more decision-making powers to federal employees who deal daily with state and local officials.

"The federal government has been assigned many new responsibilities in the last several decades — many of which it carries and many of which it fumbles," Nixon said in a statement. "Many of the disappointments and frustrations of the last several years can be blamed on the fact that the administrative performance has not kept pace with the legislative promise. This situation must be changed. The actions I announced today are important steps toward achieving such changes."

The restructuring was done by executive action.

The President pointed out that each agency now has its own set of regional offices and regional boundaries, which often means that if a director of one field operation is to meet with his counterpart in another branch of government he often must make an airplane trip to see him.

State and local officials often must go to regional federal offices in different cities on the same problem. Nixon said the new uniform regions and regional headquarters will streamline and coordinate the systems through which the government provides social and economic services.

The five divisions involved are the Labor, Health, Education and Welfare, and Housing and Urban Development departments, the Office of Economic Opportunity and the Small Business Administration.

The eight regional centers are:

Region 1, Boston—Connecticut, Maine, Massachusetts, New Hampshire, Rhode Island and Vermont.

Region 2, New York City—New York, New Jersey, Puerto Rico and the Virgin Islands.

Region 3, Philadelphia—Delaware, District of Columbia, Kentucky, Maryland, North Carolina, Pennsylvania, Virginia and West Virginia.

Region 4, Atlanta—Alabama, Florida, Georgia, Mississippi, South Carolina and Tennessee.

Region 5, Chicago—Illinois, Indiana, Minnesota, Michigan, Ohio and Wisconsin.

Region 6, Dallas-Fort Worth—Arkansas, Louisiana, New Mexico, Oklahoma and Texas.

Region 7, Denver—Colorado, Idaho, Iowa, Kansas, Missouri, Montana, Nebraska, North Dakota, South Dakota, Utah and Wyoming.

Region 8, San Francisco—Alaska, Arizona, California, Guam, Hawaii, Nevada, Oregon and Washington.

Philip S. Hughes, deputy director of the Budget Bureau, said the reorganization will mean that regional headquarters of one or more of the agencies involved will be abolished in Charlottesville, Washington, Austin, Nashville, Baltimore, New York, Jacksonville, New Orleans, Cleveland and Seattle. Congressmen representing these districts have opposed Nixon's plans.

Hughes and Daniel P. Moynihan, assistant to the President for urban affairs (since resigned—Ed.) said the order will not mean these cities will lose any substantial number of federal employees, however. They said federal offices would be maintained in each of the cities, some of which functioning as subregional headquarters. Actual movement of personnel probably will involve 1,200 people or less and will be spread over the next 18 months, they said.

Exhibit H

Statement By The President

On March 27, I announced a series of steps being taken to streamline the structure and processes of Federal agencies in the field. I am confident that these changes will greatly improve the effectiveness of Federal social and economic services.

The first of these actions was the establishment of a common pattern of regional boundaries and headquarters for the Department of Labor, the Department of Health, Education, and Welfare, the Department of Housing and Urban Development, the Office of Economic Opportunity, and the Small Business Administration.

Since the announcement we have met with congressional, state and local interests from many areas of the country and received from them a great deal of valuable information on implementing this plan.

After considering this information, I have concluded that the level of Federal service which would be required of the planned subregional offices in Kansas City and Seattle warrants their elevation to full regional status.

Three other changes are desirable. With the establishment of the new Seattle region, it is appropriate to shift Idaho to that region from the Denver region. Also, after reviewing the situation, I have concluded that the States of North Carolina and Kentucky would be better served from Atlanta than from Philadelphia.

In summary, the new alignment for the regions is as follows:

Region I (Boston)—Connecticut, Maine, Massachusetts, New Hampshire, Rhode Island, and Vermont.

Region II (New York City)—New York, New Jersey, Puerto Rico, and the Virgin Islands.

Region III (Philadelphia)–Delaware, District of Columbia, Maryland, Pennsylvania, Virginia, and West Virginia.

Region IV (Atlanta)–Alabama, Florida, Georgia, Kentucky, Mississippi, North Carolina, South Carolina, and Tennessee.

Region V (Chicago)–Illinois, Indiana, Minnesota, Michigan, Ohio, and Wisconsin.

Region VI (Dallas-Fort Worth)–Arkansas, Louisiana, New Mexico, Oklahoma, and Texas.

Region VIII (Denver)–Colorado, Montana, North Dakota, South Dakota, Utah, and Wyoming.

Region IX (San Francisco)–Arizona, California, Hawaii, and Nevada.

Region X (Seattle)–Alaska, Idaho, Oregon, and Washington.

You will note that the foregoing article calls for only eight Regions. Here someone apparently slipped up. There are twelve Federal Reserve Districts, with headquarters at Boston, New York, Philadelphia, Cleveland, Richmond, Atlanta, Chicago, St. Louis, Minneapolis, Kansas City, Dallas and San Francisco. It would seem logical, therefore, that these Regional Government Centers be the same as the centers where Federal Reserve Banks are located, which would call for the establishment of four more Regional Headquarters.

President Nixon moved toward that ultimate goal when on May 21, 1969, he named two more "Regional Capitals": Kansas City and Seattle. Because of the importance of this subject, we reprint the whole of a press release issued by the White House on May 21, 1969.

So, here is all the necessary machinery, all installed and ready to run; in the case of five federal departments Nixon wants to revamp the Cabinet structure at Washington, so that the consolidation of departments which is to be carried out at each Regional Capital, will be carried out also at the National Capital.

However, there is "a fly in the ointment."

Congress permitted the setting up of the machinery for Regional Government, but it did not provide the fuel to run the machinery; indeed, it could not without wrecking the United States Constitution which declares, in effect, that if the States are to be abolished, the States themselves must do the abolishing. We'll explain that:

The authority to set up these Regional Governments is derived from this Public Works and Economic Development Act of 1965. This Act empowers the Federal Government to set up Regional Centers but, to be Constitutional and lawful, it also stipulated that the State Governments must request the Federal Government to put this regional plan into operation. The one weapon which the Executive had to force the States to ask to be destroyed was the money weapon: Welfare funds would be withheld unless the States fell into line.

To supply additional money power, Rep. Blank introduced H.R. 2519 in January,1969 providing block grants to States if they met regional modernization conditions. In other words, to qualify for the promised bloc grant, a State would have to enact legislation at the State level which would permit the setting up of sub-regions which, in turn, would fit into the Federal Ten Region structure.

To put it bluntly, *the States would have to vote themselves into the Regional Structure if they were to qualify for Federal assistance!*

Incidentally, that bill introduced by Reuss did not pass, though several States rushed through enabling legislation in preparation for the expected bloc grant. A Maryland correspondent informs us that State passed such legislation but that it was later defeated by a referendum vote of the citizens. To complete this story of the money bill: H.R. 2519 was reintroduced as H.R. 11764 but time ran out; and it is to be reintroduced this year, revamped and giving control over $22½ billion which will be doled out for welfare, health, education, guaranteed income, etc., if the States agree to the Regional Plan.

Tied to this Regional Plan are most of the Nixon goals: Revenue sharing, Government reorganization at the Cabinet level, new health care proposals, the guaranteed annual income plan, etc. (Please note: We refer to these as "Nixon's goals;" but we do not mean this to designate Nixon the individual. A Conspiracy is difficult to explain or comprehend as an abstraction, it must be personalized; and since Nixon is the *front man* and the *public voice* of the *Conspiracy*, we speak of "Nixon's goals." Personally, Nixon may know little of how these proposals coordinate, interweave, complement each other to promote Regional Government at the National level, then Regional Government at the inter-National level, and finally Regional Government at the world level, a la 1984. But since Nixon is known to favor Atlantic Union and Rockefeller's "New Federalism," his "ignorance is no excuse," if he should happen to plead that condition in 1974).

Prof. R.J. Phillips of New York State University says "the only effective way to modernize state government is to abolish it." Then he explains what, supposedly, is on Mr. Nixon's mind:

"The plan . . . would call for substituting a number of regional governmental units for the present fifty states . . . Each region would serve in a dual capacity. On the one hand they would be administrative units of the national government, charged with the implementation of federal programs . . . On the other hand they would have the responsibility for supervising local programs. Changes in the latter area would call for a dramatic alteration of existing units of local government through the development of fewer but more viable local governments.

"With the demise of the existing states we could develop a national court system, standard suffrage legislation, a national public school system that would include higher education, uniform marriage and divorce laws, standard automobile registration and licensing, and many others . . .

"We must remove from our thinking the idea that there is something sacred about our federal system of government . . . we do not need to establish more commissions to examine ways of strengthening and revitalizing state governments . . . What we need now is the courage to embark upon a different course and to attack these problems. How long are we willing to permit the problems of an urban and industrial society to be administered by governmental machinery, developed in a rural and agrarian society of two centuries ago?" (End of quotation).

Shall we have Regional Government, whether we like it or not? This much is certain: any appeal to the President, your Senator, or U.S. Representative, if futile. But there is this hope: you may be able to interest your State and County officials in keeping their jobs!

Exhibit I

[From the *Wisconsin State Journal*, Mar. 30, 1971]

Right Wing Advocate Here-- Roberts Wants People Power

(By William R. Wineke)

Ideology, like politics, makes strange bedfellows.

For example, Arch E. Roberts, a retired Army colonel popular among right wing groups, will testify before a joint legislative committee meeting today that America must return power to the people.

Roberts, who believes an international banking conspiracy is behind most of the world's ills, assesses the current state of the nation in much the same way that college radicals do, although his solutions run opposite theirs.

"If we are to survive as a race and as a nation, the People (he capitalizes the word) must regain control over the centers of power in America," Roberts says in testimony prepared for today.

"The stark truth is that America is now passing from a constitutional republic into a totalitarian world-wide government."

Roberts does not find it upsetting that his words, if printed on a mimeographed leaflet, would be attributed to bearded radicals.

"We have a great deal in common" with the radical students, Roberts said in an interview Monday.

"We are opposed to the polarization of the American people into right and left camps . . . The student is not an instigator of revolution; he is a product of his education."

That education, in Roberts' view, relies heavily on foundation funds, and foundation funds rely heavily on enormously wealthy people who want to see American society destroyed so that the banking conspiracy can control the world.

Roberts finds other things in common with the radical young.

He scoffs at the reasons the United States government gives for its involvement in Vietnam and suggests that the real reason for that involvement is to gain control of the vast oil reserves lying under its soil.

"When that is accomplished, we will see troops pulled out and sent on to the next place of economic exploitation, probably the Mideast," Roberts predicted.

And, although Roberts was kicked out of the Army in 1962 after he charged that some American political leaders had Communist leanings (the U.S. Court of Appeals reinstated him in 1964), Roberts now maintains that he is not anti-Communist.

"The historical fact that has been concealed from the American people" is that the Soviet revolution was bankrolled by a New York banking house, he said.

The former officer believes that the conspiracy he sees wants a world society that operates on a Soviet model with a few men making all the decisions and the people obeying them.

If Roberts and radical leftists agree on many assessments of the world situation, they obviously disagree on proposals for curing the situation.

Roberts thinks violence is useless because the other side has the power; he hopes that state legislatures will expose the alleged conspiracy, pull out of regional governmental deals—which Roberts thinks lead to world government—and go back to the ideals of the founding fathers.

Roberts is an executive of the Committee to Restore the Constitution, nationally based in Ft. Collins, Colo.

He did not reveal the committee's budget, but said funding comes from individuals who send small amounts. He lives on his Army pension (he was a public information officer) and on speaking fees.

Roberts and his wife have five sons, two of whom have served in the Marines and three of whom live at home.

Exhibit J

[From the *Valley* (Minn.) *Times*, Apr. 1970]

Minnesota World Citizens in Tax Revolt

(By Jo Hindman)

Over the wires came the electrifying news, "World Citizenship has been declared over the whole State of Minnesota."

State officials gathered at St. Paul to sign The Declaration of World Citizenship of the State of Minnesota, March 25, 1971 and verified by Governor Wendell Anderson's office. These signed: The Governor, Lt. Gov. Perpich, state senators Holmquist, majority leader; Coleman, minority leader; state representatives Lindstrom, majority; Sabo, minority; Speaker Aubrey Diriam.

This is the second world unity paper signed in the state. Three years ago almost to the day, a former governor and various officials inked the Hennepin County-Minneapolis world citizenship pact, said to be almost identical with the new state document.

Governor Anderson was unavailable for comment on what the action implies.

The same question put to the chairman of the Concerned Taxpayers of Minnesota, Mrs. Joan Van Poperin, drew this: "The Declaration indicates take-over right now . . . we are in the position of citizens against World Government."

Mrs. Van Poperin sketched prior events of the week. Rep. John Bares, Jr. introduced a bill to repeal Minnesota's Regionalization Act of 1969, a radical piece of the world regionalization movement. The subcommittee hearings on March 23 were jammed with repeal citizens, many of them farmers coming from all points of the state.

A lawmaker said that he "believes in World Government." Asked why, by a constituent, the official reportedly replied that he "got new streets and new sidewalks through urban renewal."

The point is significant. Controversial urban renewal laws increasingly are attacked on the premise that they are unconstitutional, existing only because the United Nations global treaty has pre-empted the U.S. Constitution. Unprotected Americans are left defending themselves against present-day world law such as urban renewal and regional laws.

As this is written, a statewide protest march is scheduled on April 3 converging on the Minnesota capitol steps. The Governor and legislators are invited. Originally planned as a tax protest against the state legislature, the event undoubtedly will protest the world citizenship betrayal.

A press conference by CTM, 628 Stryker Ave., St. Paul 55107, dealt the cards. The words of Joan Van Poperin were picked up by TV, newspapers and radio. She said: "We have a tax crisis. Rates are 10 to 15 times what they should be. People are losing their homes. We want property taxes to be levied at one per cent (1%) of the year 1967's assessed valuation. 1967 was picked because that year the legislature passed the law to change tax base due to regionalization." (Twin Cities regional government created in 1967 consists of St. Paul, Minneapolis and seven counties).

"We urge the repeal of the statewide Regionalization Act of 1969 which followed, putting all powers under appointed officials and taking away our right to vote on those representing us on tax matters. If the April 3 protest has no effect," she said, "We shall withhold our real estate taxes."

"As for world citizenship, if it can be forcibly imposed on Minnesotans, so can it be done to all citizens in these United States!"

Exhibit K

[From the *Yakima* (Wash.) *Eagle*, Mar. 25, 1971)

States to Question United Nations Treaty

(By Jo Hindman)

The United Nations strategy to bleed and conquer is running into a groundswell of American counter-action. Significantly, the movement is state, not Washington, D.C. inspired.

The aversion against the UN and its agencies stems from countless disasters that the international trouble makers bring upon Americans within the United States and upon their soldier sons outside the U.S.A.

The advancing thrust of a citizen-sponsored campaign in Wisconsin brilliantly demonstrates how the intelligent anger of Americans is zeroing in on the root of the trouble — the UN's Charter/Treaty (1945) ratified by the U.S. Senate in ill-advised lack of prudence.

The Wisconsin Legislative & Research Committee, a citizen group, seeks to restore the U.S. Constitution and thus eliminate the UN Charter's chaotic influence on the economic, social, political, cultural, educational, and judicial institutions of the U.S.A. and Wisconsin State.

A first step — to study the injurious effects of the UN Charter — is underway, coordinated by the Wisconsin L&R Committee working through a legislative steering committee comprised of members of both houses.

Assembly Joint Resolution No. 34 (1971) will come up for hearings before the Wisconsin Legislature late in March. Technically worded, "This joint resolution establishes a special joint committee comprised of four senators and four

representatives to the assembly, to study the constitutionality of the actions of federal agencies with regard to the
United Nations, the effect of these actions on the state and
possible measures which could be taken by this state to
punish unconstitutional actions." A list of grievances is
included.

The objective is to initiate legislative action by the State
which will outlaw the United Nations Treaty-Charter and
other illegal acts of Congress within the boundaries of the
State of Wisconsin.

The legislative "first" is part of a nationwide movement
designed to help the states clean house. The legislatures of
several states must investigate the UN Charter to see if it is
pre-empting the Constitution of the United States or of the
State. When this fact has been established, then each investigating legislature will declare that the U.S. Senate has no
right to ratify the Charter. Next, each investigating state will
declare the Charter to be an act outside of the law and make
it a felony for anyone to try to enforce the provisions of the
UN Charter within the state.

Archibald E. Roberts, Lt.Col. AUS ret., author of the
state-oriented strategy, heads the nationwide Committee to
Restore the Constitution, Oak at Howes St., Fort Collins,
Colo. 80521. The Wisconsin L&R Committee is affiliated
with the national organization.

Both the national and its affiliates believe that it is necessary to inspire public awareness of the UN peril and to
encourage the voice of reason to be heard in the halls of the
State capitols.

The model legislation from which the Wisconsin joint
resolution is adapted was prepared under the direction of the
late John Janney, nationally recognized constitutional
authority and Mr. T. David Horton, counsel for the national
committee.

"Implementation of the legal instrument will go far in
probing the forces which are manipulating the American
economy, generating depression, and financing civil violence

for the revolutionary purpose of establishing a Regional Governance upon the ruins of the American civilization," according to Col. Roberts who will testify in Madison, Wis.

Ref. Wisconsin Legislative and Research Committee, Inc., Box 45, Brookfield, Wis. 53005.

Exhibit L

Revenue Sharing Opt Causes Syndicate Tiff

(By Jo Hindman)

Revenue sharing is losing its appeal among Congressmen who are hearing from taxpayers back home.

Even politically organized Syndicate 1313, staunch supporter of revenue sharing, has split on a technical issue concerning method.

Tax payers deplore the magicianship whereby the federal government would give to public tax Spenders a portion of federal income raised by taxing the earnings of individuals. The flow of grants back to the states would blatantly detour around the nationwide demand for cuts in tax spending and would make funds available for local spending projects which have been blocked or turned down by local tax payers.

Sensible government requires the spending unit of government to collect the taxes it would spend.

It is fatal nonsense to separate the tax-collecting level from the level that spends. The split levels make it impossible for tax payers to call government to account on how it uses or misuses the funds.

But Syndicate 1313, Metro, is going all out for revenue sharing.

1313's "law factory" wrote a sample bill to call Congress into a convention to graft revenue sharing into the U.S. Constitution. The tiff in 1313 developed when the National Municipal League editorially attacked the sample but without identifying the Council of State Government faction as the author. Both the NML and CSG are powerful lead units in the political 1313 conglomerate, Chicago-headquartered.

1313's mail order samples, bearing the markings LC 838 1-15-71 hit all state legislatures meeting in early 1971, ready for copying. A legislator who introduced LC 838 as a House

Joint Resolution in his state, admitted that the measure is a nationwide effort sponsored by the National Conference of State Legislative Leaders (NCSLL) and the National Society of State Legislators (NSSL).

Last year, those two organizations popped up in the company of the National Legislative Conference (NLC), the Office of Federal-State Relations of the National Governors (GC), the National Assn. of Attorneys-General (NAAG), the National Conference of Lieutenant Governors (NCLG), and the federal Advisory Commission on Intergovernmental Relations (ACIR) when those 1313 adjuncts collaborated under the CSG whip to get the U.S. Con-Con proposal on the road.

The NML supports the concept of revenue sharing; it merely objects to the U.S. Con-Con idea, fearing that revenue sharing (NML-defined as of statutory nature) will be put into the Constitution where, NML opines, only "new principles belong."

NML, claiming civic status, includes in its membership bankers, lawyers, professors, League of Women Voters, etc.; its treasury regularly receives tax exempt funds from Ford Foundation, Carnegie Corporation and other such institutions.

The CSG, composed of careerists in government, exacts annual tribute from the fifty state treasuries; its "secretariat" controls a legion of syndicate puppets, all active.

The time has come for Congress to heed the wishes of the American constituency rather than to listen to syndicate lobbyists.

It is high time for Congress to cut spending and to forget about revenue sharing which, in the long run, is merely debt-sharing (the national government has been spending more than it takes in).

Refs. NML's "State Legislatures Progress Report" Sept.-Oct. 1970, and National Civic Review Magazine Feb. 1971, both published by National Municipal League, 47 E. 68th St., N.Y. 10021.

Exhibit M

There's Only Debt to Share

(By Jo Hindman)

The tussle over so-called revenue sharing — dividing federal grants between the states — exposes two factions of the same camp maneuvering state-local governments into a fatal fiscal crunch.

The main action is taking place in Wash., D.C. The Administration's "General" sharing proposal is the force working from the top down. The blank proposal, termed "constructive alternative," is the force working from the bottom up.

The Administration, talking $5 — to $10 — billion per year, would mark 1.3 per cent of taxable personal income revenue to be returned to the state-local levels as their share. Population and state-local government's tax effort ration would determine the distribution, i.e. the heavier a state taxes its citizenry, the more federal refund it would "earn."

Using the same ratios, the blank $24-billion proposal, letting the U.S. President handle the purse, requires an additional condition: a "masterplan for modernizing" state-local governments. States not "modernizing" would be stricken from the sharing list. The mandated masterplan would implement the Metro program to eliminate *all* local governments smaller than regions.

The Administration's "Special" sharing proposals are not divulged, as this is written, but the "General" proposal stays silent on the Presidential partitioning of the 50 states into 10 regions. Done in 1969, U.S.A.'s regionalization was accomplished by one stroke at the top.

Meanwhile, Metro's bottom-to-top regionalization is running into opposition. The most recent report comes from the Texas Panhandle.

At meetings of the Panhandle Regional Planning Commission whose jurisdiction covers 26 counties, no private
citizen is allowed to address the board. Even commissioners
not members of the board, although their unit of government
is in PRPC, reportedly are likewise gagged. The meetings are
shifted all over the Panhandle, apparently to discourage
citizen attendance.

At first glance it might seem that the PRPC is following
the Metro movement's COG pattern (councils of government). These, posing as state-local advisory groups, inevitably
clamor for taxing and other powers of a full government.

At second glance, the Panhandle region looks like a new
breed, it sports a peculiarity associated with the Administration's ten (10) regional councils in federal cities — ruling
bodies composed of federal HUD, HEW, SBA, Labor and
OEO staffings, more being added each day.

OEO (Office of Economic Opportunity, "anti-poverty")
operates through Community Action Committee (CAC) at
neighborhood levels. In the Panhandle, the Texas Panhandle
Community Action Corporation has been chartered by the
state to organize in the 26 Panhandle counties. Seven counties have joined the TPCAC by passing resolutions. That is
significant. Resolutions are beyond citizen action.

Texans have sent letters to the state capitol and to the
TPCAC headquarters in Amarillo asking why the federal
government is incorporating its "give-away" programming
under the laws of Texas?

Is it possible that by so doing, a queer new administrative
conduit, from the U.S. President to state-blessed federal dis-
pensaries, would be created?

Complicating the zaniness, federal spending is still ex-
ceeding its income. Therefore, the only thing to share is debt.

If Congress approves the sharing of non-existent funds,
U.S. citizens will be forced into deeper public debt.

Ref. Congressional Records: 12-17-70, 1-25 and 26-71
"State and Local Government Modernization Act of 1971;"
CR 2-4-71-Administration's revenue sharing proposals.

Exhibit N

Metro Regions Created

(By Jo Hindman)

The United States has been divided into ten beggarly Metro regions by the pronouncement of a single man.

On the Day of Partitioning* a White House spokesman boasted, "The curious fact of the American national government is that there is only one 'single man' and he is called the President." That is the arrangement.

The reorganization powers to subordinate the American people under bondage have existed in the hands of U.S. presidents for more than 20 years reportedly. "No President has ever been willing to bite the bullet," according to the assistant to the president for urban affairs. "Now we have done so."

Virtually *every* facet of the lives of American citizens has been brought under the hand of a *single man*. The pattern is simple: He divided the United States into ten regions, named the states to comprise each region, designated ten cities as regional capitols, moved into them skeletal field forces of five federal agencies—HUD, HEW, OEO, SBA and Labor, all of which comprise the ten regional councils. More agencies will be added later.

The action established embryonic Metro governance over the U.S.A.

This is the first time in the history of the American nation that the regional boundaries of the major United Nations—chartered domestic programs have been made coterminus, under the administrative governance of the chief executive of the United States.

---

*   *White House press conference 3-27-69;*

At first, the President announced eight Metro regions fanning out from Washington, D.C. To pacify Kansas City and Seattle which desired regional capitol status, he upped the count to ten regions** Unless changed again, the new Metro alignment is as follows:

Region I (Boston): Conn., Maine, Mass., N.H., R.I., Vt.; Region II (N.Y. City): N.Y., N.J., Puerto-Rico, Virgin Islands; Region III (Philadelphia): Del., D.C., Md., Pa., Va., West Va.; Region IV (Atlanta): Ala., Fla., Ga., Ky., Miss., N.C., S.C., Tenn.; Region V (Chicago): Ill., Ind., Minn., Mich., Ohio, Wisc.; Region VI (Dallas-Fort Worth); Ark., La., N.Mex., Okla., Tex.; Region VII (Kansas City): Iowa, Kan., Mo., Nebr.; Region VIII (Denver): Colo., Mont., N.D., S.D., Utah, Wyo.; Region IX (San Francisco): Ariz., Cal., Hawaii, Nev.; Region X (Seattle): Alaska, Idaho, Ore., Washington.

A White House spokesman said that "if you broke these regions up and put them in the *United Nations Gazetteer* they would be the "8th . . . 12th . . . 14th biggest and richest countries in the world."

The Metro federal regional structure seeks to transfer administrative governance (U.N. global ruling power) FROM the single man TO ten (10) federal directors in the 10-region national field.

One of the federal money bills to finance Metro governance in the nation was H.R. 2519 introduced by Congressman Reuss, January 1969, providing bloc grants if regional modernization conditions were met by the states.

To qualify for the promised bloc grants, the states enacted legislation enabling – or mandating in some instances – the collectivizing of counties into sub-regions which, in turn, fit neatly into the federal 10-regions under the single man governance.

Following the White House 10-region coup, the same measure (H.R. 2519) was renumbered H.R. 11764 and reintroduced later 5-28-69 by the same congressman. Sections

** *Statement by the President 5-21-69.*

were added giving control over the proposed $22½ billion outlay to the "single man" – the U.S. President.

The 91st Congress, now ended, failed to approve the money bill. Watch for one like it to appear in 1971.

Exhibit O

NACo Activates 'Mein Kampf'

(By Jo Hindman)

NACo launched a 15-point assault in 1970 for "modernizing county governments." In Metro gibberish that means that the National Assn. of Counties began the United Nations chartered administrative rules system.

NACo is the political Syndicate 1313's unit assigned to revamp county government. In turn, 1313 is the political transformer designed to conduct the global government of the U.N. into domestic use.

By early 1971, NACo accomplishments disclosed that its "New County, U.S.A." national center has been established at NACo's headquarters, 1101 Connecticut Ave. NW., Washington, D.C. 20036.

The Center is furnished with a "situation room" and a "situation map." The "situations" to be uncovered by NACo surveillance on state constitutional revisons, Metro's so-called home rule charters and other attempts to metropolitanize the United States, will be accumulated in the files and pegged on the map. Through rewritten charters and regional geopolitics, Metro's takeover of the U.S.A. is being accomplished.

NACo has tightened its nationwide "grapevine" hoping for prompt responses to its queries. A national network of clipping services and daily exchange of information with organizations such as the U.S. Chamber of Commerce which is deeply involved with the Metro 1313 syndicate, will serve as NACo eyes and ears.

An advisory committee has been appointed, drawing membership from other 1313 adjuncts such as the National League of Cities (NLC) and Conference of Mayors, International City Managers Assn. (ICMA), National Municipal

League (NML), Public Administration Service (PAS), League
of Women Voters (LWV), Committee on Economic Development (CED), Urban Coalition (UC) and the "portable 1313"
within federal government, the Advisory Commission on
Intergovernmental Relations.

The latter ACIR is top contender in federal government
for the vital spot of referee in deciding which States qualify
for block federal grants. The deciding factor will depend to
what extent a State has overthrown constitutional government in favor of UN-Metro administrative rule.

Spiro T. Agnew, U.S. Vice Pres. will serve as honorary
chairman of NACo's advisory committee, a stance quite in
line with U.S. President Nixon's delineation of duties between himself and Agnew — Spiro to oversee the domestic
scene while Nixon pitches at the international level.

"New States may be admitted by the Congress into this Union; but no new State shall be formed or erected within the jurisdiction of any other State; nor any State be formed by the junction of two or more States, or parts of States, without the consent of the Legislatures of the States concerned, as well as the Congress."

UNITED STATES CONSTITUTION,
Art, IV, section 3, paragraph 1

CHAPTER FIVE

Regionalism: The Quiet Revolution

Transformation of the United States Republic to a dictatorship of the "financial elite," the New World Order fashioned for Americans by the Council on Foreign Relations, reached political reality in 1972 under the administration of President Richard M. Nixon.

Although give little publicity, the White House, on March 27, 1969, pronounced that the United States had been divided into ten Metro regions.[1]   In so doing, President Nixon and his controllers set in motion a series of pre-planned events which would, by February 12, 1972, place virtually every facet of the lives of U.S. citizens under the

---

1. Exhibit A: STATEMENT BY THE PRESIDENT ON RESTRUCTURING OF GOVERNMENT SERVICE SYSTEMS, The White House, March 27, 1969.

domination of socialist planners.

Flouting the prohibitions of Article IV, United States Constitution, Mr. Nixon, in his statement of 1969, "Restructuring of Government Service Systems," purported to "streamline" the Department of Labor, the Department of Health, Education and Welfare, the Department of Housing and Urban Development, the Office of Economic Opportunity, and the Small Business Administration by establishing "uniform boundaries and regional office locations."

Significantly, regional boundaries and the boundaries of major United Nations programs, and Federal Reserve System areas, in the United States were made co-terminus.

Few realized then, or comprehend now, that regional governance is a new form of government which has been covertly engineered to replace the city, county, state, and school district system. Boundary lines of these familiar political subdivisions are to be dropped and a new set of geo-political lines followed.[2]

Under regional government there are now ten U.S. provinces, or regions. Each province has a designated "capitol" to handle all matters within that particular province. Offices of HUD, OEO, SBA, and Labor were moved into the new capitols of each province, with more agencies added later. The objective is to establish the mechanics for controlling the lives and ambitions of the people from a central authority in Washington, and to direct their efforts into channels ordered by a Bureaucratic Civil Service.

An examination of the type of government proposed under regional government shows that it is a government by

2. Exhibit B: PRESS CONFERENCE OF DANIEL P. MOYNIHAN, ASSISTANT TO THE PRESIDENT FOR URBAN AFFAIRS; PHILIP S. HUGHES, DEPUTY DIRECTOR, BUREAU OF THE BUDGET; AND RON ZIEGLER, PRESS SECRETARY TO THE PRESIDENT, Office of the White House Press Secretary, March 27, 1969.

appointed rather than elected officials. Under regional government dis-franchised U.S. Citizens are to be held in bondage, in perpetuity, as producers and servers for a self-appointed Oligarchy.

The ten new political subdivisions to which the fifty States have been allocated by this unconstitutional decree are:

REGION I — Capitol: Boston
Connecticut, Maine, Massachusetts, New Hampshire, Rhode Island, Vermont.

REGION II — Capitol: New York City
New York, New Jersey, Puerto Rico, Virgin Islands

REGION III — Capitol: Philadelphia
Delaware, Maryland, Pennsylvania, Virginia, West Virginia, District of Columbia

REGION IV — Capitol: Atlanta
Alabama, Florida, Georgia, Kentucky, Mississippi, North Carolina, South Carolina, Tennessee

REGION V — Capitol: Chicago
Illinois, Indiana, Michigan, Minnesota, Ohio, Wisconsin

REGION VI — Capitol: Dallas-Fort Worth
Arkansas, Louisiana, New Mexico, Oklahoma, Texas

REGION VII — Capitol: Kansas City
Iowa, Kansas, Missouri, Nebraska

REGION VIII — Capitol: Denver
Colorado, Montana, North Dakota, South Dakota, Utah, Wyoming

REGION IX — Capitol: San Francisco
Arizona, California, Hawaii, Nevada

REGION X — Capitol: Seattle
Alaska, Oregon, Washington, Idaho

One of the federal money bills designed to finance Metro governance in the nation was H.R. 2519, introduced by Congressman Reuss, January, 1969. This bill was to provide bloc grants if regional "modernization" conditions were met by the States.

To qualify for the promised grants the States were required to enact legislation enabling, or mandating in some instances, the collectivizing of counties into sub-regions which would fit neatly into the federal ten-region governance formed by Presidential proclamation.

Following the White House pronouncement of March 27, 1969, the same measure was renumbered H.R. 11764 and reintroduced on May 28 by the same congressman. Sections were added to give control over twenty-two and a half billion tax dollars for Metro funding to one man, President Nixon.

On February 12, 1972, Mr. Nixon dropped the other shoe.

By Executive Order 11647, Federal Regional Councils, (Federal Register No. 30) the President authorized staffing of the ten regional capitols, and effected appointment of a chairman, or commissar for each province.[3]

"Three years ago," said Mr. Nixon in his order, "I directed the senior regional officials of certain of the grant-making agencies to convene themselves in regional councils to better coordinate their services to Governors, Mayors, and the Public.

---

3. **Exhibit C:** EXECUTIVE ORDER 11647, "Federal Regional Councils," The President, Federal Register No. 30, February 12, 1972.

"Now, therefore, by virtue of the authority vested in me as President of the United States it is hereby ordered as follows:

"SECTION 1, Federal Regional Councils. (a) There is hereby established a Federal Regional Council for each of the ten standard Federal regions. Each Council shall be composed of the directors of the regional offices of the Department of Labor, Health, Education, and Welfare, and Housing and Urban Development, the Secretarial Representative of the Department of Transportation, and the directors of the regional offices of the Office of Economic Opportunity, and the Environmental Protection Agency, and the Law Enforcement Assistance Administration. The President shall designate one member of each such Council as Chairman of that Council and such Chairman shall serve at the pleasure of the President. Representatives of the Office of Management and Budget may participate in any deliberations of each Council."

It is intended, of course, that regional council members will assume all real authority over State govenments and the people they represent. The people and the States will be reduced to political impotency.

The image of a police state becomes chillingly real under the provisions of Executive Order 11490, "Assigning Emergency Preparedness Functions to Federal Departments" (Federal Register, October 30, 1969). By this order regional council members, under color of law, can control all food supply, money and credit, transportation, communications, public utilities and other facets of the lives of every citizen.[4, 5, 6, 7]

---

4. Exhibit D: STATE OF NATIONAL EMERGENCY AND EXECUTIVE ORDERS, Hon. John R. Rarick, The Congressional Record, September 27, 1972.
5. Exhibit E: EXECUTIVE ORDER 11615, "Providng for the stabilization of prices, rents, wages, and salaries," (From the Federal Register, Vol. 36, No. 159, August 17, 1971) Hon. John R. Rarick, The Congressional Record, September 27, 1971.
6. Exhibit F: EXECUTIVE ORDER 11490, "Assigning Emergency Preparedness Functions To Federal Departments and Agencies," (From the Federal Register, vol. 34, No. 209, October 30, 1969) Hon. John R. Rarick, The Congressional Record, September 27, 1971.
7. Exhibit G: STATE OF NATIONAL EMERGENCY LEGALIZES THE EXECUTIVE ORDERS, by Archibald E. Roberts, Lt.Col., AUS, ret (from the Borger (Tex) News Herald, Sept. 19, 1971) Entered in the Congressional Record, September 27, 1971, by the Hon. John R. Rarick.

Seizure of private property [homes, businesses, and farms] via the ploy of reassessment under United Nations tax guidelines is a concurrent objective of the madmen who now direct national policy.

Robert C. Weaver, former Chief, Department of Housing and Urban Development, said of Metro governance:

"Regional government means absolute Federal control over all property and its development regardless of location, anywhere in the United States, to be administered on the Federal official's determination. It [regional government] would supersede state and local laws ... Through this authority we seek to recapture control of the use of land, most of which the government has already given to the people."

World government planners hope to achieve federalization of all land, resources and production facilities under regional government authority without serious public challenge. Self-rule and self-determination are to be phased out of the society, the Constitution overthrown, and the citizen made an economic serf in the country that once was his.

President Nixon, in his plea for cooperation in "revenue sharing" (another technique for financing Metro governance) admitted that we are experiencing a "New American Revolution." Proof that the "New American Revolution" is an actual revolution is born out by evidence from "Hearings Before the Subcommittee on Urban Affairs of the Joint Economic Committee," United States Congress, May 19-26, 1917:

"REGIONALISM: The Quiet Revolution

"Local government is changing itself in an effort to better meet the needs of the people. Across the nation, cities, counties, towns, and school districts that serve a common area are joining together in a regional effort to solve mutual problems. In a quiet way, regionalism is a revolution in the structure of our Federal system."

The impact of Metro governance on the freedoms of person and property formerly guaranteed to the people by the Constitution is obvious.

Interlocking subversion in government departments can, however, be successfully challenged by an informed electorate motivated to act within the authority of the U.S. Constitution.

The law involved is the fundamental law of agency: Actions of an agent are not binding on the principal if those actions are not authorized by the principal Constitutionally, States are Principals and federal departments are Agents of the State.

To escape the "New World Order" being prepared for us by the Council on Foreign Relations and the aristocracy of finance[8] Americans must demand that their State lawmakers investigate the illegal actions of federal agents who attempt to abridge the U.S. Constitution in violation of their oath of office.

8. Exhibit H: THE "NEW LOOK" OF THE COUNCIL ON FOREIGN RELATIONS, **Don Bell Reports** May 5, 1972.

Exhibit A

Statement by the President on
Restructuring of Government Service Systems

(DELETED: See Exhibit C, page 94.)

Exhibit B

Press Conference of Daniel P. Moynihan, Assistant to the President for Urban Affairs; Philip S. Huges, Deputy Director, Bureau of the Budget and Ron Ziegler, Press Secretary to the President

(DELETED: See Exhibit D. page 99.)

Exhibit C

THE PRESIDENT
EXECUTIVE ORDER 11647
Federal Regional Councils

The proper functioning of Government requires the development of closer working relationships between major Federal grantmaking agencies and State and local government and improved coordination of the categorical grant system.

I have heretofore directed the Domestic Council to:

(1) receive and develop information necessary for assessing national domestic needs and defining national domestic goals, and to develop for the President alternative proposals for reaching those goals;

(2) collaborate with the Office of Management and Budget and others in the determination of national domestic priorities for the allocation of available resources;

(3) collaborate with the Office of Management and Budget and others to assure a continuing review of ongoing programs from the standpoint of their relative contributions to national goals as compared with their use of available resources; and

(4) provide policy advice to the President on domestic issues.

Furthermore, I have assigned to the Office of Management and Budget the responsibility for assisting the President in developing efficient coordinating mechanisms to implement Government activities and to expand interagency cooperation. Three years ago I directed that the senior regional officials of certain of the grantmaking agencies convene themselves in *regional councils* to better coordinate their services to Governors, Mayors, and the public.

I have now determined that the measures prescribed by this Order would assure improved service to the public.

NOW, THEREFORE, by virtue of the authority vested in

me as President of the United States, it is hereby ordered as follows:

SECTION 1. *Federal Regional Councils.* (a) There is hereby established a *Federal Regional Council* for each of the *ten* standard Federal regions. Each Council shall be composed of the directors of the regional offices of the Departments of Labor, Health, Education, and Welfare, and Housing and Urban Development, the Secretarial Representative of the Department of Transportation, and the directors of the regional offices of the Office of Economic Opportunity, the Environmental Protection Agency, and the Law Enforcement Assistance Administration. The President shall designate one member of each such Council as Chairman of that Council and such Chairman shall serve *at the pleasure of the President.* Representatives of the Office of Management and Budget may participate in any deliberations of each Council.

(b) Each member of each Council may designate an alternate who shall serve as a member of the Council involved whenever the regular member is unable to attend any meeting of the Council.

(c) When the Chairman determines that matters which significantly affect the interests of Federal agencies which are not represented on any such Council are to be considered by that Council, he shall invite the regional director or other appropriate representative of the agency involved to participate in the deliberations of the Council.

SEC. 2. *Functions of the Councils.* Each Federal Regional Council shall be constituted as a body within which the participating agencies will, under the general policy formulation of the Under Secretaries Group, and to the maximum extent feasible, conduct their grantmaking activities in concert through:

(1) the development of short-term regional interagency strategies and mechanicms for program delivery;

(2) the development of integrated program and funding

plans with Governors and local chief executives;

(3) the encouragement of joint and complementary grant applications for related programs;

(4) the expeditious resolution of interagency conflicts and coordination problems;

(5) the evaluation of programs in which two or more member agencies participate;

(6) the development of *long-term regional* interagency and intergovernmental *strategies* for *resource allocations* to better respond to the needs of States and local communities;

(7) the supervision of regional interagency program coordination mechanisms; and

(8) the development of administrative procedures to facilitate day-to-day interagency and intergovernmental cooperation.

SEC. 3. *Under Secretaries Group for Regional Operations.* There is hereby established an "Under Secretaries Group for Regional Operations" which shall be composed of the Under Secretaries of Labor, Health, Education, and Welfare, Housing and Urban Development, and Transportation, the Administrator of the Law Enforcement Assistance Administration, the Deputy Director of the Office of Economic Opportunity, the Deputy Administrator of the Environmental Protection Agency, and the Associate Director of the Office of Management and Budget, who shall serve as the Chairman of the Group. When the Chairman determines that matters which significantly affect the interest of Federal agencies which are not represented on the Group are to be considered by the Group, he shall invite an appropriate representative of the agency involved to participate in the deliberations of the Group. The Under Secretaries Group for Regional Operations shall, consistent with the objectives and priorities established by the President and the Domestic Council, establish policy with respect to Federal Regional Council matters, provide guidance to the Councils, respond to their initiatives, and seek to resolve policy issues referred to it by the Councils. The Under Secretaries Group, under the Chairmanship of the Associate Director of the Office of Management and Budget, shall be responsible for the proper functioning of the system established by this Order.

SEC. 4. *Construction.* Nothing in this Order shall be construed as subjecting any department, establishment, or other instrumentality of the executive branch of the Federal Government or the head thereof, or any function vested by law in or assigned pursuant to law to any such agency or head to the authority of any other such agency or head or as abrogating, modifying, or restricting any such function in any manner.

THE WHITE HOUSE   *(Signed) Richard Nixon*

February 10, 1972
[FR Doc.72–2332 Filed 2-11-71; 12:14 pm]

Exhibit D

THE STATE OF NATIONAL EMERGENCY AND EXECUTIVE ORDERS

HON. JOHN R. RARICK

OF LOUISIANA

IN THE HOUSE OF REPRESENTATIVES

Monday, September 27, 1971

Mr. RARICK. Mr. Speaker, the declaration of a state of national emergency by the President of the United States, like a declaration of war, should be an historical event which a free press should be expected to bring to public attention with banner headlines. Yet, the recent declaration of a national emergency proclaimed by President Nixon on August 15, 1971, through proclamation No. 4074 (F.R. vol. 36, No. 159, Aug. 17, 1971) strangely went almost without comment by the Nation's press.

In an article entitled "State of National Emergency Legalizes Executive Orders" appearing in the Borger Texas News Herald, Lt. Col. Archibald E. Roberts, AUS, retired, national director of the Committee To Restore the Constitution, points out:

The state of "national emergency" declared by President Nixon in August "legalized" the imposition of Executive Orders and other socialist directives under the guise of a "time of increased tension, and economic and financial crisis."

The Executive orders of 1962 through

1966 referred to in Roberts' article, with the exception of Executive Order 11051, were among 21 Executive orders and two defense mobilization orders that were consolidated in an all-inclusive Presidential directive, Executive Order 11490, signed by President Nixon on October 28, 1969, entitled "Assigning Emergency Preparedness Functions to Federal Departments and Agencies." (F.R. vol. 34, No. 209, Oct. 30, 1969.) Assignments to departments and agencies were adjusted to conform to changes in organization which occurred subsequent to the issuance of the earlier Executive orders and defense mobilization orders. Executive orders effectuated by the President's proclamation of August 15, 1971, would be under Executive Order 11490.

Because of the vast powers which, without further congressional approval, Executive Order 11490 places in the hands of the President and his heads of departments and agencies over food supply, money and credit, transportation, communications, public utilities, and other facets of the lives of our people; and in order that our colleagues may have this vital information more readily available for themselves and their constituents, I insert in the RECORD at this point the President's 1971 Proclamation No. 4074, its companion Executive Order 11615, the 1969 Executive Order 11490, and a newsclipping from the Borger Texas News Herald:

[From the Federal Register, vol. 36, No. 159, Aug. 17, 1971]

PROCLAMATION 4074: IMPOSITION OF SUPPLE-
MENTAL DUTY FOR BALANCE-OF-PAYMENTS
PURPOSES

(A proclamation by the President of the United States of America)

Whereas, there has been a prolonged decline in the international monetary reserves of the United States, and our trade and international competitive position is seriously threatened and, as a result, our continued ability to assure our security could be impaired;

Whereas, the balance of payments position of the United States requires the imposition of a surcharge on dutiable imports;

Whereas, pursuant to the authority vested in him by the Constitution and the statutes, including, but not limited to, the Tariff Act of 1930, as amended (hereinafter referred to as "the Tariff Act"), and the Trade Expansion Act of 1962 (hereinafter referred to as "the TEA"), the President entered into, and proclaimed tariff rates under, trade agreements with foreign countries;

Whereas, under the Tariff Act, the TEA and other provisions of law, the President may, at any time, modify or terminate, in whole or in part, any proclamation made under his authority;

Now, therefore, I, Richard Nixon, President of the United States of America, acting under the authority vested in me by the Constitution and the statutes, including, but not limited to, the Tariff Act, and the TEA, respectively, do proclaim as follows:

A. I hereby declare a national emergency during which I call upon the public and private sector to make the efforts necessary to strengthen the international economic position of the United States.

B. (1) I hereby terminate in part for such period as may be necessary and modify prior Presidential Proclamations which carry out trade agreements insofar as such proclamations are inconsistent with, or proclaim duties different from, those made effective pursuant to the terms of this Proclamation.

(2) Such proclamations are suspended only insofar as is required to assess a surcharge in the form of a supplemental duty amounting to 10 percent ad valorem. Such supplemental duty shall be imposed on all dutiable articles imported into the customs territory of the United States from outside thereof, which are entered, or withdrawn from warehouse, for consumption after 12:01 a.m., August 16, 1971, provided, however, that if the imposition of an additional duty of 10 percent ad valorem would cause the total duty or charge payable to exceed the total duty or charge payable at the rate prescribed in column 2 of the Tariff Schedules of the United States, then the column 2 rate shall apply.

C. To implement section B of this Proclamation, the following new subpart shall be inserted after subpart B of part 2 of the Appendix to the Tariff Schedules of the United States:

SUBPART C—TEMPORARY MODIFICATIONS FOR
BALANCE-OF-PAYMENTS PURPOSES

Subpart C headnotes:

1. This subpart contains modifications of the provisions of the tariff schedules proclaimed by the President in Proclamation 4074.

2. *Additional duties imposed*—The duties provided for in this subpart are cumulative

duties which apply in addition to the duties otherwise imposed on the articles involved. The provisions for these duties are effective with respect to articles entered on and after 12:01 a.m., August 16, 1971, and shall continue in effect until modified or terminated by the President or by the Secretary of the Treasury (hereinafter referred to as the Secretary) in accordance with headnote 4 of this subpart.

3. *Limitation on additional duties*—The additional 10 percent rate of duty specified in rate of duty column numbered 1 of item 948.00 shall in no event exceed that rate which, when added to the column numbered 1 rate imposed on the imported article under the appropriate item in schedules 1 through 7 of these schedules, would result in an aggregated rate in excess of the rate provided for such article in rate of duty column numbered 2.

4. For the purposes of this subpart—

(a) *Delegation of authority to Secretary*— The Secretary may from time to time take action to reduce, eliminate or reimpose the rate of additional duty herein or to establish exemption therefrom, either generally or with respect to an article which he may specify either generally or as the product of a particular country, if he determines that such action is consistent with safeguarding the balance of payments position of the United States.

(b) *Publication of Secretary's actions*— All actions taken by the Secretary hereunder shall be in the form of modifications of this subpart published in the Federal Register. Any action reimposing the additional duties on an article exempted therefrom by the Secretary shall be effective only with respect to articles entered on and after the date of publication of the action in the Federal Register.

(c) *Authority to prescribe rules and regulations*—The Secretary is authorized to prescribe such rules and regulations as he determines to be necessary or appropriate to carry out the provisions of this subpart.

5. *Articles exempt from the additional duties*—In accordance with determinations made by the Secretary in accordance with headnote 4(a), the following described articles are exempt from the provisions of this subpart:

*   *   *   *   *

THE PRESIDENT

Item	Article	Rates of duty	
		1	2
948.00	Articles, except as exempted under headnote 5 of this subpart, which are not free of duty under these schedules and which are the subject of tariff concessions granted by the United States in trade agreements.	10% ad val. (See headnote 3 of this subpart.)	No change.

D. This Proclamation shall be effective 12:01 a.m., August 16, 1971.

In witness whereof, I have hereunto set my hand this fifteenth day of August in the year of our Lord nineteen hundred and seventy-one, and of the Independence of the United States of America the one hundred and ninety-sixth.

RICHARD NIXON.

Exhibit E

[From the Federal Register, vol. 36, No. 159, Aug. 17, 1971]

EXECUTIVE ORDER 11615 (Providing for stabilization of prices, rents, wages, and salaries)

Whereas, in order to stabilize the economy, reduce inflation, and minimize unemployment, it is necessary to stabilize prices, rents, wages, and salaries; and

Whereas, the present balance of payments situation makes it especially urgent to stabilize prices, rents, wages, and salaries in order to improve our competitive position in world trade and to protect the purchasing power of the dollar:

Now, therefore, by virtue of the authority vested in me by the Constitution and statutes of the United States, including the Economic Stabilization Act of 1970 (P.L. 91–379, 84 Stat. 799), as amended, it is hereby ordered as follows:

SECTION 1. (a) Prices, rents, wages, and salaries shall be stabilized for a period of 90 days from the date hereof at levels not greater than the highest of those pertaining to a substantial volume of actual transactions by each individual, business, firm or other entity of any kind during the 30-day period ending August 14, 1971, for like or similar commodities or services. If no transactions occurred in that period, the ceiling will be the highest price, rent, salary or wage in the nearest preceding 30-day period in which transactions did occur. No person shall charge, assess, or receive, directly or indirectly in any transaction prices or rents in any form higher than those permitted hereunder, and no person shall, directly or indirectly, pay or agree to pay in any transaction wages or salaries in any form, or to use any means to obtain payment of wages and salaries in any form, higher than those permitted hereunder, whether by retroactive increase or otherwise.

(b) Each person engaged in the business of selling or providing commodities or services shall maintain available for public inspection a record of the highest prices or rents charged for such or similar commodities or services during the 30-day period ending August 14, 1971.

(c) The provisions of sections 1 and 2 hereof shall not apply to the prices charged for raw agricultural products.

SEC. 2. (a) There is hereby established the Cost of Living Council which shall act as an agency of the United States and which is hereinafter referrer to as the Council.

(b) The Council shall be composed of the following members: The Secretary of the Treasury, the Secretary of Agriculture, the the Secretary of Commerce, the Secretary of Labor, the Director of the Office of Management and Budget, the Chairman of the Council of Economic Advisers, the Director of the Office of Emergency Preparedness, and the Special Assistant to the President for Consumer Affairs. The Secretary of the Treasury shall serve as Chairman of the Council and the Chairman of the Council of Economic Advisers shall serve as Vice Chairman. The Chairman of the Board of Governors of the Federal Reserve System shall serve as adviser to the Council.

(c) Under the direction of the Chairman of the Council a Special Assistant to the President shall serve as Executive Director of the Council, and the Executive Director is authorized to appoint such personnel as may be necessary to assist the Council in the performance of its functions.

SEC. 3. (a) Except as otherwise provided herein, there are hereby delegated to the Council all of the powers conferred on the President by the Economic Stabilization Act of 1970.

(b) The Council shall develop and recommend to the President additional policies, mechanisms, and procedures to maintain economic growth without inflationary increases in prices, rents, wages, and salaries after the expiration of the 90-day period specified in Section 1 of this Order.

(c) The Council shall consult with representatives of agriculture, industry, labor and the public concerning the development of policies, mechanisms and procedures to maintain economic growth without inflationary increases in prices, rents, wages, and salaries.

(d) In all of its actions the Council will be guided by the need to maintain consistency of price and wage policies with fiscal, monetary, international and other economic policies of the United States.

(e) The Council shall inform the public, agriculture, industry, and labor concerning the need for controlling inflation and shall encourage and promote voluntary action to that end.

Sec. 4. (a) The Council, in carrying out the provisions of this Order, may (i) prescribe definitions for any terms used herein, (ii) make exceptions or grant exemptions, (iii) issue regulations and orders, and (iv) take such other actions as it determines to be necessary and appropriate to carry out the purposes of this Order.

(b) The Council may redelegate to any

agency, instrumentality or official of the United States any authority under this Order, and may, in administering this Order, utilize the services of any other agencies, Federal or State, as may be available and appropriate.

(c) On request of the Chairman of the Council, each Executive department or agency is authorized and directed, consistent with law, to furnish the Council with available information which the Council may require in the performance of its functions.

(d) All Executive departments and agencies shall furnish such necessary assistance as may be authorized by section 214 of the Act of May 3, 1945 (59 Stat. 134; 31 U.S.C. 691).

SEC. 5. The Council may require the maintenance of appropriate records or other evidence which are necessary in carrying out the provisions of this Order, and may require any person to maintain and produce for examination such records or other evidence, in such form as it shall require, concerning prices, rents, wages, and salaries and all related matters. The Council may make such exemptions from any requirement otherwise imposed as are consistent with the purposes of this Order. Any type of record or evidence required under regulations issued under this Order shall be retained for such period as the Council may prescribe.

SEC. 6. The expenses of the Council shall be paid from such funds of the Treasury Department as may be available therefor.

SEC. 7. (a) Whoever willfully violates this Order or any order or regulation issued under authority of this Order shall be fined not more than $5,000 for each such violation.

(b) The Council shall in its discretion request the Department of Justice to bring actions for injunctions authorized under Section 205 of the Economic Stabilization Act of 1970 whenever it appears to the Council that any person has engaged, is engaged, or is about to engage in any acts or practices constituting a violation of any regulation or order issued pursuant to this Order.

RICHARD NIXON.

THE WHITE HOUSE, *August 15, 1971.*

Exhibit F

[From the Federal Register, vol. 34, No. 209, Oct. 30, 1969]

EXECUTIVE ORDER 11490 ASSIGNING EMERGENCY PREPAREDNESS FUNCTIONS TO FEDERAL DEPARTMENT AND AGENCIES

Whereas our national security is dependent upon our ability to assure continuity of government, at every level, in any national emergency type situation that might conceivably confront the nation; and

Whereas effective national preparedness planning to meet such an emergency, including a massive nuclear attack, is essential to our national survival; and

Whereas effective national preparedness planning requires the identification of functions that would have to be performed during such an emergency, the assignment of responsibility for developing plans for performing these functions, and the assignment of responsibility for developing the capability to implement those plans; and

Whereas the Congress has directed the development of such national emergency preparedness plans and has provided funds for the accomplishment thereof; and

Whereas this national emergency preparedness planning activity has been an established program of the United States Government for more than twenty years:

Now, therefore, by virtue of the authority

vested in me as President of the United States, and pursuant to Reorganization Plan No. 1 of 1958 (72 Stat. 1799), the National Security Act of 1947, as amended, the Defense Production Act of 1950, as amended, and the Federal Civil Defense Act, as amended, it is hereby ordered as follows—

PART 1—PURPOSE AND SCOPE

SECTION 101 *Purpose.* This order consolidates the assignment of emergency preparedness functions to various departments and agencies heretofore contained in the 21 Executive orders and 2 Defense Mobilization orders listed in Section 3015 of this order. Assignments have been adjusted to conform to changes in organization which have occurred subsequent to the issuance of those Executive orders and Defense Mobilization orders.

SEC. 102 *Scope.* (a) This order is concerned with the emergency national planning and preparedness functions of the several departments and agencies of the Federal Government which complement the military radiness planning responsibilities of the Department of Defense; together, these measures provide the basic foundation for our overall national preparedness posture, and are fundamental to our ability to survive.

(b) The departments and agencies of the Federal Government are hereby severally charged with the duty of assuring the continuity of the Federal Government in any national emergency type situation that might confront the nation. To this end, each department and agency with essential functions, whether expressly identified in this order or not, shall develop such plans and take such actions, including but not limited to those specified in this order, as may be necessary to assure that it will be able to perform its essential functions, and continue as a viable part of the Federal Government, during an emergency that might conceivably occur. These include plans for maintaining the continuity of essential functions of the department or agency at the seat of government and elsewhere, through programs concerned with: (1) succession to office; (2) predelegation of emergency authority; (3) safekeeping of essential records; (4) emergency relocation sites supported by communications and required services; (5) emergency action steps; (6) alternate headquarters or command facilities; and (7) protection of Government resources, facilities, and personnel. The continuity of Government activities undertaken by the departments and agencies shall be in accordance with guidance provided by, and subject to evaluation by, the Director of the Office of Emergency Preparedness.

(c) In addition to the activities indicated above, the heads of departments and agencies described in Parts 2 through 29 of this order shall: (1) prepare national emergency plans, develop preparedness programs, and attain an appropriate state of readiness with respect to the functions assigned to them in this order for all conditions of national emergency; (2) give appropriate consideration to emergency preparedness factors in the conduct of the regular functions of their agencies, particularly those functions considered essential in time of emergency, and (3) be prepared to implement, in the event of an emergency, all appropriate plans developed under this order.

SEC. 103 *Presidential Assistance.* The Director of the Office of Emergency Preparedness, in accordance with the provisions of Executive Order No. 11051 of September 27, 1962, shall advise and assist the President in determining national preparedness goals and policies for the performance of functions under this order and in coordinating the performance of such functions with the total national preparedness program.

SEC. 104. *General and Specific Functions.* The functions assigned by Part 30, General Provisions, apply to all departments and agencies having emergency preparedness responsibilities. Specific functions are assigned to departments and agencies covered in Parts 2 through 29.

SEC. 105. *Construction.* The purpose and legal effect of the assignments contained in this order do not constitute authority to implement the emergency plans prepared pursuant to this order. Plans so developed may be effectuated only in the event that authority for such effectuation is provided by a law enacted by the Congress or by an order or directive issued by the President pursuant to statutes or the Constitution of the United States.

PART 2—DEPARTMENT OF STATE

SECTION 201 *Functions.* The Secretary of State shall prepare national emergency plans and develop preparedness programs to permit modification or expansion of the activities of the Department of State and agencies, boards, and commissions under his jurisdiction in order to meet all conditions of national emergency, including attack upon the United States. The Secretary of State shall provide to all other departments and agencies overall foreign policy direction, coordination, and supervision in the formulation and execution of those emergency preparedness activities which have foreign policy implications, affect foreign relations, or depend directly or indirectly, on the policies and capabilities of the Department of State. The Secretary of State shall develop policies, plans, and procedures for carrying out his responsibilities in the conduct of the foreign relations of the United States under conditions of national emergency, including, but not limited to (1) the formulation and implementation, in consultation with the Department of Defense and other appropriate agencies, and the negotiation of contingency and post-emergency plans with our allies and of the intergovernmental agreements, and arrangements required by such plans; (2) formulation, negotiation, and execution of policy affecting the relationships of the United States with neutral States; (3) formulation and execution of political strategy toward hostile or enemy States, including the definition of war objectives and the political means for achieving those objectives; (4) maintenance of diplomatic and consular representation abroad; (5) reporting and advising on conditions overseas which bear upon the national emergency; (6) carrying out or proposing economic measures with respect to other nations, including coordination with the export control functions of the Secretary of Commerce; (7) mutual assistance activities such as ascertaining requirements of the civilian economies of other nations, making recommendations to domestic resource agencies for meeting such requirements, and determining the availability of and making arrangements for obtaining foreign resources required by the United States; (8) providing foreign assistance, including continuous supervision and general direction of authorized economic and military assistance programs, and determination of the value thereof; (9) protection or evacuation of American citizens and nationals abroad and safeguarding their property; (10) protection and/or control of international organization and foreign diplomatic, consular, and other official personnel and property, or other assets, in the United States; (11) documentary control of persons seeking to enter or leave the United States; and (12) regulation and control of exports of items on the munitions list.

PART 3—DEPARTMENT OF THE TREASURY

SECTION 301. *Functions.* The Secretary of the Treasury shall develop policies, plans, and procedures for the performance of emergency functions with respect to (1) stabilization aspects of the monetary, credit, and financial system; (2) stabilization of the dollar in relation to foreign currencies; (3) collection of revenue; (4) regulation of financial institutions; (5) supervision of the Federal depository system; (6) direction of transactions in government securities; (7) tax and debt policies; (8) participation in bilateral and multilateral financial arrangements with foreign governments; (9) regulation of foreign assets in the United States and of foreign financial dealings (in consultation with the Secretaries of State and Commerce); (10) development of procedures for the manufacture and/or issuance and redemption of securities, stamps, coins, and currency; (11) development of systems for the issuance and payment of Treasury checks; (12) maintenance of the central government accounting and financial reporting system; (13) administration of customs laws, tax laws, and laws on control of alcohol, alcoholic beverages, tobacco, and firearms; (14) suppression of counterfeiting and forgery of government securities, stamps, coins, and currency; (15) protection of the President and the Vice President and other designated persons; (16) granting of loans (including participation in or guarantees of loans) for the expansion of capacity, the development of technological processes, or the production of essential material; and (17) to the extent that such functions have not been transferred to the Secretary of Transportation, enforcement of marine inspection and navigation laws.

SEC. 302. *Financial Coordination.* The Secretary shall assume the initiative in developing plans for implementation of national policy on sharing war losses and for the coordination of emergency monetary, credit, and Federal benefit payment programs of those departments and agencies which have responsibilities dependent on the policies or capabilities of the Department.

PART 4—DEPARTMENT OF DEFENSE

SECTION 401. *Functions.*—In addition to the civil defense functions assigned to the Secretary of Defense by Executive Order No. 10952, the Secretary of Defense shall perform the following emergency preparedness functions:

(1) Provide specific strategic guidance as required for emergency preparedness planning and programming, including, for example, guidance regarding such factors as accessibility of foreign sources of supply and estimated shipping loss discounts and aircraft losses in the event of war.

(2) Develop and furnish quantitative and time-phased military requirements for selected end-items, consistent with defined military concepts, and supporting requirements for materials, components, production facilities, production equipment, petroleum, natural gas, solid fuels, electric power, food, transportation, and other services needed to carry out specified Department of Defense current and mobilization procurement, construction, research and development, and production programs. The items and supporting resources to be included in such re-

quirements, the periods to be covered, and the dates for their submission to the appropriate resource agency will be determined by mutual agreement between the Secretary of Defense and the head of the appropriate resource agency.

(3) Advise and assist the Office of Emergency Preparedness in developing a national system of production urgencies.

(4) Advise and assist the Office of Emergency Preparedness in developing a system, in conjunction with the Department of State, for the international allocation of critical materials and products among the United States and the various foreign claimants in the event of an emergency, including an attack on the United States.

(5) Plan for and administer priorities and allocations authority delegated to the Department of Defense. Authorize procurement and production schedules and make allotments of controlled materials pursuant to program determinations of the Office of Emergency Preparedness.

(6) Assist the Department of Commerce and other appropriate agencies in the development of the production and distribution controls plans for use in any period of emergency.

(7) Develop with industry, plans for the procurement and production of selected military equipment and supplies needed to fulfill emergency requirements, making maximum use of plants in dispersed locations, and, where essential and appropriate, providing for alternative sources of supply in order to minimize the effects of enemy attack.

(8) Develop with industry, plans and programs for minimizing the effect of attack damage to plants producing major items of military equipment and supply.

(9) Recommend to the Office of Emergency Preparedness measures for overcoming potential deficiencies in production capacity to produce selected military supplies and equipment needed to fulfill emergency requirements, when necessary measures cannot be effected by the Department of Defense.

(10) Furnish information and recommendations, when requested by the Office of Emergency Preparedness, for purposes of processing applications for defense loans under Title II of the Defense Production Act of 1950, as amended.

(11) Furnish advice and assistance on the utilization of strategic and critical materials in defense production, including changes that occur from time to time.

(12) Analyze problems that may arise in maintaining an adequate mobilization production base in military-product industries and take necessary actions to overcome these problems within the limits of the authority and funds available to the Department of Defense.

(13) Assist the Secretary of Commerce with respect to the identification and evaluation of facilities important to the national defense.

(14) Advise and assist the Office of Emergency Preparedness in the development and review of standards for the strategic location and physical security of industries, services, government, and other activities for which continuing operation is essential to national security, and exercise physical security cognizance over the facilities assigned to him for such purpose.

(15) Develop and operate damage assessment systems and assist the Office of Emergency Preparedness and other departments and agencies in their responsibilities as

stated in Section 3002(2); participate with the Office of Emergency Preparedness in the preparation of estimates of potential damage from enemy attack.

(16) Advise and assist the Office of Emergency Preparedness in the development of over-all manpower policies to be instituted in the event of an emergency, including an attack on the United States, including the provision of information relating to the size and composition of the Armed Forces.

(17) Advise on existing communications facilities and furnish military requirements for commercial communications facilities and services in planning for and in event of an emergency, including an attack on the United States.

(18) Furnish military requirements for all forms of transportation and transportation facilities in planning for and in the event of emergency, including an attack upon the United States.

(19) Assist the Office of Emergency Preparedness in preparation of legislative programs and plans for coordinating nonmilitary support of emergency preparedness programs.

(20) Develop plans and procedures for the Department of Defense utilization of non-industrial facilities in the event of an emergency in order to reduce requirements for new construction and to provide facilities in a minimum period of time.

(21) Advise and assist the Office of Emergency Preparedness in (1) determining what key foreign facilities and operating rights thereto are important enough to the security of the United States, and (2) obtaining through appropriate channels protection against sabotage.

(22) Develop plans and procedures to carry out Department of Defense responsibilities stated in the National Censorship Agree-

ment between the Department of Defense and the Office of Emergency Preparedness.

(23) Advise and assist the Department of State in planning for the evacuation of dependents from overseas areas, United States teachers and administrators in the overseas dependents schools, and such other United States citizens as may be working for United States schools overseas.

(24) Develop plans for implementation of approved Department of State/Department of Defense policies and procedures for the protection and evacuation of United States citizens and certain designated aliens abroad.

(25) Develop plans and procedures for the provision of logistical support to members of foreign forces, their employees and dependents as may be present in the United States under the terms of bilateral or multilateral agreements which authorize such support in the event of a national emergency.

(26) Develop with the Department of Transportation and Federal Communications Commission plans and programs for the control of air traffic, civil and military, during an emergency.

(27) Develop with the Federal Communications Commission and the Office of Telecommunications Management (OEP) plans and programs for the emergency control of all devices capable of emitting electromagnetic radiation.

PART 5—DEPARTMENT OF JUSTICE

Section 501. *Functions.* The Attorney General shall perform the following emergency preparedness functions:

(1) *Emergency documents and measures.* Provide advice, as appropriate, with respect to any emergency directive or procedure prepared by a department or agency as a part of its emergency preparedness function.

(2) *Industry support.* As appropriate, review the legal procedures developed by the Federal agencies concerned to be instituted if it becomes necessary for the Government to institute extraordinary measures with respect to vital production facilities, public facilities, communications systems, transportation systems, or other facility, system, or service essential to national survival.

(3) *Judicial and legislative liaison.* In cooperation with the Office of Emergency Preparedness, maintain liaison with Federal courts and with the Congress so there will be mutual understanding of Federal emergency plans involving law enforcement and the exercise of legal powers during emergencies of various magnitudes.

(4) *Legal advice.* Develop emergency plans for providing legal advice to the President, the Cabinet, and the heads of Executive departments and agencies wherever they may be located in an emergency, and provide emergency procedures for the review as to form and legality of Presidential proclamations, Executive orders, directives, regulations, and documents, and of other documents requiring approval by the President or by the Attorney General which may be issued by authorized officers after an armed attack.

(5) *Alien control and control of entry and departure.* Develop emergency plans for the control of alien enemies and other aliens within the United States and, in consultation with the Department of State and Departmnt of the Treasury, develop emergency plans for the control of persons attempting to enter or leave the United States. These plans shall specifically include provisions for the following:

(a) The location, restraint, or custody of alien enemies.

(b) Temporary detention of alien enemies and other persons attempting to enter the United States pending determination of their admissibility.

(c) Apprehension of deserting alien crewmen and stowaways.

(d) Investigation and control of aliens admitted as contract laborers.

(e) Control of persons entering or departing from the United States at designated ports of entry.

(f) Increased surveillance of the borders to preclude prohibited crossings by persons.

(6) *Alien property.* Develop emergency plans, in consultation with the Department of State, for the seizure and administration of property of alien enemies under provisions of the Trading with the Enemy Act.

(7) *Security standards.* In consultation with the Department of Defense and with other executive agencies, to the extent appropriate, prepare plans for adjustment of security standards governing the employment of Federal personnel and Federal contractors in an emergency.

(8) *Drug Control.* Develop emergency plans and procedures for the administration of laws governing the import, manufacture, and distribution of narcotics. Consult with and render all possible aid and assistance to the Office of Emergency Preparedness, the Department of Health, Education, and Welfare, and the General Services Administration in the allocation, distribution, and, if necessary, the replenishment of Government stockpiles of narcotic drugs.

SEC. 502. *Civil Defense Functions.* In consonance with national civil defense programs developed by the Department of Defense, the Attorney General shall:

(1) *Local law enforcement.* Upon request, consult with and assist the Department of

Defense to plan, develop, and distribute materials for use in the instruction and training of law enforcement personnel for civil defense emergency operations; develop and carry out a national plan for civil defense instruction and training for enforcement officers, designed to utilize to the maximum extent practicable the resources and facilities of existing Federal, State, and local police schools, academies, and other appropriate institutions of learning; and assist the States in preparing for the conduct of intrastate and interstate law enforcement operations to meet the extraordinary needs that would exist for emergency police services under conditions of attack or imminent attack.

(2) *Penal and correctional institutions.* Develop emergency plans and procedures for the custoday and protection of prisoners and the use of Federal penal and correctional institutional resources, when available, for cooperation with local authorities in connection with mass feeding and housing, for the storage of standby emergency equipment, for the emergency use of prison hospitals and laboratory facilities, for the continued availability of prison-industry products, and, in coordination with the Department of Labor, for the development of Federal prisoner skills to appropriately augment the total supply of manpower, advise States and their political subdivisions regarding the use of State and local prisons, jails, and prisoners for the purpose of relieving local situations and conditions arising from a state of emergency.

(3) *Identification and location of persons.* Develop emergency plans and procedures for the use of the facilities and personnel of the Department of Justice in assisting the Department of Health, Education, and Welfare with the development of plans and procedures for the identification of the dead and

the reuniting of families during a civil defense emergency.

PART 6—POST OFFICE DEPARTMENT

SECTION 601 *Functions*. The Postmaster General shall prepare plans and programs for emergency mail service and shall cooperate with indicated Federal agencies, in accordance with existing agreements or directives, in the following national emergency programs:

(1) *Registering of persons.* Assist the Department of Health, Education, and Welfare in planning a national program and developing technical guidance for States, and directing Post Office activities concerned with registering persons and families for the purpose of receiving and answering welfare inquiries and reuniting families in civil defense emergencies. The program shall include procurement, transportation, storage, and distribution of safety notification and emergency change of address cards in quantities and localities jointly determined by the Department of Defense and the Post Office Department.

(2) *Other emergency programs.* (a) Censorship of international mails. (Department of Defense; Department of the Treasury; Office of Emergency Preparedness).

(b) Provision for emergency mail service to Federal agencies at both regular and emergency sites. (General Services Administration)

(c) Emergency registration of Federal employees. (Civil Service Commission)

(d) Emergency leasing of space for Federal agencies. (General Services Administration)

(e) Registration of enemy aliens. (Department of Justice)

PART 7—DEPARTMENT OF THE INTERIOR

SECTION 701 *Résumé of Responsibilities.*

The Secretary of the Interior shall prepare national emergency plans and develop preparedness programs covering (1) electric power; (2) petroleum and gas; (3) solid fuels; (4) minerals; and (5) water, as defined in Section 702 of this part.

SEC. 702 *Definitions.* As used in this part:

(1) "Electric power" means all forms of electric power and energy, including the generation, transmission, distribution, and utilization thereof.

(2) "Petroleum" means crude oil and synthetic liquid fuel, their products, and associated hydrocarbons, including pipelines for their movement and facilities specially designed for their storage.

(3) "Gas" means natural gas (including helium) and manufactured gas, including pipelines for their movement and facilities specially designed for their storage.

(4) "Solid fuels" means all forms of anthracite, bituminous, subbituminous, and lignitic coals, coke, and coal chemicals produced in the coke-making process.

(5) "Minerals" means all raw materials of mineral origin (except petroleum, gas, solid fuels, and source materials as defined in the Atomic Energy Act of 1954, as amended) obtained by mining and like operations and processed through the stages specified and at the facilities designated in an agreement between the Secretary of the Interior and the Secretary of Commerce as being within the emergency preparedness responsibilities of the Secretary of the Interior.

(6) "Water" means water from all sources except water after its withdrawal into a community system, or an emergency system for treatment, storage, and distribution for public use.

SEC. 703. *Resource functions.* With respect to the resources defined in Section 702, the

Secretary of the Interior shall:

(1) *Minerals development.* Develop programs and encourage the exploration, development, and mining of strategic and critical minerals for emergency purposes.

(2) *Production.* Provide guidance and leadership to assigned industries in the development of plans and programs to insure the continuity of production in the event of an attack, and cooperate with the Department of Commerce in the identification and evaluation of essential facilities.

(3) *Water.* Develop plans with respect to water, including plans for the treatment and disposal, after use, of water after its withdrawal into a community system or an emergency system for treatment, storage, and distribution for public use. In developing any plans relating to water for use on farms and in food facilities, assure that those plans are in consonance with plans and programs of the Department of Agriculture.

(4) *Electric power and natural gas.* In preparedness planning for electric power and natural gas, the Federal Power Commission shall assist the Secretary of the Interior as set forth in Section 1901 of this order.

PART 8—DEPARTMENT OF AGRICULTURE

SECTION 801 *Résumé of Responsibilities.* The Secretary of Agriculture shall prepare national emergency plans and develop preparedness programs covering: (1) food resources, farm equipment, fertilizer, and food resource facilities as defined below; (2) lands under the jurisdiction of the Secretary of Agriculture; (3) rural fire control; (4) defense against biological and chemical warfare and radiological fall out pertaining to agricultural activities; and (5) rural defense information and education.

SEC. 802 *Definitions.* As used in this part:

(1) "Food resources" means all commodities and products, simple, mixed, or compound, or complements to such commodities or products, that are capable of being eaten or drunk, by either human beings or animals, irrespective of other uses to which such commodities or products may be put, at all stages of processing from the raw commodity to the products thereof in vendible form for human or animal consumption. For the purposes of this order, the term "food resources" shall also include all starches, sugars, vegetable and animal fats and oils, cotton, tobacco, wool, mohair, hemp, flax fiber, and naval stores, but shall not include any such material after it loses its identity as an agricultural commodity or agricultural product.

(2) "Farm equipment" means machinery, equipment, and repair parts manufactured primarily for use on farms in connection with the production or preparation for market or use of "food resources".

(3) "Fertilizer" means any product or combination of products for plant nutrition in form for distribution to the users thereof.

(4) "Food resource facilities" means plants, machinery, vehicles (including on farm), and other facilities (including farm housing) for the production, processing, distribution, and storage (including cold storage) of food resources, and for domestic distribution of farm equipment and fertilizer.

SEC. 803. *Functions.* With respect to food resources, food resource facilities, lands under the jurisdiction of the Secretary, farm equipment, and fertilizer, the Secretary of Agriculture shall:

(1) *Production, processing, storage, and distribution.* Develop plans for priorities, al-

locations, and distribution control systems
and related plans, including control of use
of facilities designed to provide adequate and
continuing production, processing, storage,
and distribution of essential food resources
in an emergency, and to provide for the
domestic distribution of farm equipment and
fertilizer.

(2) *Stockpiles*. In addition to the food
stockpile functions identified in Executive
Order No. 10958, take all possible measures
in the administration of Commodity Credit
Corporation inventories of food resources to
assure the availability of such inventories
when and where needed in an emergency.
The Secretary shall also develop plans and
procedures for the proper utilization of agricultural items stockpiled for survival
purposes.

(3) *Land management*. Develop plans and
direct activities for the emergency protection, management, and utilization of the
lands, resources, and installations under the
jurisdiction of the Secretary of Agriculture
and assist in the development of plans for the
emergency operation, production, and
processing of forest products in cooperation
with other Federal, State, and private
agencies.

SEC. 804   *Civil Defense Functions*. In consonance with national civil defense programs
developed by the Development of Defense,
the Secretary of Agriculture shall:

(1) *Rural fire defense*. In cooperation with
Federal, State, and local agencies, develop
plans for a national program and direct
activities relating to the prevention and control of fires in the rural areas of the United
States caused by the effects of enemy attack.

(2) *Biological, chemical, and radiological
warfare defense*. Develop plans for a national
program, direct Federal activities, and fur-

nish technical guidance to State and local authorities concerning (a) diagnosis and strengthening of defensive barriers and control or eradication of diseases, pests, or chemicals introduced as agents of biological or chemical warfare against animals, crops, or products thereof; (b) protective measures, treatment, and handling of livestock, including poultry, agricultural commodities on farms or ranches, agricultural lands, forest lands, and water for agricultural purposes, any of which have been exposed to or affected by radiation. Plans shall be developed for a national program and direction of Federal activities to assure the safety and wholesomeness and to minimize losses from biological and chemical warfare, radiological effects, and other emergency hazards of livestock, meat and meat products, poultry and poultry products in establishments under the continuous inspection of the Department of griculture, and agricultural commodities and products owned by the Commodity Credit Corporation or by the Department of Agriculture.

(3) *Defense information and education.* Conduct a defense information and education program in support of the Department's emergency responsibilties.

PART 9—DEPARTMENT OF COMMERCE

SECTION 901 *Résumé of Responsibilities.* The Secretary of Commerce shall prepare national emergency plans and develop preparedness programs covering:

(1) The production and distribution of all materials, the use of all production facilities (except those owned by, controlled by, or under the jurisdiction of the Department of Defense or the Atomic Energy Commission), the control of all construction materials, and the furnishing of basic industrial services ex-

cept those involving the following:

(a) Production and distribution of and use of facilities for petroleum, solid fuels, gas, electric power, and water;

(b) Production, processing, distribution, and storage of food resources and the use of food resource facilities for such production, processing, distribution, and storage;

(c) Domestic distribution of farm equipment and fertilizer;

(d) Use of communications services and facilities, housing and lodging facilities, and health, education, and welfare facilities;

(e) Production, and related distribution, of minerals as defined in Subsection 702(5), and source materials as defined in the Atomic Energy Act of 1954, as amended; and the construction and use of facilities designated as within the responsibilities of the Secretary of the Interior;

(f) Distribution of items in the supply systems of, or controlled by, the Department of Defense and the Atomic Energy Commission;

(g) Construction, use, and management of civil aviation facilities; and

(h) Construction and use of highways, streets, and appurenant structures.

(2) Federal emergency operational control responsibilities with respect to ocean shipping, ports, and port facilities, except those owned by, controlled by, or under the jurisdiction of the Department of Defense, and except those responsibilities of the Department of the Treasury with respect to the entrance and clearance of vessels. The following definitions apply to this part:

(a) "Ocean shipping" includes all overseas, coastwise, intercoastal, and Great Lakes shipping except that solely engaged in the transportation of passengers and cargo between United States ports on the Great

Lakes.

(b) "Port" or "port area" includes any zone contiguous to or associated in the traffic network of an ocean or Great Lakes port, or outport location, including beach loading sites, within which facilities exist for transshipment of persons and property between domestic carriers and carriers engaged in coastal, intercoastal, and overseas transportation.

(c) "Port facilities" includes all port facilities, port equipment including harbor craft, and port services normally used in accomplishing the transfer or interchange of cargo and passengers between ocean-going vessels and other media of transportation, or in connection therewith (including the Great Lakes).

(3) Scientific and technological services and functions, essential to emergency preparedness plans, programs, and operations of the Federal departments and agencies, in which the Department of Commerce has the capability, including, but not limited to:

(a) Meteorological and related services;

(b) Preparation, reproduction, and distribution of nautical and aeronautical charts, geodetic, hydrogrraphic, and oceanographic data, and allied services for nonmilitary purposes;

(c) Standards of measurement and supporting services; and,

(d) Research, development, testing, evaluation, application, and associated services and activities in the various fields and disciplines of science and technology in which the Department has special competence.

(4) Collection, compilation, and reporting of census information and the provision of statistical and related services, as required, for emergency planning and operations.

(5) Regulation and control of exports and imports, under the jurisdiction of the Department of Commerce, in support of national security, foreign policy, and economic stabilization objectives.

(6) Regulation and control of transfers of capital to, and reinvestment of earnings of, affiliated foreign nationals pursuant to authority conferred by Executive Order No. 11387 of January 1, 1968.

SEC. 902 *Production Functions*. Within the areas designated in section 901(1) hereof, the Secretary of Commerce shall:

(1) *Priorities and allocations*. Develop control systems for priorities, allocation, production, and distribution, including provisions for other Federal departments and agencies, as appropriate, to serve as allotting agents for materials and other resources made available under such systems for designated programs and the construction and operation of facilities assigned to them.

(2) *New construction*. Develop procedures by which new production facility construction proposals will be reviewed for appropriate location in light of such area factors as locational security, availability of labor, water, power, housing, and other support requirements.

(3) *Industry evaluation*. Identify and evaluate the national security essentiality of those products and services, and their producing or supporting facilities, which are of exceptional importance to mobilization readiness, national defense, or post-attack survival and recovery.

(4) *Production capability*. Analyze potential effects of attack on actual production capability, taking into account the entire production complex, including shortages of resources, and conduct studies as a basis for recommending pre-attack measures that

would strengthen capabilities for post-attack production.

(5) *Loans for plant modernization.* Develop plans, in coordination with the Small Business Administration, for providing emergency assistance to essential small business establishments through direct loans or participation loans for the financing of production facilities and equipment.

SEC. 903 *Maritime Functions.* Within the areas designated in section 901(2) of this part, the Secretary of Commerce shall develop plans and procedures in consonance with international treaties, under coordinating authority of the Secretary of Transportation and in cooperation with other appropriate Federal agencies and the States and their political subdivisions, to provide for Federal operational control of ocean ports and shipping, including:

(1) *Shipping allocation.* Allocation of specific ocean shipping to meet the national requirements, including those for military, foreign assistance, emergency procurement programs, and those essential to the civilian economy.

(2) *Ship acquisition.* Provision of ships for ocean shipping by purchase, charter, or requisition, by breakout from the national defense reserve fleet, and by construction.

(3) *Operations.* Operation of ocean shipping, directly or indirectly.

(4) *Traffic control.* Provisions for the control of passengers anu cargo through port areas to assure an orderly and continuous flow of such traffic.

(5) *Traffic priority.* Administration of priorities for the movement of passengers and cargo through port areas.

(6) *Port allocation.* Allocation of specific ports and port facilities to meet the needs of the Nation and our allies.

(7) *Support activities*. Performance of supporting activities needed to carry out the above-described functions, such as: ascertaining national support requirements for ocean shipping, including those for support of military and other Federal programs and those essential to the civil economy; maintenance, repair, and arming of ships; recruiting, training, and assigning of officers and seamen; procurement, warehousing, and issuance of ships' stores, supplies, equipment, and spare parts; supervision of stevedoring and bunkering; management of terminals, shipyards, repair, and other facilities; and provision, maintenance, and restoration of port facilities.

SEC. 904 *Census Functions*. Within the area designated in section 901(4) hereof, the Secretary of Commerce shall:

(1) Provide for the collection and reporting of census information on the status of human and economic resources, including population, housing, agriculture, manufacture, mineral industries, business, transportation, foreign trade, construction, and governments, as required for emergency planning purposes.

(2) Plan, create, and maintain a capability for the conduct of post-attack surveys to provide information on the status of surviving populations and resources as required for the programs of the Office of Emergency Preparedness.

(3) Provide for and maintain the ability to make estimates of attack effects on industry, population, and other resources for use within the Department of Commerce.

SEC. 905 *Civil Defense Functions*. In consonance with national civil defense programs developed by the Department of Defense, the Secretary of Commerce shall:

(1) *Weather functions.* Prepare and issue currently, as well as in an emergency, forecasts and estimates of areas likely to be covered by radiological fallout in event of attack and make this information available to Federal, State, and local authorities for public dissemination.

(2) *Geodetic, hydrographic, and oceanographic data.* Provide geodetic, hydrographic, and oceanographic data and services to the Department of Defense and other governmental agencies, as appropriate.

PART 10—DEPARTMENT OF LABOR

SECTION 1001 *Résumé of Responsibilities.* The Secretary of Labor shall have primary responsibility for preparing national emergency plans and developing preparedness programs covering civilian manpower mobilization, more effective utilization of limited manpower resources, including specialized personnel, wage and salary stabilization, worker incentives and protection, manpower resources and requirements, skill development and training, research, labor-management relations, and critical occupations.

SEC. 1002 *Functions.* The Secretary of Labor shall:

(1) *Civilian manpower mobilization.* Develop plans and issue guidance designed to utilize to the maximum extent civilian manpower resources, such plans and guidance to be developed with the active participation and assistance of the States and local political subdivisions thereof, and of other organizations and agencies concerned with the mobilization of the people of the United States. Such plans shall include, but not necessarily be limited to:

(a) *Manpower management.* Recruitment, selection and referral, training, employment stabilization (including appeals procedures), proper utilization, and determination of the skill categories critical to meeting the labor requirements of defense and essential civilian activities;

(b) *Priorities.* Procedures for translating survival and production urgencies into manpower priorities to be used as guides for allocating available workers; and

(c) *Improving mobilization base.* Programs for more effective utilization of limited manpower resources, and, in cooperation with other appropriate agencies, programs for recruitment, training, allocation, and utilization of persons possessing specialized competence or aptitude in acquiring such competence.

(2) *Wage and salary stabilization.* Develop plans and procedures for wage and salary stabilization and for the national and field organization necessary for the administration of such a program in an emergency, including investigation, compliance, and appeals procedures; statistical studies of wages, salaries, and prices for policy decisions and to assist operating stabilization agencies to carry out their functions.

(3) *Worker incentives and protection.* Develop plans and procedures for wage and salary compensation and death and disability compensation for authorized civil defense workers and, as appropriate, measures for unemployment payments, re-employment rights, and occupational safety, and other protection and incentives for the civilian labor force during an emergency.

(4) *Skill development and training.* Initiate current action programs to overcome or offset present or anticipated manpower deficiencies, including those identified as a result of resource and requirements studies.

(5) *Labor-management relations.* Develop after consultation with the Department of

Commerce, the Department of Transportation, the Department of Defense, the National Labor Relations Board, the Federal Mediation and Conciliation Service, the National Mediation Board, and other appropriate agencies and groups, including representatives of labor and management, plans and procedures, including organization plans for the maintenance of effective labor-management relations during a national emergency.

PART 11—DEPARTMENT OF HEALTH, EDUCATION, AND WELFARE

SECTION 1101 *Résumé of Responsibilities.* In addition to the medical stockpile functions identified in Executive Order No. 10958, the Secretary of Health, Education, and Welfare shall prepare national emergency plans and develop preparedness programs covering health services, civilian health manpower, health resources, welfare services, social security benefits, credit union operations, and educational programs as defined below.

SEC. 1102 *Definitions.* As used in this part:

(1) "Emergency health services" means medical and dental care for the civilian population in all of their specialties and adjunct therapeutic fields, and the planning, provision, and operation of first aid stations, hospitals, and clinics; preventive health services, including detection, identification and control of communicable diseases, their vectors, and other public health hazards, inspection and control of purity and safety of food, drugs, and biologicals; vital statistics services; rehabilitation and related services for disabled survivors; preventive and curative care related to human exposure to radiological, chemical, and biological warfare agents; sanitary aspects of disposal of the dead; food and milk sanitation; community solid waste disposal; emergency public water supply; and

the determination of the health significance
of water pollution and the provision of other
services pertaining to health aspects of water
use and water-borne wastes as set forth in an
agreement between the Secretary of Health,
Education, and Welfare and the Secretary of
the Interior, approved by the President, pursuant to Reorganization Plan No. 2 of 1966,
which plan placed upon the Secretary of the
Interior responsibilities for the prevention
and control of water pollution. It shall be
understood that health services for the purposes of this order, however, do not encom-
pass the following areas for which the Department of Agriculture has responsibility:
plant and animal diseases and pest prevention, control, and eradication, wholesomeness
of meat and meat products, and poultry and
poultry products in establishments under
continuous inspection service by the Department of Agriculture, veterinary biologicals,
agricultural commodities and products owned
by the Commodity Credit Corporation or the
Secretary of Agriculture, livestock, agricultural commodities stored or harvestable on
farms and ranches, agricultural lands and
water, and registration of pesticides.

(2) "Health manpower" means physicians
(including osteopaths); dentists; sanitary
engineers; registered professional nurses; and
such other occupations as may be included in
the List of Health Manpower Occupations
issued for the purposes of this part by the
Director of the Office of Emergency Preparedness after agreement by the Secretary of
Labor and the Secretary of Health, Education, and Welfare.

(3) "Health resources" means manpower,
material, and facilities required to prevent
the impairment of, improve, and restore the
physical and mental health conditions of the
civilian population.

(4) "Emergency welfare services" means feeding; clothing; lodging in private and congregate facilities; registration; locating and reuniting families; care of unaccompanied children, the aged, the handicapped, and other groups needing specialized care or services; necessary financial or other assistance; counseling and referral services to families and individuals; aid to welfare institutions under national emergency or post-attack conditions; and all other feasible welfare aid and services to people in need during a civil defense emergency. Such measures include organization, direction, and provision of services to be instituted before attack, in the event of strategic or tactical evacuation, and after attack in the event of evacuation or of refuge in shelters.

(5) "Social security benefits" means the determination of entitlement and the payment of monthly insurance benefits to those eligible, such as workers who have retired because of age or disability and to their dependent wives and children, and to the eligible survivors of deceased workers. It also includes determinations of eligibility and payments made on behalf of eligible individuals to hospitals, home health agencies, extended care facilities, physicians, and other providers of medical services.

(6) "Credit union operations" means the functions of any credit union, chartered either by a State or the Federal Government, in stimulating systematic savings by members, the investment and protection of those savings, providing loans for credit union members at reasonable rates, and encouraging sound credit and thrift practices among credit union members.

(7) "Education" or "training" means the organized process of learning by study and instruction primarily through public and

private systems.

SEC. 1103 *Health Functions.* With respect to emergency health services, as defined above, and in consonance with national civil defense plans, programs, and operation of the Department of Defense under Executive Order No. 10952, the Secretary of Health, Education, and Welfare shall:

(1) *Professional training.* Develop and direct a nationwide program to train health manpower both in professional and technical occupational content and in civil defense knowledge and skills. Develop and distribute health education material for inclusion in the curricula of schools, colleges, professional schools, government schools, and other educational facilities throughout the United States. Develop and distribute civil defense information relative to health services to States, voluntary agencies, and professional groups.

(2) *Emergency public water supply.* Prepare plans to assure the provision of usable water supplies for human consumption and other essential community uses in an emergency. This shall include inventorying existing community water supplies, planning for other alternative sources of water for emergency uses, setting standards relating to human consumption, and planning community distribution. In carrying on these activities, the Department shall have primary responsibility but will make maximum use of the resources and competence of State and local authorities, the Department of the Interior, and other Federal agencies.

(3) *Radiation.* Develop and coordinate programs of radiation measurement and assessment as may be necessary to carry out the responsibilities involved in the provision of emergency helath services.

(4) *Biological and chemical warfare.* Develop and coordinate programs for the prevention, detection, and identification of human exposure to chemical and biological warfare agents as may be necessary to carry out the responsibilities involved in the provision of emergency health services, including the provision of guidance and consultation to Federal, State, and local authorities on measures for minimizing the effects of biological or chemical warfare.

(5) *Food, drugs, and biologicals.* Plan and direct national programs for the maintenance of purity and safety in the manufacture and distribution of food, drugs, and biologicals in an emergency.

(6) *Disabled survivors.* Prepare national plans for emergency operations of vocational rehabilitation and related agencies, and for measures and resources necessary to rehabilitate and make available for employment those disabled persons among the surviving population.

SEC. 1104 *Welfare Functions.* With respect to emergency welfare services as defined above, and in consonance with national civil defense plans, programs, and operations of the Department of Defense under Executive Order No. 10952, the Secretary of Health, Education, and Welfare shall:

(1) *Federal support.* Cooperate in the development of Federal support procedures, through joint planning with other departments and agencies, including but not limited to the Post Office Department, the Department of Labor, and the Selective Service System, the Department of Housing and Urban Development, and resource agencies, including the Department of Agriculture, the Department of the Interior, and the Department of Commerce, for logistic support of State and community welfare in an emer-

gency.

(2) *Emergency welfare training.* Develop and direct a nationwide program to train emergency welfare manpower for the execution of the functions set forth in this part, develop welfare educational materials, including self-help program materials for use with welfare organizations and professional schools, and develop and distribute civil defense information relative to emergency welfare services to States, voluntary agencies, and professional groups.

(3) *Financial Aid.* Develop plans and procedures for financial assistance to individuals injured or in want as a result of an enemy attack and for welfare institutions in need of such assistance in an emergency.

(4) *Non-combatant evacuees to the Continental United States.* Develop plans nad procedures for assistance, at ports of entry to U.S. personnel evacuated from overseas areas, their onward movement to final destination, and follow-up assistance after arrival at final destination.

SEC. 1105 *Social Security Functions.* With respect to social security, the Secretary of Health, Education, and Welfare shall:

(1) *Social Security benefits.* Develop plans for the continuation or restoration of benefit payments to those on the insurance rolls as soon as possible after a direct attack upon the United States, and prepare plans for the acceptance and disposition of current claims for social security benefits.

(2) *Health insurance.* Develop plans for the payment of health insurance claims for reimbursement for items or services provided by hospitals, physicians, and other providers of medical services submitted by or on behalf of individuals who are eligible under the Medicare program.

SEC. 1106 *Credit Union Functions.* With respect to credit union functions, the Secretary of Health, Education, and Welfare shall:

(1) *Credit union operations.* Provide instructions to all State and Federally chartered credit unions for the development of emergency plans to be put into effect as soon as possible after an attack upon the United States in order to guarantee continuity of credit union operations.

(2) *Economic stabilization.* Provide guidance to credit unions that will contribute to stabilization of the Nation's economy by helping to establish and maintain a sound economic base for combating inflation, maintaining confidence in public and private financial institutions, and promoting thrift.

SEC. 1107 *Education Functions.* With respect to education, the Secretary of Health, Education, and Welfare shall:

(1) *Program guidance.* Develop plans and issue guidance for the continued function of educational systems under all conditions of national emergency. Although extraordinary circumstances may require the temporary suspension of education, plans should provide for its earliest possible resumption.

(2) *Educational adjustment.* Plan to assist civilian educational institutions, both public and private, to adjust to demands laid upon them by a large expansion of government activities during any type of emergency. This includes advice and assistance to schools, colleges, universities, and other educational institutions whose facilities may be temporarily needed for Federal, State, or local government programs in an emergency or whose faculties and student bodies may be affected by the demands of a sudden or long-standing emergency.

(3) *Post-attack recovery.* Develop plans for the rapid restoration and resumption of education at all levels after an attack. This includes assistance to educators and educational institutions to locate and use surviving facilities, equipment, supplies, books, and educational personnel. Particular emphasis shall be given to the role of educational institutions and educational leadership in reviving education and training in skills needed for post-attack recovery.

(4) *Civil defense education.* In consonance with national civil defense plans, programs, and operations of the Department of Defense, develop and issue instructional materials to assist schools, colleges, and other educational institutions to incorporate emergency protective measures and civil defense concepts into their programs. This includes assistance to various levels of education to develop an understanding of the role of the individual, family, and community for civil defense in the nuclear age.

PART 12—DEPARTMENT OF HOUSING AND URBAN DEVELOPMENT

SECTION 1201 *Résumé of Responsibilities.* The Secretary of Housing and Urban Development shall prepare national emergency plans and develop preparedness programs covering all aspects of housing, community facilities related to housing, and urban development (except that housing assets under the jurisdiction and control of the Department of Defense, other than those leased for terms not in excess of one year, shall be and remain the responsibility of the Department of Defense).

SEC. 1202. *Definition.* As used in this part:

(1) "Emergency housing" means any and all types of accommodations used as dwellings in an emergency.

(2) "Community facilities related to housing" means installations necessary to furnish water, sewer, electric, and gas services between the housing unit or project and the nearest practical source or servicing point.

(3) "Urban development" means the building or restoration of urban community, suburban, and metropolitan areas (except transportation facilities).

SEC. 1203. *Housing and Community Facilities Functions.* The Secretary of Housing and Urban Development shall:

(1) *New housing.* Develop plans for the emergency construction and management of new housing and the community facilities related thereto to the extent that it is determined that it may be necessary to provide for such construction and management with public funds and through direct Federal action, and to the extent that such construction of new housing may have to be provided through Federal financial or credit assistance.

(2) *Community facilities.* Develop plans to restore community facilities related to housing affected by an emergency through the repair of damage, the construction of new facilities, and the use of alternate or back-up facilities.

SEC. 1204 *Urban Development Functions.* The Secretary of Housing and Urban Development shall:

(1) *Regional cooperation.* Encourage regional emergency planning and cooperation among State and local governments with respect to problems of housing and metropolitan development.

(2) *Vulnerability and redevelopment.* In cooperation with the Office of Emergency Preparedness, develop criteria and provide guidance for the design and location of housing and community facilities related to housing to minimize the risk of loss under various

emergency situations. Develop criteria for determining which areas should be redeveloped in the event of loss or severe damage resulting from emergencies.

SEC. 1205 *Civil Defense Functions.* In consonance with national civil defense plans, programs, and operations of the Department of Defense under Executive Order No. 10952, the Secretary of Housing and Urban Development shall:

(1) *Transitional activities.* Develop plans for the orderly transfer of people from fallout shelters and from billets to temporary or permanent housing, including advice and guidance for State and local government agencies in the administration thereof. These plans shall be coordinated with national plans and guidance for emergency welfare services of the Department of Health, Education, and Welfare.

(2) *Temporary housing.* Develop plans for the emergency repair and restoration for use of damaged housing, for the construction and management of emergency housing units and the community facilities related thereto, for the emergency use of tents and trailers, and for the emergency conversion for dwelling use of non-residential structures, such activities to be financed with public funds through direct Federal action or through financial or credit assistance.

(3) *Shelter.* In conformity with national shelter policy, assist in the development of plans to encourage the construction of shelters for both old and new housing, and develop administrative procedures to encourage the use of low-cost design and construction techniques to maximize protection in connection with national programs.

PART 13—DEPARTMENT OF TRANSPORTATION

SECTION 1301 *Résumé of Responsibilities.*

The Secretary of Transportation, in carrying out his responsibilities to exercise leadership in transportation matters affecting the national defense and those involving national or regional transportation emergencies, shall prepare emergency plans and develop preparedness programs covering:

(1) Preparation and promulgation of overall national policies, plans, and procedures related to providing civil transportation of all forms—air, ground, water, and pipelines, including public storage and warehousing (except storage of petroleum and gas and agricultural food resources including cold storage): *Provided* that plans for the movement of petroleum and natural gas through pipelines shall be the responsibility of the Secretary of the Interior except to the extent that such plans are a part of functions vested in the Secretary of Transportation by law;

(2) Movement of passengers and materials of all types by all forms of civil transportation;

(3) Determination of the proper apportionment and allocation for control of the total civil transportation capacity, or any portion thereof, to meet over-all essential civil and military needs;

(4) Determination and identification of the transportation resources available and required to meet all degrees of national emergencies and regional transportation emergencies;

(5) Assistance to the various States, the local poiltical subdivisions thereof, and nongovernmental organizations and systems engaged in transportation activities in the preparation of emergency plans;

(6) Rehabilitation and recovery of the Naton's transportation systems; and

(7) Provisions for port security and safety, for aids to maritime navigation, and for search and rescue and law enforcement over, upon, and under the navigable waters of the United States and the high seas.

SEC. 1302. *Transportation Planning and Co-ordination Functions.*

In carrying out the provisions of Section 1301, the Secretary of Transportation, with assistance and support of other Federal, State and local governmental agencies, and the transport industries, as appropriate, shall:

(1) Obtain, assemble, analyze, and evaluate data on current and projected emergency requirements of all claimants for all forms of civil transportation to meet the needs of the military and of the civil economy, and on current and projected civil transportation resources—of all forms—available to the United States to move passengers or materials in an emergency.

(2) Develop plans and procedures to provide—under emergency conditions—for the collection and analysis of passenger and cargo movement demands as they relate to the capabilities of the various forms of transport, including the periodic assessment of over-all transport resources available to meet emergency requirements.

(3) Conduct a continuing analysis of transportation requirements and capabilities in relation to economic projections for the purpose of initiating actions and/or recommending incentive and/or regulatory programs designed to stimulate government and industry improvement of the structure of the transportation system for use in an emergency.

(4) Develop systems for the control of the movement of passengers and cargo by all forms of transportation, except for those re-

sources owned by, controlled by, or under the jurisdiction of the Department of Defense, including allocation of resources and assignment of priorities, and develop policies, standards, and procedures for emergency enforcement of these controls.

SEC. 1303. *Departmental Emergency Transportation Preparedness.* Except for those resources owned by, controlled by, or under the jurisdiction of the Department of Defense, the Secretary of Transportation shall prepare emergency operational plans and programs for, and develop a capability to carry out, the transportation operating responsibilities assigned to the Department, including but not limited to:

(1) Allocating air carrier civil air transportation capacity and equipment to meet civil and military requirements.

(2) Emergency management, including construction, reconstruction, and maintenance of the Nation's civil airports, civil aviation operating facilities, civil aviation services, and civil aircraft (other than air carrier aircraft), except manufacturing facilities.

(3) Emergency management, of all Federal, State, city, local, and other highways, roads, streets, bridges, tunnels, and appurtenant structures, including:

(a) The adaptation, development, construction, reconstruction, and maintenance of the Nation's highway and street systems to meet emergency requirements;

(b) The protection of the traveling public by assisting State and local authorities in informing them of the dangers of travel through hazardous areas; and

(c) The regulation of highway traffic in an emergency through a national program in cooperation with all Federal, State, and local governmental units or other agencies concerned.

(4) Emergency plans for urban mass transportation, including:

(a) Providing guidance to urban communities in their emergency mass transportation planning efforts, either directly or through State, regional, or metropolitan agencies;

(b) Coordinating all such emergency planning with the Department of Housing and Urban Development to assure compatibility with emergency plans for all other aspects of urban development;

(c) Maintaining an inventory of urban mass transportation systems.

(5) Maritime safety and law enforcement over, upon, and under the high seas and waters, subject to the jurisdiction of the United States, in the following specific programs:

(a) Safeguarding vessels, harbors, ports, and waterfront facilities from destruction, loss or injury, accidents, or other causes of a similar nature.

(b) Safe passage over, upon, and under the high seas and United States waters through effective and reliable systems of aids to navigation and ocean stations.

(c) Waterborne access to ice-bound locations in furtherance of national economic, scientific, defense, and consumer needs.

(d) Protection of lives, property, natural resources, and national interests through enforcement of Federal law and timely assistance.

(e) Safety of life and property through regulation of commercial vessels, their officers and crew, and administration of maritime safety law.

(f) Knowledge of the sea, its boundaries, and its resources through collection and analysis of data in support of the national interest.

(g) Operational readiness for essential wartime functions.

(6) Planning for the emergency management and operation of the Alaska Railroad, and for the continuity of railroad and petroleum pipeline safety programs.

(7) Planning for the emergency operation and maintenance of the United States-controlled sections of the Saint Lawrence Seaway.

PART 14—ATOMIC ENERGY COMMISSION

SECTION 1401. *Functions.* The Atomic Energy Commission shall prepare national emergency plans and develop preparedness programs for the continuing conduct of atomic energy activities of the Federal Government. These plans and programs shall be designed to develop a state of readiness in these areas with respect to all conditions of national emergency, including attack upon the United States and, consistent with applicable provisions of the Atomic Energy Act of 1954, as amended, shall be closely coordinated with the Department of Defense and the Office of Emergency Preparedness. The Atomic Energy Commission shall:

(1) *Production.* Continue or resume in an emergency essential (a) manufacture, development, and control of nuclear weapons and equipment, except to the extent that the control over such weapons and equipment shall have been transferred to the Department of Defense; (b) development and technology related to reactors; (c) process development and production of feed material, special nuclear materials, and other special products; (d) related raw materials procurement, processing, and development; and (e) repair, maintenance, and construction related to the above.

(2) *Regulation.* Continue or resume in an emergency (a) controlling the possession, use, transfer, import, and export of atomic materials and facilities; and (b) ordering the operation or suspension of licensed facilities, and recapturing from licensees, where necessary, special nuclear materials whether related to military support or civilian activities.

(3) *Public health and safety.* Shut down, where required, in anticipation of an imminent enemy attack on the United States, and maintain under surveillance, all Commission-owned facilities which could otherwise constitute a significant hazard to public health and safety, and insure the development of appropriate emergency plans for nuclear reactors and other nuclear activities licensed by the Commission whether privately-owned or Government-owned.

(4) *Scientific, technical, and public atomic energy information.* Organize, reproduce, and disseminate appropriate public atomic energy information and scientific and technical reports and data relating to nuclear science research, development, engineering, applications, and effects to interested Government agencies, the scientific and technical communities, and approved, friendly, and cooperating foreign nations.

(5) *International atomic energy affairs.* Maintain, in consultation with the Department of State, essential liaison with foreign nations with respect to activities of mutual interest involving atomic energy.

(6) *Health services.* Assist the Department of Health, Education, and Welfare, consistent with the above requirements, in integrating into civilian health programs in an emergency the Commission's remaining health manpower and facilities not required for the performance of the Commission's essential emergency functions.

(7) *Priorities and allocations.* Plan for the administration of any priorities and allocations authority delegated to the Atomic Energy Commission. Authorize procurement and production schedules and make allotments of controlled materials pursuant to program determinations of the Office of Emergency Preparedness.

PART 15—CIVIL AERONAUTICS BOARD

SECTION 1501. *Definitions.* As used in this part:

(1) "War Air Service Program" (hereinafter referred to as WASP) means the program designed to provide for the maintenance of essential civil air routes and services, and to provide for the distribution and redistribution of air carrier aircraft among civil air transport carriers after withdrawal of aircaft allocated to the Civil Reserve Air Fleet.

(2) "Civil Reserve Air Fleet" (hereinafter referred to as CRAF) means those air carrier aircraft allocated by the Secretary of Transportation to the Department of Defense to meet essential military needs in the event of an emergency.

SEC. 1502 *Functions.* The Civil Aeronautics Board, under the coordinating authority of the Secretary of Transportation, shall:

(1) *Distribution of aircraft.* Develop plans and be prepared to carry out such distribution and redistribution of all air carrier civil aircraft allocated by the Secretary of Transportation among the civil air transport carriers as may be necessary to assure the maintenance of essential civil routes and services under WASP operations after the CRAF requirements have been met.

(2) *Economic regulations.* Develop plans covering route authorizations and operations, tariffs, rates, and fares charged the public, mail rates, government compensation and

subsidy, and accounting and contracting procedures essential to WASP operations.

(3) *Operational controls and priorities.* Developed plans and procedures for the administration of operational controls and priorities of passenger and cargo movements in connection with the utilization of air carrier aircraft for WASP purposes in an emergency.

(4) *Investigation.* Maintain the capability to investigate violations of emergency economic regulations affecting air carrier operations.

(5) *Contracting.* Prepare to perform as a contracting agency, if such an agency is necessary, in connection with distribution and redistribution of aircraft for WASP.

PART 16—EXPORT-IMPORT BANK OF THE UNITED STATES

SECTION 1601 *Functions.* (a) Under guidance of the Secretary of the Treasury, the Export-Import Bank shall develop plans for the utiliation of the resources of the Bank, or other resources made available to the Bank, in expansion of productive capacity abroad for essential materials, foreign barter arrangements, acquisition of emergency imports, and in support of the domestic economy, or any other plans designed to strengthen the relative position of the Nation and its allies.

(b) In carrying out the guidance functions described above, the Secretary of the Treasury shall consult with the Secretary of State and the Secretary of Comemrce as appropriate.

PART 17—FEDERAL BANK SUPERVISORY AGENCIES

SECTION 1701 *Financial Plans and Programs.* The Board of Governors of the Federal Reserve System, the Comptroller of the Currency, the Federal Home Loan Bank Board, the Farm Credit Administration, and the Fedral Deposit Insurance Corporation shall participate with the Office of Emergency Preparedness, the Department of the Treasury, and other agencies in the formulation of emergency financial and stabilization policies. The heads of such agencies shall, as appropriate, develop emergency plans, programs, and regulations, in consonance with national emergency financial and stabilization plans and policies, to cope with potential economic effects of mobilization or an attack, including, but not limited to, the following:

(1) *Money and credit.* Provision and regulation of money and credit in acocrdance with the needs of the economy, including the acquisition, decentralization, and distribution of emergency supplies of currency; the collection of cash items and non-cash items; and the conduct of fiscal agency and foreign operations.

(2) *Financial institutions.* Provision for the continued or resumed operation of banking, savings and loan, and farm credit institutions, including measures for the re-creation of evidence of assets or liabilities destroyed or inaccessible.

(3) *Liquidity.* Provision of liquidity necessary to the continued or resumed operation of banking, savings and loan, credit unions, and farm credit institutions, including those damaged or destroyed by enemy action.

(4) *Cash withdrawals and credit transfers.* Regulation of the withdrawal of currency and the transfer of credits including deposit and share account balances.

(5) *Insurance.* Provision for the assumption and discharge of liability pertaining

to insured deposits and insured savings accounts or withdrawable shares in banking and savings and loan institutions destroyed or made insolvent.

SEC. 1702 *Sharing of war losses.* Heads of agencies shall, as appropriate, participate with the Office of Emergency Preparedness and the Department of the Treasury in the development of policies, plans, and procedures for implementation of national policy on sharing war losses.

PART 18—FEDERAL COMMUNICATIONS COMMISSION

SECTION 1801 *Definitions.* As used in this part:

(1) "Common carrier" means any person subject to Commission regulation engaged in providing, for use by the public, for hire, interstate or foreign communications facilities or services by wire or radio; but a person engaged in radio broadcasting shall not, insofar as such person is so engaged, be deemed a common carrier.

(2) "Broadcast facilities" means those stations licensed by the Commission for the dissemination of radio communications intended to be received by the public directly or by the intermediary of relay stations.

(3) "Safety and special radio services" includes those non-broadcast and non-common carrier services which are licensed by the Commission under the generic designation "safety and special radio services" pursuant to the Commission's Rules and Regulations.

SEC. 1802 *Functions.* The Federal Communications Commission shall develop policies, plans, and procedures, in consonance with national telecommunications plans and policies developed pursuant to Executive Order No. 10705, Executive Order No. 10995, Executive Order No. 11051, the Presidential Memorandum of August 21, 1963, "Establishment of the National Communications System", and other appropriate authority, covering:

(1) *Common carrier service.* (a) Extension, discontinuance, or reduction of common carrier facilities or services, and issuance of appropriate authorizations for such facilities, services, and personnel in an emergency; and control of all rates, charges, practices, classifications, and regulations for service to Government and non-Government users during an emergency, in consonance with overall national economic stabilization policies.

(b) Development and administration of priority systems for public correspondence and for the use and resumption of leased inter-city private line service in an emergency.

(c) Use of common carrier facilities and services to overseas points to meet vital needs in an emergency.

(2) *Broadcasting service.* Construction, activation, or deactivation of broadcasting facilities and services, the continuation or suspension of broadcasting services and facilities, and issuance of appropriate authorizations for such facilities, services, and personnel in an emergency.

(3) *Safety and special radio service.* Authorization, operation, and use of safety and special radio services, facilities, and personnel in the national interest in an emergency.

(4) *Radio frequency assignment.* Assignment of radio frequencies to, and their use by, Commission licensees in an emergency.

(5) *Electromagnetic radiation.* Closing of any radio station or any device capable of emitting electromagnetic radiation or sus-

pension or amending any rules or regulations applicable thereto, in any emergency, except for those belonging to, or operated by, any department or agency of the United States Government.

(6) *Investigation and enforcement.* Investigation of violations of pertinent law and regulations in an emergency, and development of procedures designated to initiate, recommend, or otherwise bring about appropriate enforcement actions required in the interest of national security.

PART 19—FEDERAL POWER COMMISSION

SECTION 1901 *Functions.* The Federal Power Commission shall assist the Department of the Interior, in conformity with Part 7, in the preparation of national emergency plans and the development of preparedness programs for electric power and natural gas in the areas as set forth in the Memorandum of Agreement dated August 9, 1962, between the Secretary of the Interior and the Chairman of the Federal Power Commission.

PART 20—GENERAL SERVICES ADMINISTRATION

SECTION 2001 *Résumé of Responsibilities.* The Administrator of General Services shall prepare national emergency plans and develop preparedness programs designed to permit modification or expansion of the activities of the General Services Administration under the Federal Property and Administrative Services Act of 1949, as amended and other statutes prescribing the duties and responsibilities of the Administrator. These plans and programs shall include, but not be limited to: (1) operation, maintenance, and protection of Federal buildings and their sites; construction, alteration, and repair of public buildings; and acquisition, utilization, and disposal of real and personal properties; (2) public utilities service management for Federal agencies; (3) telecommunications to meet the essential requirements of civilian activities of executive departments and agencies; (4) transportation management to meet the traffic service requirements of civilian activities of Federal agencies; (5) records management; (6) Emergency Federal Register; (7) Government-wide supply support; (8) service to survival items stockpiles; (9) national industrial reserve; (10) guidance and consultation to Government agencies regarding facilities protection measures; (11) administration of assigned functions under the Defense Production Act; and (12) administration and operation of the stockpile of strategic and critical materials in accordance with policies and guidance furnished by the Office of Emergency Preparedness.

SEC. 2002 *Functions*. The Administrator of General Services shall:

(1) *Public buildings*. Develop emergency plans and procedures for the operation, maintenance, and protection of both existing and new Federally-owned and Federally-occupied buildings, and construction, alteration, and repair of public buildings. Develop emergency operating procedures for the control, acquisition, assignment, and priority of occupancy of real property by the Federal Government and by State and local governments to the extent they may be performing functions as agents of the Federal Government.

(2) *Public utility service management*. Develop emergency operational plans and procedures for the claimancy, procurement, and use of public utility services for emergency activities of executive agencies of the Government.

(3) *Communications.* Plan for and provide, operate, and maintain appropriate telecommunications facilities designed to meet the essential requirements of Federal civilian departments and agencies during an emergency within the framework of the National Communications System. Plans and programs of the Administrator shall be in consonance with national telecommunications policies, plans and programs developed pursuant to Executive Order No. 10705, Executive Order No. 10995, Executive Order No. 11051, and the Presidential Memorandum of August 21, 1963, "Establishment of the National Communications System," or other appropriate authority.

(4) *Transportation.* Develop plans and procedures for providing: (a) general transportation and traffic management services to civilian activities of Federal agencies in connection with movement of property and supplies, including the claimancy, contracting, routing, and accounting of Government shipments by commercial transportation in time of emergency; and (b) motor vehicle service to meet the administrative needs of Federal agencies, including dispatch and scheduled Government motor service at and between headquarters, field offices, relocation sites, and other installations of the Federal and State governments.

(5) *Records.* Provide instructions and advice on appraisal, selection, preservation, arrangement, reference, reproduction, storage, and salvage of essential records needed for the operation of the Federal Government after attack, on an emergency basis, including a decentralized system.

(6) *Federal Register.* Develop emergency procedures for providing and making available, on a decentralized basis, a Federal

Register of Presidential Proclamations and Executive Orders, Federal administrative regulations, Federal emergency notices and actions, and Acts of Congress during a national emergency.

(7) *Government-wide procurement and supply.* Prepare plans and procedures for the coordination and/or operation of Government-wide supply programs to meet the requirements of Federal agencies under emergency conditions, including the development of policies, methods, and procedures for emergency procurement and for emergency requisitioning of private property when authorized by law and competent authority; identification of essential civil agency supply items under the Federal catalog system; development of emergency Federal specifications and standards; determination of sources of supply; procurement of personal property and non-personal services; furnishing appropriate inspection and contract administration services; and establishment, coordination, and/or operation of emergency storage and distribution facilities.

(8) *Survival item stockpiles.* Assist the Department of Health, Education, and Welfare, insofar as civil defense medical stockpile items under its jurisdiction are concerned, and the Department of Defense, insofar as survival items under its jurisdiction are concerned, informulating plans and programs for service activity support relating to stockpiling of such supplies and equipment. The Administrator shall arrange for the procurement, storage, maintenance, inspection, survey, withdrawal, and disposal of supplies and equipment in accordance with the provisions of interagency agreements with the departments concerned.

(9) *National industrial reserve and ma-*

chine tool program. Develop plans for the custody of the industrial plants and production equipment in the national industrial reserve and assist the Department of Defense, in collaboration with the Department of Commerce, in the development of plans and procedures for the disposition, emergency reactivation, and utilization of the plants and equipment of this reserve in the custody of the Administrator.

(10) *Excess and surplus real and personal property.* Develop plans and emergency operating procedures for the utilization of excess and surplus real and personal property by Federal Government agencies with emergency assignments or by State and local governmental units as directed, including review of the property holdings of Federal agencies which do not possess emergency functions to determine the availability of property for emergency use, and including the disposal of real and personal property and the rehabilitation of personal property.

(11) *Facilities protection and building and shelter manager service.* In accordance with the guidance from the Department of Defense, promote, with respect to Federal buildings and installations, a Government-wide program (a) to stimulate protection, preparedness, and control in emergencies in order to minimize the effects of overt or covert attack, including disposal of facilities; and (b) to establish shelter manager organizations, including safety and service personnel, shelter manager service, first aid, police, and evacuation service.

Sec. 2003 *Defense Production.* The Administrator of General Services shall assist the Office of Emergency Preparedness in the formulation of plans and programs relating to the certification of procurement programs, subsidy payments, and plant improvement programs provided by the Defense Production Act of 1950, as amended.

SEC. 2004 *Strategic and Critical Material Stockpiles.* The Administrator of General Services shall assist the Office of Emergency Preparedness in formulating plans, programs, and reports relating to the stockpiling of strategic and critical materials. Within these plans and programs, the Administrator shall provide for the procurement (for this purpose, procurement includes upgrading, rotation, and benefication), storage, security, maintenance, inspection, withdrawal, and disposal of materials, supplies, and equipment.

PART 21—INTERSTATE COMMERCE COMMISSION

SEC. 2101. *Résumé of Responsibilities.* The Chairman of the Interstate Commerce Commission, under the coordinating authority of the Secretary of Transportation, shall prepare national emergency plans and develop preparedness programs covering railroad utilization, reduction of vulnerability, maintenance, restoration, and operation in an emergency (other than for the Alaska Railroad—see Section 1303(6)); motor carrier utilization, reduction of vulnerability, and operation in an emergency; inland waterway utilization of equipment and shipping, reduction of vulnerability, and operation in an emergency; and also provide guidance and consultation to domestic surface transportation and storage industries, as defined below, regarding emergency preparedness measures, and to States regarding development of their transportation plans in assigned areas.

SEC. 2102 *Definitions.* As used in this part:

(1) "Domestic surface transportation and storage" means rail, motor, and inland water

transportation facilities and services and public storage;

(2) "Public storage" includes warehouses and other places which are used for the storage of property belonging to persons other than the persons having the ownership or control of such premises;

(3) "Inland water transportation" includes shipping on all inland waterways and Great Lakes shipping engaged solely in the transportation of passengers or cargo between United States ports on the Great Lakes;

(4) Specifically excluded, for the purposes of this part, are pipelines, petroleum and gas storage, agricultural food resources storage, including the cold storage of food resources. the St. Lawrence Seaway, ocean ports and Great Lakes ports and port facilities, highways, streets, roads, bridges, and related appurtenances, maintenance of inland waterways, and any transportation owned by or pre-allocated to the militray.

SEC. 2103 *Transportation Functions.* The Interstate Commerce Commission shall:

(1) *Operational control.* Develop plans with appropriate private transportation and storage organizations and associations for the coordination and direction of the use of domestic surface transportation and storage facilities for movement of passenger and freight traffic.

(2) *Emergency operations.* Develop and maintain necessary orders and regulations for the operation of domestic surface transport and storage industries in an emergency.

PART 22—NATIONAL AERONAUTICS AND SPACE
ADMINISTRATION

SECTION 2201 *Functions.* The Administrator of the National Aeronautics and Space Administration shall:

(1) *Research and development.* Adapt and

utilize the scientific and technological capability of the National Aeronautics and Space Administration, consistent with overall requirements, to meet priority needs of the programs of the Federal Government in an emergency. This will include the direction and conduct of essential research and development activities relating to (a) aircraft, spacecraft, and launch vehicles, (b) associated instrumentation, guidance, control and payload, propulsion, and communications systems, (c) scientific phenomena affecting both manned and unmanned space flights, (d) the life sciences (biology, medicine, and psychology) as they apply to aeronautics and space, and (e) atmospheric and geophysical sciences.

(2) *Military support*. Provide direct assistance as requested by the Department of Defense and other agencies in support of the military effort. This may include (a) undertaking urgent projects to develop superior aircraft, spacecraft, launch vehicles, and weapons systems, (b) developing methods to counter novel or revolutionary enemy weapons systems, (c) providing technical advice and assistance on matters involving air and space activities, and (d) furnishing personnel and facilities to assist in emergency repairs of equipment deficiencies and for other essential purposes.

PART 23—NATIONAL SCIENCE FOUNDATION

SECTION 2301 *Functions*. The Director of the National Science Foundation shall:

(1) *Manpower functions*. Assist the Department of Labor in sustaining readiness for the mobilization of civilian manpower by: (a) maintaining the Foundation's register of scientific and technical personnel in such form and at such locations as will assure maximum usefulness in an emergency; (b)

being prepared for rapid expansion of the Foundation's current operation as a central clearing house for information covering all scientific and technical personnel in the United States and its possessions; and (c) developing, in consultation with the Department of Labor, the Selective Service System, the Department of Defense, and the Office of Science and Technology, plans and procedures to assure the most effective distribution and utilization of the Nation's scientific and engineering manpower in an emergency.

(2) *Special functions.* (a) Provide leadership in developing, with the assistance of Federal and State agencies and appropriate nongovernmental organizations, the ability to mobilize scientists, in consonance with over-all civilian manpower mobilization programs, to perform or assist in performance of special tasks, including the identification of and defense against unconventional warfare; (b) advance the national radiological defense capability by including, in consulation with appropriate agencies, pertinent scientific information and radiological defense techniques in the Foundation's scientific institute program for science, mathematics, and engineering teachers; (c) assemble data on the location and character of major scientific research facilities, including non-governmental as well as government facilities, and their normal inventories of types of equipment and instruments which would be useful in identification and analysis of hazards to human life in the aftermath of enemy attack; and (d) prepare to carry on necessary programs for basic research and for training of scientific manpower.

PART 24—RAILROAD RETIREMENT BOARD

SECTION 2401 *Functions.* The Railroad Retirement Board shall:

(1) *Manpower functions.* Within the frame work of the over-all manpower plans and programs of the Department of Labor, assist in the mobilization of civilian manpower in an emergency by developing plans for the recruitment and referral of that segment of the Nation's manpower resources subject to the Railroad Retirement and Railroad Unemployment Insurance Acts.

(2) *Benefit payments.* Develop plans for administering, under emergency conditions, the essential aspects of the Railroad Retirement Act and Railroad Unemployment Insurance Act consistent with overall Federal plans for the continuation of benefit payment after an enemy attack.

PART 25—SECURITIES AND EXCHANGE COMMISSION

SECTION 2501 *Functions.* The Securities and Exchange Commission shall collaborate with the Secretary of the Treasury in the development of emergency financial control plans, programs, procedures, and regulations for:

(1) *Stock trading.* Temporary closure of security exchanges, suspension of redemption rights, and freezing of stock and bond prices, if required in the interest of maintaing economic controls.

(2) *Modified trading.* Development of plans designed to reestablish and maintain a stable and orderly market for securities when the situation permits under emergency conditions.

(3) *Protection of securities.* Provision of a national records system which will make it possible to establish current ownership of securities in the event major trading centers and depositories are destroyed.

(4) *Flow of capital.* The control of the

formation and flow of private capital as it relates to new securities offerings or expansion of prior offerings for the purpose of establishing or reestablishing industries in relation to the Nation's needs in or following a national emergency.

(5) *Flight of capital.* The prevention of the flight of capital outside this country, in coordination with the Secretary of Commerce, and the impounding of securities in the hands of enemy aliens.

PART 26—SMALL BUSINESS ADMINISTRATION

SECTION 2601 *Functions.* The Administrator of the Small Business Administration shall:

(1) *Prime contract authority.* Develop plans to administer a program for the acquisition of prime contracts by the Administration and, in turn, for negotiating or otherwise letting of subcontracts to capable small business concerns in an emergency.

(2) *Resource information.* Provide data on facilities, inventories, and potential production capacity of small business concerns to all interested agencies.

(3) *Procurement.* Develop plans to determine jointly with Federal procurement agencies, as appropriate, which defense contracts are to go to small business concerns and to certify to the productive and financial ability of small concerns to perform specific contracts, as required.

(4) *Loans for plant modernization.* Develop plans for providing emergency assistance to essential individual industrial establishments through direct loans or participation loans for the financing of production facilities and equipment.

(5) *Resource pools.* Develop plans for encouraging and approving small business defense production and research and development pools.

(6) *Financial assistance.* Develop plans to make loans, directly or in participation with private lending institutions, to small business concerns and to groups or pools of such concerns, to small business investment companies, and to State and local development companies to provide them with funds for lending to small business concerns, for defense and essential civilian purposes.

PART 27—TENNESSEE VALLEY AUTHORITY

SECTION 2701   *Functions.* The Board of Directors of the Tennessee Valley Authority shall:

(1) *Electric power.* Assist the Department of the Interior in the development of plans for the integration of the Tennessee Valley Authority power system into national emergency programs and prepare plans for the emergency management, operation, and maintenance of the system and for its essential expansion.

(2) *Waterways.* Assist the Interstate Commerce Commission, under the coordinating authority of the Secretary of Transportation, in the development of plans for integration and control of inland waterway transportation systems and, in cooperation with the Department of Defense and the Department of the Interior, prepare plans for the management, operation, and maintenance of the river control system in the Tennessee River and certain of its tributaries for navigation during an emergency.

(3) *Flood control.* Develop plans and maintain its river control operations for the prevention or control of floods caused by natural phenomena or overt and covert attack affecting the Tennessee River System and, in so doing, collaborate with the Department of Defense with respect to the control of water in the lower Ohio and Mississippi Rivers.

(4) *Emergency health services and sanitary water supplies.* Assist the Department of Health, Education, and Welfare in the development of plans and programs covering emergency health services, civilian health manpower, and health resources in the Tennessee Valley Authority area and, in collaboration with the Department of the Interior and the Department of Health, Education, and Welfare, prepare plans for the management, operation, and maintenance of the Tennessee River System consistent with the needs for sanitary public water supplies, waste disposal, and vector control.

(5) *Coordination of water use.* Develop plans for determining or proposing priorities for the use of water by the Tennessee Valley Authority in the event of conflicting claims arising from the functions listed above.

(6) *Fertilizer.* Assist the Department of Agriculture in the development of plans for the distribution and claimancy of fertilizer; assist the Department of Commerce and the Department of Defense in the development of Tennessee Valley Authority production quotas and any essential expansion of production facilities, and prepare plans for the management, operation, and maintenance of its facilities for the manufacture of nitrogen and phosphorous fertilizers.

(7) *Munitions production.* Perform chemical research in munitions as requested by the Department of Defense, maintain standby munitions production facilities, and develop plans for converting and utilizing fertilizer facilities as required in support of the Department of Defense's munitions program.

(8) *Land management.* Develop plans for the maintenance, management, and utilization of Tennessee Valley Authority-con-

trolled lands in the interest of an emergency economy.

(9) *Food and forestry.* Assist the Department of Agriculture in the development of plans for the harvesting and processing of fish and game, and the Department of Commerce in the development of plans for the production and processing of forest products.

(10) *Coordination with Valley States.* Prepare plans and agreements wth Tennessee Valley States, consistent with Federal programs, for appropriate integration of Tennessee Valley Authority and State plans for the use of available Tennessee Valley Authority resources.

PART 28—UNITED STATES CIVIL SERVICE COMMISSION

SECTION 2801 *Functions.* The United States Civil Service Commission shall:

(1) *Personnel system.* Prepare plans for adjusting the Federal civilian personnel system to simplify administration and to meet emergency demands.

(2) *Utilization.* Develop policies and implementing procedures designed to assist Federal agencies in achieving the most effective utilization of the Federal Government's civilian manpower in an emergency.

(3) *Manpower policies.* As the representative of the Federal Government as an employer, participate, as appropriate, in the formulation of national and regional manpower policies as they affect Federal civilian personnel and establish implementing policies as necessary.

(4) *Manpower administration.* Prepare plans, in consonance with national manpower policies and programs, for the administration of emergency civilian manpower and employment policies within the execu-

tive branch of the Government, including
the issuance and enforcement of regulations
to implement such policies.

(5) *Wage and salary stabilization.* Participate, as appropriate, with the Office of
Emergency Preparedness and the Department of Labor in the formulation of national and regional wage and salary stabilization policies as they affect Federal civilian
personnel. Within the framework of such
policies, prepare plans for the implementation of such policies and controls established
for employees within the executive branch
of the Government, including the issuance
and enforcement of necessary regulations.

(6) *Assistance.* Develop plans for rendering
personnel management and staffing assistance to new and expanding Federal agencies.

(7) *Recruiting.* Develop plans for the coordination and control of civilian recruiting
policies and practices by all Federal agencies
in order to increase the effectiveness of the
total recruitment efforts during an emergency and to prevent undesirable recruitment practices.

(8) *Reassignment.* Develop plans to facilitate the reassignment or transfer of Federal civilian employees, including the movement of employees from one agency or location to another agency or location, in order to meet the most urgent needs of the
executive branch during an emergency.

(9) *Registration.* Develop plans and procedures for a nationwide system of post-
attack registration of Federal employees to
provide a means for locating and returning
to duty those employees who become physically separated from their agencies after an
enemy attack, and to provide for the maximum utilization of the skills of surviving
employees.

(10) *Deferment*. Develop plans and procedures for a system to control Government requests for the selective service deferment of employees in the executive branch of the Federal Government and in the municipal government of the District of Columbia.

(11) *Investigation*. Prepare plans, in coordination with agencies having responsibilities in the personnel security field, for the conduct of national agency checks and inquiries, limited suitability investigations, and full field investigations under emergency conditions.

(12) *Salaries, wages, and benefits*. Develop plans for operating under emergency conditions the essential aspects of salary and wage systems and such benefit systems as the Federal Employees Retirement System, the Federal Employees Group Life Insurance Program, the Federal Employees and Retired Federal Employees Health Benefits Programs, and the Federal Employees Compensation Program.

(13) *Federal manpower mobilization*. Assist Federal agencies in establishing manpower plans to meet their own emergency manpower requirements; identify major or special manpower problems of individual Federal agencies and the Federal Government as a whole in mobilizing a civilian work force to meet essential emergency requirements; identify sources of emergency manpower supply for all agencies where manpower problems are indicated; and develop Government-wide plans for the use of surplus Federal civilian manpower.

(14) *Distribution of manpower*. Participate in the formulation of policies and decisions on the distribution of the nation's civilian manpower resources, obtain appropriate civilian manpower data from Federal agencies,

and establish necessary implementing policies and procedures within the Executive Branch.

(15) *Training.* Develop, organize, and conduct, as appropriate, interagency training programs in emergency personnel management for Federal employes.

PART 29—VETERANS' ADMINISTRATION

SECTION 2901 *Functions.* The Administrator of Veterans Affairs shall develop policies, plans, and procedures for the performance of emergency functions with respect to the continuation or restoration of authorized programs of the Veterans Administration under all conditions of national emergency, including attack upon the United States. These include:

(1) The emergency conduct of inpatient and outpatient care and treatment in Veterans Administration medical facilities and participation with the Departments of Defense and Health, Education, and Welfare as provided for in interagency agreements.

(2) The emergency conduct of compensation, pension, rehabilitation, education, and insurance payments consistent with over-all Federal plans for the continuation of Federal benefit payments.

(3) The emergency performance of insurance and loan guaranty functions in accordance with indirect stabilization policies and controls designed to deal with various emergency conditions.

PART 30—GENERAL PROVISIONS

SECTION 3001 *Resource Management.* In consonance with the national preparedness, security, and mobilization readiness plans, programs, and operations of the Office of Emergency Preparedness under Executive Order No. 11051 of September 27, 1962, and subject to the provisions of the preceding parts, the head of each department and agency shall:

(1) *Priorities and allocations.* Develop systems for the emergency application of priorities and allocations to the production, distribution, and use of resources for which he has been assigned responsibility.

(2) *Requirements.* Assemble, develop as appropriate, and evaluate requirements for assigned resources, taking into account estimated needs for military, atomic energy, civilian, and foreign purposes. Such evaluation shall take into consideration geographical distribution of requirements under emergency conditions.

(3) *Evaluation.* Assess assigned resources in order to estimate availability from all sources under an emergency situation, analyze resource availabilities in relation to estimated requirements, and develop appropriate recommendations and programs, including those necessary for the maintenance of an adequate mobilization base. Provide data and assistance before and after attack for national resource analysis purposes of the Office of Emergency Preparedness.

(A) *Claimancy.* Prepare plans to claim from the appropriate agency supporting materials, manpower, equipment, supplies, and services which would be needed to carry out assigned responsibilities and other essential functions of his department or agency, and cooperate with other agencies in developing programs to insure availability of such resources in an emergency.

SEC. 3002. *Facilities protection and warfare effects monitoring and reporting.* In consonance with the national preparedness, security, and mobilization readiness plans, programs, and operations of the Office of

Emergency Preparedness under Executive
Order No. 11051, and with the national civil
defense plans, programs, and operations of
the Department of Defense under Executive Order No. 10952, the head of each department and agency shall:

(1) *Facilities protection.* Provide facilities
protection guidance material adapted to the
needs of the facilities and services concerned
and promote a national program to stimulate
disaster preparedness and control in order to
minimize the effects of overt or covert attack
on facilities or other resources for which he
has management responsibility. Guidance
shall include, but not be limited to, organization and training of facility employees,
personnel shelter, evacuation plans, records
protection, continuity of management, emergency repair, dispersal of facilities, and
mutual aid associations for an emergency.

(2) *Welfare effects monitoring and reporting.* Maintain a capability, both at national
and field levels, to estimate the effects of attack on assigned resources and to collaborate
with and provide data to the Office of Emergency Preparedness, the Department of Defense, and other agencies, as appropriate, in
verifying and updating estimates of resource status through exchanges of data
and mutual assistance, and provide for the
detection, identification, monitoring and reporting of such warfare effects at selected
facilities under his operation or control.

(3) *Salvage and rehabilitation.* Develop
plans for salvage, decontamination, and rehabilitation of facilities involving resources
under his jurisdiction.

(4) *Shelter.* In conformity with national
shelter policy, where authorized to engage in
building construction, plan, design, and construct such buildings to protect the public to
the maximum extent feasible against the

hazards that could result from an attack upon the United States with nuclear weapons; and where empowered to extend Federal financial assistance, encourage recipients of such financial assistance to use standards for planning design and construction which will maximize protection for the public.

SEC. 3003 *Critical skills and occupations*. (a) The Secretaries of Defense, Commerce, and Labor shall carry out the mandate of the National Security Council, dated February 15, 1968, to "maintain a continuing surveillance over the Nation's manpower needs and identify any particular occupation or skills that may warrant qualifying for deferment on a uniform national basis." In addition, the Secretaries of Defense, Commerce, Labor, and Health, Education, and Welfare shall carry out the mandate of the National Security Council to "maintain a continuing surveillance over the Nation's manpower and education needs to identify any area of graduate study that may warrant qualifying for deferment in the national interest." In carrying out these functions, the Secretaries concerned shall consult with the National Science Foundation with respect to scientific manpower requirements.

(b) The Secretaries of Commerce and Labor shall maintain and issue, as necessary, lists of all essential activities and critical occupations that may be required for emergency preparedness purposes.

SEC. 3004 *Research*. Within the framework of research policies and objectives established by the Office of Emergency Preparedness, the head of each department and agency shall supervise or conduct research in areas directly concerned with carrying out emergency preparedness responsibilities, designate representatives for necessary ad hoc or task force groups, and provide advice and assistance to other agencies in planning for research in areas involving each agency's interest.

SEC. 3005 *Stockpiles*. The head of each department and agency, with appropriate emergency responsibilities, shall assist the Office of Emergency Preparedness in formulating and carrying out plans for stockpiling of strategic and critical materials, and survival items.

SEC. 3006 *Direct Economic Controls*. The head of each department and agency shall cooperate with the Office of Emergency Preparedness and the Federal financial agencies in the development of emergency preparedness measures involving emergency financial and credit measures, as well as price, rent, wage and salary stabilization, and consumer rationing programs.

SEC. 3007 *Financial Aid*. The head of each department and agency shall develop plans and procedures in cooperation with the Federal financial agencies for financial and credit assistance to those segments of the private sector for which he is responsible in the event such assistance is needed under emergency conditions.

SEC. 3008 *Functional Guidance*. The head of each department and agency in carrying out the functions assigned to him by this order, shall be guided by the following:

(1) *National program guidance.* In consonance with the national preparedness, security, and mobilization readiness plans, programs, and operations of the Office of Emergency Preparedness under Executive Order No. 11051, and with the national civil defense plans, programs, and operations of the Department of Defense, technical guidance shall be provided to State and local governments and instrumentalities thereof, to the end that all planning concerned with functions assigned herein will be effectively

coordinated. Relations with the appropriate segment of the private sector shall be maintained to foster mutual understanding of Federal emergency plans.

(2) *Interagency coordination.* Emergency preparedness functions shall be coordinated by the head of the department or agency having primary responsibility with all other departments and agencies having supporting functions related thereto.

(3) *Emergency preparedness.* Emergency plans, programs, and an appropriate state of readiness, including organizational readiness, shall be developed as an integral part of the continuing activities of each department or agency on the basis that that department or agency will have the responsibility for carrying out such plans and programs during an emergency. The head of each department or agency shall be prepared to implement all appropriate plans developed under this order. Modifications and temporary organizational changes, based on emergency conditions, shall be in accordance with policy determinations by the President.

(4) *Professional liaison.* Mutual understanding and support of emergency preparedness activities shall be fostered, and the National Defense Executive Reserve shall be promoted by maintaining relations with the appropriate non-governmental sectors.

SEC. 3009 *Training.* The head of each department and agency shall develop and direct training programs which incorporate emergency preparedness and civil defense training and information programs necessary to insure the optimum operational effectiveness of assigned resources, systems, and facilities.

SEC. 3010 *Emergency Public Information.* In consonance with such emergency public information plans and central program decisions of the Office of Emergency Prepared-

ness, and with plans, programs, and procedures established by the Department of Defense to provide continuity of programming
for the Emergency Broadcast System, the
head of each department and agency shall:

(1) Obtain and provide information as to
the emergency functions or assignments of
the individual department or agency for dissemination to the American people during
the emergency, in accordance with arrangements made by the Office of Emergency Preparedness.

(2) Determine requirements and arrange
for prerecordings to provide continuity of
program service over the Emergency Broadcast System so that the American people can
receive information, advice, and guidance
pertaining to the implementation of the civil
defense and emergency preparedness plans
or assignments of each individual department
or agency.

SEC. 3011. *Emergency Actions.* This order
does not confer authority to put into effect
any emergency plan, procedure, policy, program, or course of action prepared or developed pursuant to this order. Plans so developed may be effectuated only in the event
that authority for such effectuation is provided by a law enacted by the Congress or
by an order or directive issued by the President pursuant to statutes or the Constitution of the United States.

SEC. 3012 *Redelegation.* The head of each
department and agency is hereby authorized to redelegate the functions assigned to
him by this order, and to authorize succes-
sive redelegations to agencies or instrumentalities of the United States, and to officers
and employees of the United States.

SEC. 3013 *Transfer of Functions.* Any emergency preparedness function under this order, or parts thereof, may be transferred from

one department or agency to another with the consent of the heads of the organizations involved and with the concurrence of the Director of the Office of Emergency Preparedness. Any new emergency preparedness function may be assigned to the head of a department or agency by the Director of the Office of Emergency Preparedness by mutual consent.

SEC. 3014 *Retention of Existing Authority.* Except as provided in Section 3015, nothing in this order shall be deemed to derogate from any now existing asignment of functions to any department or agency or officer thereof made by statute. Executive order or Presidential directives, including Memoranda

SEC. 3015 *Revoked Orders.* The following are hereby revoked:

(1) Defense Mobilization Order VI–2 of December 11, 1953.

(2) Defense Mobilization Order I–12 of October 5, 1954.

(3) Executive Order No. 10312 of December 10, 1951.

(4) Executive Order No. 10346 of April 17, 1952.

(5) Executive Order No. 10997 of February 16, 1962.

(6) Executive Order No. 10998 of February 16, 1962.

(7) Executive Order No. 10999 of February 16, 1962.

(8) Executive Order No. 11000 of February 16, 1962.

(9) Executive Order No. 11001 of February 16, 1962.

(10) Executive Order No. 11002 of February 16, 1962.

(11) Executive Order No. 11003 of February 16, 1962.

(12) Executive Order No. 11004 of February 16, 1962.

(13) Executive Order No. 11005 of February 16, 1962.

(14) Executive Order No. 11087 of February 26, 1963.

(15) Executive Order No. 11088 of February 26, 1963.

(16) Executive Order No. 11089 of February 26, 1963.

(17) Executive Order No. 11090 of February 26, 1963.

(18) Executive Order No. 11091 of February 26, 1963.

(19) Executive Order No. 11092 of February 26, 1963.

(20) Executive Order No. 11093 of February 26, 1963.

(21) Executive Order No. 11094 of February 26, 1963.

(22) Executive Order No. 11095 of February 26, 1963.

(23) Executive Order No. 11310 of October 11, 1966.

THE WHITE HOUSE, *October 28, 1969.*

RICHARD NIXON.

Exhibit G

[From the Borger (Tex.) News Herald,
Sept. 19, 1971]

STATE OF NATIONAL EMERGENCY LEGALIZES THE
EXECUTIVE ORDERS: THE NATIONAL EMER-
GENCY

(By Archibald E. Roberts, Lt. Col.
AUS. ret.)

The state of "national emergency" declared
by President Nixon in August "legalized" the
imposition of Executive Orders and other
socialist directives under the guise of a "time
of increased international tension, and economic and financial crisis."

When published in the Federal Register
Executive Orders, without any concurring
action by the Congress, become law. In combination these documents achieve the objective of those who have long sought to
dismantle the Constitution and erect a socialist state upon the ruins of the Republic.

The implications of "national emergency"
may be best understood by examining a few
of the Executive Orders published in the Federal Register during February and September,
1962:

Executive Order No. 11051 Details responsibility of the Office of Emergency Planning
and gives authorization to put all Executive
Orders into effect in times of increased international tensions and economic or financial
crisis.

Executive Order No. 10995 Provides for the take over of communication media.

Executive Order No. 10997 Provides for the take over of all electrical power, gas, petroleum, fuels, and minerals.

Executive Order No. 10998 Provides for the take over of food resources and farms.

Executive Order No. 10990 Provides for the take over of all modes of transportation and control of highways, seaports, etc.

Executive Order No. 11000 Provides for mobilization of civilians into work brigades under government supervision.

Executive Order No. 11001 Provides for government take over of health, education, and welfare functions.

Executive Order No. 11002 Designates the Postmaster General to operate a national registration of all persons.

Executive Order No. 11003 Provides for the government take over of airports and aircraft.

Executive Order No. 11004 Provides for the Housing and Finance Authority to relocate communities, build new housing with public funds, designate areas to be abandoned, and established new locations for populations.

Executive Order No. 11005 Provides for the government to take over railroads, inland waterways, public storage facilities.

Executive Order No. 11310 Published in the Federal Register, 11 October, 1966, grants authority to the Department of Justice to enforce the plans set out in Executive Orders, to institute industry support, to establish judicial and legislative liaison, to control all aliens, to operate penal and correctional institutions, and to advise and assist the President.

In all respects the Attorney General will be an all powerful commissar with life and death authority over virtually all aspects of

American life.

In a public speech at Casper, Wyoming, 7 March, 1969, I predicted that, "America is within two years of being taken over by an international cartel," and, "Nixon will be the one to lead us into total world government."

"An international monetary crisis will be the tipoff to the takeover of the world by an organization of large bankers and business-men intent on power," I said.

Contemporary events confirm our worst apprehensions.

On 15 August, 1971, President Richard M. Nixon, in Proclamation No. 4074, announced, "I hereby declare a national emergency," thus effecting delivery of the Untied States to a cabal of international money lenders and in-dustrialists. Pressures of economic coercion spelled out in Executive Order No. 11615 of the same date, are intended to expedite the transfer of Americans into an Orwilian, 1984, animal farm.

The Order of "Stabilization of Prices, Rents, Wages, and Salaries," which is the title of Executive Order 11615, reveals that Arthur F. Burns, Chairman of the Board of Gover-nors, Federal Reserve System, is the advisor (controller) of the Council.

The Federal Reserve System is a private banking cartel which controls the American economy by regulating the flow of Federal Reserve notes in circulation, by controlling interest rates, the stock market, and other facets of American life.

The Council (read Federal Reserve System) is also charged under the Order with the re-sponsibility for developing additional policies, mechanism, and procedures to control prices, rents, wages, and salaries "after the expira-tion of the 90-day period.

In consonance with the provisions of Executive Order 11310 dated 11 October, 1966, the Order of 15 August, 1971, directs the Department of Justice to "bring actions for injunctions whenever it appears that any person has violated the regulations set out by the Council (F.R.S.).

It will take a little time for the loose ends to be tidied up—three months say the planners—but ultimately all of us will experience the crunch of a controlled society.

The die is cast in Proclamation 4074 and companion Executive Order 11615.

Through these acts, and certain other Executive Orders published during the Kennedy and Johnson Administrations, one man, on behalf of hidden sponsors, has completely ignored the Constitution, the authority of Congress, and the people.

By implementing Executive Orders a dictatorship can be imposed on the American people.

This is the political reality of Mr. Nixon's declaration of a state of "national emergency."

All else is rhetoric.

The success of the conspiracy can, however, be temporary . . . if the people will it. Covert control of the Federal Government is dependent upon secrecy until full consolidation of power is achieved.

The moment an aroused and indignant people commit themselves to exposing and neutralizing the Financial "Elite" who pull the strings the "Day of the Wizard" will end.

Ref: "Proclamation 4074," and "Executive Order 1615," the Federal Register, Vol. 36, No. 159, Tuesday, August 17, 1971, pp. 15724–15729.

Exhibit H

Don Bell Reports

A WEEKLY COMMENTARY

Year Nineteen - - - - - - - - Number Eighteen - - - - - May 5, 1972

THE "NEW LOOK" OF THE
COUNCIL ON FOREIGN RELATIONS

BROTHERHOOD BECOMES BISEXUAL – The prestigious, puissant and pelf-packed Council on Foreign Relations, often called *The Invisible Government* and known by its members as the most exclusive club in the United States, did a new thing in 1971. After fifty-two years of patrician chauvinism and esoteric oligarchy, the Council decided it would expire of senility unless it brought in new blood. It determined that it must invite selected *young* men to join the patrician complot, and—with the greatest of reluctance—seek out women who were worthy to take positions of covert command, and invite them, too, to become members of the Elite Inner Circle.

As a result, there has been an increase in membership – about 1500 now belong to CFR – and a number of changes in the old membership list. Consequently, we were pleased when Congressman John R. Rarick obtained an up-to-date list of CFR members, so that we might pass along to our subscribers, that new compilation of America's Unelected Rulers.

In making public this new membership list, Representative Rarick said:

". . . The Council on Foreign Relations — dedicated to one-world government, financed by a number of the largest tax-exempt foundations, and wielding such power and influence over our lives in the areas of finance, business, labor, military, education, and mass communication media — should be familiar to every American concerned with good government and with preserving and defending the U.S. Constitution and our free enterprise system.

"Yet the Nation's 'right-to-know-machinery' — the news media — usually so aggressive in exposures to inform our people, remain conspicuously silent when it comes to the CFR, its members, and their activities. And I find that few university students and graduates have even heard of the Council on Foreign Relations. "The CFS is *the establishment*. Not only does it have influence and power in key decision-making positions at the highest levels of government to apply pressure from above, but it also finances and uses individuals and groups to bring pressure from below, to justify the high level decisions for converting the United States from a sovereign Constitutional Republic into a servile member state of a one-world dictatorship."

In addition to its influence *upon* the government from above and below, there also is the serious matter of the CFR's influence from *within* the government. The Network of Patriotic Letter Writers of Pasadena, California compiled a list of 110 members of the CFR who have been nominated and appointed to government posts by President Nixon. Out of a total membership of 1500, this is an enormous number of members of this one exclusive, semi-secret organization to be in positions of influence within the Federal Government! In presenting this list, NPLW observed that "The goal of the CFR is simply to abolish the United States with its

Constitutional guarantees of liberty. And they don't even try to hide it. *Study No. 7*, published by the CFR on November 25, 1959 openly advocates 'building a new international order (which) must be responsibe to world aspirations for peace (and) for social and economic change. . . . an international order . . . including states labelling themselves as Socialist . . .'

This "new international order" that CFR is building, involves the recognition of three co-equal superpowers: U.S.A., U.S.S.R., and P.R.C., the three forming a Troika, or "Triangular Constellation" which is to divide and rule the world. Hence the new "One China" policy, the division of Pakistan into two separate countries, the current controversy over the Berlin-Moscow treaties, and CFR-member Kissinger's arrangements for Peking and Moscow Summit Meetings. (Text continues on page 7 of this two-part letter).

COUNCIL ON FOREIGN RELATIONS
MEMBERSHIP LIST – 1972

RESIDENT MEMBERS

Abel, Elie
Abram, Morris B.
Akers, Anthony B.
Albrecht-Carrier, Rene
Aldrich, Winthrop W.
Alexander, Archibald S.
Alexander, Robert J.
Allan, F. Aley
Allen, Philip E.
Alley, James B.
Allport, Alexander W.
Alpern, Alan N.
Altschul, Arthur G.
Altschul, Frank
Ames, Amyas
Ammidon, Hoyt
Anderson, Robert B.
Anschuetz, Norbert L.
Armour, Norman
Armstrong, Hamilton Fish
Armstrong, Wilis C.
Ascoli, Max
Attwood, William
Ault, Bromwell

Backer, George
Baird, Charles F.
Baldwin, Robert H.B.
Ball, George W.
Ballard, Allen B.
Bancroft, Harding F.
Banks, Louis L.
Barber, Charles F.
Barber, Joseph
Barker, Robert R.
Barlow, William E.
Barnds, William J.
Barnes, Robert G.
Barnett, Frank R.
Barrand, Harry P. Jr.
Barrett, Edward W.
Barzun, Jacques
Bassow, Whitman
Bastedo, Philip
Bator, Peter A.
Becker, Loftus E.
Beebe, Frederick S.
Beinecke, William S.
Bell, David E.

Benjamin, Robert S.
Benton, William
Beplat, Tristan E.
Berger, Peter L.
Bernstein, Peter L.
Bessie, Simon Michael
Bienstock, Abraham L.
Bingham, Jonathan B.
Birkelund, John P.
Black, Joseph E.
Black, Peter
Blough, Roger M.
Blough, Roy
Blum, John A.
Bogdan, Norbert A.
Bolte, Charles G.
Bonsal, Dudley B.
Borch, Fred J.
Borton, Hugh
Bowers, John Z.
Boyd, Hugh N.
Boyd, William H. 2nd
Bradshaw, Thornton F.
Braxton, Carter M.

Breck, Henry C.
Brennan, Donald G.
Brisco, Milo M.
Brittenham, Raymond L.
Bronk, Detlev W.
Brooks, John W.
Brown, Courtney C.
Brown, Irving
Brown, Walter L.
Brownell, George A.
Brzezinski, Zbigniew
Bullock, Hugh
Bundy, McGeorge
Burden, William A.M.
Burgess, Carter L.
Burkhardt, Frederick
Burnett, John G.
Burns, Patrick Owen
Bush, Donald F.
Bush, George H.W.
Bushner, Rolland H.
Butcher, Willard C.
Butler, William F.
Buttenweiser, Benjamin J.

Cabell, Richard A.
Cahill, Jane P.
Calder, Alexander, Jr.
Calhoun, Alexander D.
Camp, Hugh D.
Campbell, John C.
Campbell, John Franklin
Campbell, Nicholas J., Jr
Canfield, Cass
Canfield, Franklin O.
Carey, Andrew G.
Carroll, Mitchell B.
Carter, George E.
Carter, William D.
Cary, William L.
Case, John C.
Cates, John M.
Chace, James C.
Chase, W. Howard
Chittenden, George H.
Christopher, Robert C.
Chubb, Hendon, 2nd
Chubb, Percy 2nd
Church, Adgar M.
Clay, Gen. Lucius D.

Cleveland, Harold van B.
Coffin, Edmund
Cohen, Jerome B.
Cohen, Stephen B.
Coles, James S.
Collado, Emilio G.

Colwell, Kent G.
Conant, James B.
Conant, Melvin A.
Conner, John T.
Considine, Rev. John J.
Cook, Howard A.
Coolidge, Nicholas J.
Coombs, Charles A.
Cordier, Andrew W.
Costanzo, G.A.
Cotter, William R.
Coughran, Tom B.
Cousins, Norman
Cowan, Louis G.
Cowles, Gardner
Crassweller, Robert D.
Creel, Dana S.
Cummings, Robert L.
Curtis, Gerald L.
Cusick, Peter

Darlington, Charles F.
Darrell, Norris
Davidson, Ralph K.
Davis, John A.
Davison, W. Phillips
Dean, Arthur H.
Debevoise, Eli Whitney
DeCubas, Jose
De Lima, Oscar A.
Deming, Frederick L.
Dennison, Charles S.
De Rosso, Alphonse
Derryck, Vivian L.
De Vries, Henry P.
Diebold, John
Diebold, William Jr.
Dillon, Clarence
Dillon, Douglas
Dilworth, J. Richardson
Dodge, Cleveland E.
Dolin, Arnold
Donahue, Donald J.
Donnell, Ellsworth

Donovan, Ellsworth
Donovan, Hedley
Dorr, Goldthwaite H.
Dorwin, Oscar John
Douglas, Lewis W.
Douglas, Paul W.
Dubinsky, David
Duffy, James H.
Durkee, William P.

Eagle, Vernon A.
Eaton, Frederick M.

Edelman, Albert I.
Edelstein, Julius C. C.
Edwards, Howard L.
Eichelberger, Clark M.
Elliot, L.W.
Elliott, Osborn
Elson, Robert T.
Emmet, Christopher
Engel, Irving M.
Ewing, Sherman
Ewing, William Jr.
Exter, John

Feer, Mark C.
Field, William Osgood, Jr.
Finger, Seymour M.
Finlay, Luke W.
Finletter, Thomas K.
Finn, James
Finney, Paul B.
Fleck, G. Peter
Ford, Nevil
Forrestal, Michael V.
Fowler, Henry H.
Fox, Joseph C.
Fox, William T.R.
Frankel, Charles
Franklin, George S. Jr.
Frasche, Dean F.
Fredericks, J. Wayne
Frelinghuysen, Peter H.B.
French, John
Freudenthal, David M.
Freund, Gerald
Friele, Berent
Friendly, Henry J.
Frye, William R.
Fuerbringer, Otto
Fuller, C. Dale
Funkhouser, E.N. Jr.

Gage, Harlow W.
Gallatin, James P.
Gardner, Richard N.
Garretson, Albert H.
Garrison, Lloyd K.
Garvin, Clifton C.
Garvy, George
Garwin, Richard L.
Gates, Thomas S.
Gelb, Richard L.
Geneen, Harold S.
Gideonse, Harry D.
Gillespie, S. Hazard
Gilpatric, Howell L.
Golden, William T.

Goldin, Harrison J.
Goldstone, Harmon H.
Goodrich, Leland M.
Gordon, Albert H.
Grace, J. Peter
Graff, Robert D.
Granville, Maurice F.
Grazier, Joseph A.
Greenfield, James L.
Griffith, Thomas
Grimm, Peter
Gross, Ernest A.
Groover, Allen
Gruson, Sydney
Gurfein, Murray I-

Hager, Eric H.
Haight, George W.
Halaby, Najeeb E.
Halberstam, David
Hall, Floyd D.
Hamilton, Edward K.
Hamilton, Fowler
Hance, William A.
Harari, Maurice
Harrar, J.G.
Haskell, Broderick
Hauge, Gabriel
Hauser, Rita E.
Hayes, Alfred

Hayes, Samuel P.
Haynes, Ulric Jr.
Haywood, Oliver G.
Hazard, John N.
Heath, Donald R.
Heckscher, August

Helander, Robert C.
Hellman, Warren
Helm, Harold H.
Henderson, William
Henkin, Louis
Herod, W. Rogers

Herzog, Paul M.
Hester, James M.
Hickey, William M.
Highet, Keith
Hill, James T.
Hilsman, Roger
Hochschild, Harold K.
Hochschild, Walter
Hoffman, Paul G.

Hoglund, Elis S.
Hoguet, Robert L.
Honenberg, John
Holland, Kenneth

Holmes, Alan R.
Holt, L. Emmett, Jr.
Homer, Sidney
Hoover, Lyman
Horn, Garfield H.
Horton, Philip C.
Hottelet, Richard C.
Houghton, Arthur A. Jr.
Hovey, Allan, Jr.
Howard, John B.
Howell, John I.
Hughes, Thomas L.
Hurewitz, J.C.
Hyde, Henry B.
Hyde, James N.

Inglis, John B.
Ireland, R.L. 3rd
Isaacs, Norman E.
Iselin, O'Donnell
Issawi, Charles

Jackson, Elmore
Jackson, William E.
James, George F.
Jamieson, J.K.
Jaretzki, Alfred, Jr.
Jastrow, Robert
Javits, Jacob K.
Jessup, Alpheus W.
Jessup, John K.
Jessup, Philip C.
Johnson, Joseph E.
Jones, David J.
Jones, Gilbert E.
Josephson, William H.

Kahn, Herman
Kaminer, Peter H.
Kane, R. Keith
Kassof, Allen H.
Katzenbach, Nicholas de B
Keezer, Dexter M.
Keisef, David M.
Kempner, Maximillian W.
Kenney F. Donald
Keppel, Francis
Kerr, Harry F.
Kettaneh, Francis A.
King, Frederic R.
Kirk, Grayson
Kleiman, Robert
Knight, Douglas
Knight, Robert Huntington
Knoppers, Antonie T.
Knowlton, Winthrop

Koenig, Robert P.
Korbonski, Andrzej
Kreidler, Robert N.
Kristol, Irving

Labouisse, Henry R.
Lacy, Dan
Landry, Lionel
Larkin, Arthur E., Jr.
Larmon, Sigurd S.
LaRoche, Chester J.
Lary, Hal B.
Laukhuff, Perry
LeBaron, Eugene
Lehman, John R.
Lehman, Orin
Lehrman, Hal
Leonard, James G.
Leroy, Norbert G.
Leslie, John C.
Levy, Walter J.
Lewis, Flora
Lieberman, Henry R.
Lilienthal, David E.
Lilley, A.N.
Lindquist, Warren T.
Lindsay, George N.
Lindsay, John V.
Linen, James A.
Lissitzyn, Oliver J.
Locke, Edwin A., Jr.
Lockwood, John E.
Loeb, John L.
Loft, George
Loomis, Alfred L.
Loos, Rev. A. William
Lowenfield, Andreas F.
Loy, Frank E.
Lubar, Robert A.
Lubin, Isador
Luce, Charles F.
Luckey, E. Hugh
Ludt, R.E.
Luke, David L. 3rd.
Lyford, Joseph P.

McCance, Thomas
McCarthy, John G.
McCloy, John J.
McCloy, John J. 2nd.
McColough, C. Peter
McDermott, Walsh
McKee, James W. Jr.
McKeever, Porter
McClean, John G.
MacEachron, David W.

MacGregor, Ian K.
MacIntyre, Malcolm A.
Macomber, John D.
Maffry, August
Manning, Bayless
Manshel, Warren D.
Mark, Rev. Julius
Markel, Lester
Marron, Donald B.
Martinuzzi, Leo S., Jr.
Masten, John E.
Mathews, Edward J.
Mattison, Graham D.
Mayer, Gerald M. Jr.
Menke, John R.

Metzger, Herman A.
Meyer, John M., Jr.
Meyer, John R.
Millard, Mark J.
Model, Leo
Moe, Sherwood G.
Moore, George S.
Moore, Maurice T.
Moore Rt. Rev. Paul, Jr.
Moore, Walden
Moore, William T.
Moorman, Elliott D.
Morgan, Henry S.

Morganthau, Hans J.
Morley, James William
Morris, Grinnell
Morrisett, Lloyd N.
Morse, David A.
Mosely, Philip E.
Moyers, Bill D.
Muir, Malcolm
Mulford, David C.
Munroe, George B.
Munroe, Vernon, Jr.
Munyan, Winthrop B.
Murden, Forrest D.
Murphy, Grayson M.P.
Murphy, J. Morden
Muse, Martha T.

Nagorski, Zygmunt, Jr.
Neal, Alfred C.
Nelson, Clifford C.
Nelson, Merlin E.
Newton, Quigg, Jr.
Nichols, Thomas S.
Nielsen, Waldemar A.
Nimitz, Chester W., Jr.
Nolte, Richard H.
Nolting, Frederick E., Jr.

Notestein, Frank W.
Novak, Michael
Noyes, Charles Phelps

Oakes, John B.
Ogden, Alfred
Olmstead, Cecil J.
O'Neill, Michael J.
Osborn, Earl D.
Osborn, Frederick H.
Osborne, Stanley de J.
Ostrander, F. Taylor, Jr.
Overby, Andrew N.
Overton, Douglas W.

Pace, Frank, Jr.
Page, Howard W.
Page, John H.
Page, Walter H.
Paley, William S.
Palfrey, John G.
Parker, Philo W.
Passin, Herbert
Patterson, Ellmore C.
Patterson, Frederick D.
Patterson, Herbert P.
Paul, Roland A.
Payne, Frederick B.
Payne, Samuel B.
Payson, Charles Shipman
Pearson, John E.
Pennoyer, Robert M.
Perkins, James A.
Perkins, Roswell B.
Perry, Hart
Petersen, Gustav H.
Petschek, Stephen R.
Pfaff, William W., 3rd.
Philip, Nicholas W.
Phillips, Christopher H.

Picker, Harvey
Pickering, James V.
Piel, Gerard
Pierce, William C.
Piercy, George T.
Pierre, Andrew J.
Pierson, Warren Lee
Pifer, Alan
Pike, H. Harvey
Place, John B.M.
Platten, Donald C.
Plimpton, Calvin H.
Plimpton, Francis T.P.
Polk, Judd
Poor, J. Sheppard
Potter, Robert S.

Powers, Joshua B.
Pratt, H. Irving
Probst, George E.
Pulling, Edward
Pusey, Nathan M.

Quigg, Philip W.

Rabi, Isidor I.
Reber, Samuel
Reed, J.V.
Reed, Philip D.
Reid, Ogden R.
Reid, Whitelaw
Resor, Stanley R.
Reston, James B.
Rheinstein, Alfred
Richardson, Arthur Berry
Riegleman, Harold
Riesel, Victor
Riordan, James Q.
Robbins, Donald G., Jr.
Roche, James M.
Rockefeller, David
Rockefeller, John D. 3rd.
Rockefeller, Nelson A.
Rockefeller, Rodman C.
Rockhill, Victor E.
Rodriguez, Vincent A.
Roosa, Robert V.
Root, Oren
Rosenstiel, Lewis
Rosenthal, A.M.
Rosenwald, William
Rosin, Axel G.
Ross, T.J.
Ruebausen, Oscar M.
Russell, T.W., Jr.
Rustow, Dankworth A.

Sachs, Alexander
Salisbury, Harrison E.
Saltzman, Charles E.
Sargeant, Howland H.
Schachter, Oscar
Schaffner, Joseph Halle
Schiff, John M.
Schiller, A. Arthur
Schilling, Warner R.
Schlesinger, Arthur, Jr.
Schmidt, Herman J.
Schwartz, Harry
Schwarz, Frederick A.O.
Schwarz, Frederick A.O., Jr.
Scott, John
Stuart, N.

Seagrave, Norman P.
Seibold, Frederick C., Jr.
Seitz, Frederick
Seligman, Eustace
Seymour, Whitney North
Shapiro, Isaac
Sharp, George C.
Sharp, James H.
Sheean, Vincent
Sheeline, Paul C.
Shepard, David A.
Shepard, Frank P.
Shulman, Marshall D.
Shute, Benjamin R.
Silvers, Robert B.
Silvert, K.H.
Sims, Albert G.
Slater, Joseph E.
Slawson, John
Smith, Carleton Sprague
Smith, Datus C., Jr.
Smith, David S.
Smith, Hayden N.
Smith, W. Mason
Solbert, Peter A.O.
Sommers, Davidson
Sorensen, Theodore C.
Soubry, E.E.
Spofford, Charles M.
Stackpole, Stephen H.
Stamas, Stephen
Stanton, Frank
Staples, Eugene S.
Steadman, Richard C.
Stebbins, James H.
Stebbins, Richard P.
Steel, Ronald
Stein, Howard
Steinger, Edward L.
Stern, Fritz
Stern, H. Peter
Stewart, Robert McLean
Stoddard, George D.
Stoessinger, John G.
Stokes, Isaac N.P.
Stone, Robert G., Jr.
Straka, Jerome A.
Stratton, Julius A.
Straus, Donald B.
Straus, Jack I.
Straus, Oscar C.
Straus, Ralph I.
Straus, R. Peter
Strauss, Simon D.
Streibert, Theodore C.
Strong, Benjamin

Sulzberger, Arthur Ochs
Sutton, Francis X.
Swing, John Temple
Swinton, Stanley M.

Talbot, Phillips
Tavoulareas, William P.
Taylor, Arthur R.
Thomas, Evan
Thomas, H. Gregory
Thompson, Earle S.
Thompson, Kenneth W.
Todaro, Michael P.
Tomlinson, Alexander C.
Topping, Seymour
Townsend, Edward
Trager, Frank N.
Traphagen, J.C.
Travis, Martin B., Jr.
Trees, James F.
Trippe, Juan Terry
Trowbridge, Alexander B.
Tuchman, Barbara
Tweedy, Gordon B.

Uzielli, Giorgio

Vance, Cyrus R.
Vila, George R.
Von Klemperer, Alfred H.
Von Mehren, Robert B.
Voorhees, Tracy S.

Walker, A. Lightfoot
Walker, George G.
Walkowicz, T.F.
Wallace, Martha R.
Warburg, Eric M.
Ward, F. Champion
Warfield, Ethelbert
Warner, Rawleigh, Jr.
Wasson, Donald
Watson, Thomas J., Jr.
Watts, John H. 3rd.
Wauchope, Vice Adm. George
Webster, Bethuel M.
Wells, Richard C.
Wernimont, Kenneth
Whidden, Howard P.
Whipple, Taggart
White, Frank X.
White, Theodore H.
Whitney, John Hay
Whitridge, Arnold
Wilbur, C. Martin
Wilkins, Roger W.
Wilkinson, Theodore L.

Williams, Franklin H.
Wilson, Donald M.
Wilson, John D.
Wingate, Henry S.
Winslow, Richard S.
Wood, Thomas A.
Woodward, Donald B.
Woolley, Knight
Wriggins, W. Howard
Wriston, Henry M.
Wriston, Walter B.
Wyle, Frederic S.

Yarmolinsky, Adam
Yost, Charles W.
Young, Edgar B.
Young, John M.
Young, Kenneth T., Jr.

Zagoria, Donald S.
Zorthian, Barry
Zurcher, Arnold J.

NON-RESIDENT MEMBERS

Abegglen, James C.
Abelson, Philip H.
Acheson, Dean G.
Achilles, Theodore C.
Adams, Ruth Salzman
Allen, Charles E.
Allen, Raymond B.
Allison, Graham T.
Amory, Robert Jr.
Anderson, Dillon
Anderson, Adm. George W.,
Anderson, Robert O.
Anderson, Roger E.
Angell, James W.
Apter, David E.
Armstrong, Gen. DeWitt C.
Armstrong, John A.
Asher, Robert E.
Austin, Vice Adm. B.L.

Babcock, Gen. C. Stanton
Badeau, John S.
Baldwin, Hanson
Ballou, George T.
Barco, James W.
Barger, Thomas C.
Barghoorn, Frederick C.
Barker, James M.
Barker, Robinson F.

Donnelly, Gen. Harold C.
Dorr, Russell H.
Dorsey, Bob Rawls
Doty, Paul M. Jr.
Douglas, Donald W. Jr.
Dowling, Walter
Draper, William H Jr.
Dreter, John C.
Drummond, Roscoe
Ducas, Robert
Duke, Angier Biddle
Duncan, Ralph A.
Durdin, F. Tillman

Eberle, W.D.
Eckstein, Alexander
Edwards, A.R.
Edwards, Robert H.
Edwards, William H.
Einaudi, Marlo
Eliot, Theodore L. Jr.
Elliot, Byron K
Elliot, Randle
Elliot, William V.
Ellsberg, Daniel
Emeny, Brooks
Emerson, Rupert
Enders, Thomas O.
Enthoven, Alain C.
Eppert, Ray R.
Ernst, Albert E.
Estabrook, Robert H.
Evans, John K.
Everton, John Scott.

Fahs, Charles B.
Fainsod, Merle
Fairbank, John King
Fairbank, Douglas
Falk, Richard A.
Farmer, Garland R.
Farmer, Rhomas L.
Feis, Herbert
Fenn, William P.
Ferguson, Glenn W.
Fifield, Russell H.
Finkelstein, Lawrence S.
Firestone, Harvey S. Jr.
Fishel, Wesley R.
Fisher, Adrian S.
Fisher, Roger
Flanigan, Peter M.
Florinsky, Michael T.
Ford, Thomas K.
Forkner, Claude E.

Fosdick, Raymond B.
Foster, William C.
Frampton, George T. Jr.
Frank, Charles R.
Frank, Isaiah
Frankel, Max
Free, Lloyd A.
Freeman, Fulton
Frey, Donald N.
Fried, Edward R.
Friedman, Irving S.
Fuller, Carlton P.
Fuller, Robert G.

Gallagher, Charles F.
Gallagher, John F.
Ganoe, Charles S.
Gant, George F.
Gardner, John W.
Garthoff, Raymond L.
Gaud, William S.
Gaylord, Bradley
Geertz, Clifford
Geier, Paul E.
Geiger, Theodore
George, W.H. Krome
Gerhardt, Gen. H.A.
Gerhart, Gen. John K.
Gibney, Frank B.
Griffin, Gen. Sidney F.
Gil, Peter P.
Gilbert, Carl J.
Gilbert, H.N.
Gilchrist, Huntington
Gilpatric, Chadbourne
Gilpin, Robert G.
Ginsburgh, Gen. Robert N.
Gleason, E. Everett
Glennan, T. Keith
Goheen, Robert F
Goldberg, Arthur J.
Goldberger, Marvin L.
Goldman, Guido
Goldman, Marshall I.
Goodhart, Arthur L.
Goodpaster, Gen. A.J.
Gordon, Kermit
Gordon, Lincoln
Gornick, Alan L.
Gorter, Wytze
Graham, Katharine
Grant, James P.
Graubard, Stephan R.
Gray, Gordon
Green, Joseph C.
Greene, James C.

Greene, Gen. M.J.L.
Greenwald, Joseph A.
Griffith, Gen. S.B. 2nd.
Griffith, William E.
Grondahl, Teg. C.
Gruenther, Gen. Alfred M.
Guillion, Edmund A.
Gurganus, William R.

Hall, John W.

Halle, Louis J. Jr.
Halperin, Morton H.
Hamilton, Thomas J.
Hanes, John W. Jr.
Hansell, Gen. H.S.
Harbison, Frederick
Hare, Raymond A.
Hargrove, John L.
Harriman, W. Averrell
Harris, Irving B.
Harris, James T. Jr.
Harris, Patricia Roberts
Harsch, Joseph C.
Hart, Augustin S.
Hart, Parker T.
Hartley, Fred L.
Haskins, Caryl P.
Haviland, H. Field
Haynes, Gen. Fred
Hays, Brooks
Heintzen, Harry L.
Heinz, Henry J. Jr.
Heldring, Frederick
Henderson, Julia
Henderson, L.J. Jr.
Henderson, Loy W.
Herter, Christian A. Jr.
Hesburgh, Rev. Theodore M.
Hewitt, William A.
Hill, George Watts
Hills, Robert C.
Hinshaw, Randall
Hirschman, Albert O.
Hitch, Charles J.
Hobby, William P. Jr.
Hofer, Philip
Hoffman, Michael L.
Hoffman, Stanley
Holbrooke, Richard C.
Holst, Willem
Holt, Pat M.
Hoopes, Townsend W.
Hoover, Herbert W. Jr.
Hopkins, D. Luke
Hopper, Bruce C.
Hormats, Robert D.
Horton, Alan W.

Hoskins, Harold B.
Houghton, Amory
Houghton, Amory Jr.
Hovde, Frederick L.
Huglin, H.C.
Huizenga, John W.
Humphrey, Hunert H.
Hunsberger, Warren S.
Hunt. James Ramsey
Hunter, Clarence E.
Huntington, Samuel P.
Irwin, John N. 2nd
Iverson, Kenneth R.

Jacobson, Harold K.
Jaffe, Sam A.
Jansen, Marius B.
Jenney, John K.
Jessup, Philip C. Jr.
Johnson, Gen. H.K.
Johnson, Howard C.
Johnson, Howard W.
Johnson, James A.
Johnston, Henry R.
Johnstone, W.H.
Jones, Peter T.
Jones, Thomas V.
Jordan, Col. Amos A. Jr.
Jorden, William J.

Kahin, George McT.
Kaiser, Philip M.
Kalinski, Felix A.
Karmack, Andrew M.
Katz, Milton
Katzenbach, Edward L. Jr.
Kaufmann, William W.
Kaysen, Carl
Kearns, Doris
Kelly, George Armstrong
Kempner, Frederick C.
Kenen. Peter B.
Keniston, Kenneth
Kennan, George F.
Killefer, Tom
Killiam, James R. Jr.
Kimberly, John R.
King, James E. Jr.
King, John A. Jr.
Kintner, Col. W.R.
Kissinger, Henry A.
Kitchen, Jeffrey C.
Knorr, Klaus
Knowlton, Gen. W.A.
Kohler, Foy D.
Kohler, Walter J.
Korbel, Josef
Korry, Edward M.

Kotschnig, Walter M.
Kraft, Joseph

Lacy, Alex S.
Ladejinsky, Wolf
La Farge, Francis W.
Laing, R. Stanley
Laise, Carol C.
Lake, William A.K.
Lamontagne, Rayomnd A.
Lampert, Gen. James B.
Lamson, Roy Jr.
Lang, Robert E.
Langer, Paul F.
Langer, William L.
Langsam, Walter Consuelo
Lanham, Gen. E.G.
Larry, R. Heath
Lasswell, Harold D.
Lawrence, William H.
Laybourne, Lawrence E.
Laylin, John G.
Lazarus, Ralph
Leddy, John M.
Lee, Charles Henry
Lee, Adm. John M.
Leghorn, Richard S.
Leich, John F.
Lemnitzer, Gen. Lyman L.
Lerner, Michael
Le Sueur, Larry
Levine, Irving R.
Levy, Marion J. Jr.
Lewis, John P.
Lincoln, Gen. G.A.
Linder, Harold F.
Lindley, Ernest K.
Lindsay, Franklin A.
Lingle, Walter L. Jr.
Linowitz, Sol M.

Lipson, Leon
Little, David
Little, L.K.
Lockard, Derwood W.
Lockwood, Manice DeF 3rd
Lockwood, William W.
Lodge, George Cabot
Lodge, Henry Cabot
Long, Franklin A.
Longstreet, Victor M.
Loomis, Henry
Loucks, Harold H.
Lovestone, Jay
Lynch, Edward S.
Lyon, E. Wilson

McCabe, Thomas B.
McClintock, Robert M.

McCone, John Alex
McCormack, Gen. James
McCracken, Paul W.
McCutcheon, John D.
McDaniel, Josepg M. Jr.
McDougal, Myres S.
McFarland, Ross A.
McGee, Gale W.
McGhee, George S.
McGiffert, David E.
McHenry, Donald F.
McKay, Vernon
McKinnery, Robert M.
McLaughlin, Donald H.
McLean, Donald H. Jr.
McNamara, Robert S.
McNeill, Robert L.
McQuade, Lawrence C.
MacArthur, Douglas 2nd
MacChesney, A. Brunson
MacDonald, Gordon J.F.
MacDonald, J. Carlisle
MacIver, Murdoch
MacLaury, Bruce K.
MacVeagh, Lincoln

Machold, William F.
Maddox, William P.
Mallinson, Harry
Mallory, George W.
Mallory, Walter H.
Malmgren, Harald B.
Manning, Robert J.
Mansager, Felix N.
Marcy, Carl
Marshall, Burke
Marshall, C. Burton
Martin, Edwin M.
Martin, Malcolm W.
Martin, William McC. Jr.
Marvel, William W.
Mason, Edward S.
May, Ernest R.
Mayer, Ferdinand L.
Mayer, Gerald M.
Meagher, Robert F.
Meck, John F.
Merchant, Livingston T.
Merillat, H.C.L.
Merriwether, Duncan
Metcalf, George B.
Meyer, Albert J.
Meyer, Charles A.
Meyer, Cord Jr.
Mickelson, Sig
Milbank, Robbins
Miller, Col. F.P.
Miller, J. Irwin
Miller, William J.
Mills, Bradford

Mladek, Jan V.
Molina, Edgar R.
Montias, J. Michael
Moore, Ben T.
Moore, Hugh
Morgan, Cecil
Morgan, George A.
Morgenstern, Oskar
Morse, F. Bradford
Morton, Louis
Mudd, Henry T.
Muller, Steven.
Munger, Edwin S.
Munoz Marin, Lewis
Munro, Dana G.
Murphy, Robert D.
Myers, Denys P.

Nason, John W.
Nathan, Robert R.
Nelson, Fred M.
Neustadt, Richard E.
Newman, Richard T.
Nichols, Calvin J.
Nichols, Lauris
Nover, Barnet
Noyes, W. Albert Jr.
Nye, Joseph S.

O'Connor, Roderic L.
Oelman, R.S.
Oliver, Cobey T.
Olson, Lawrence
Olson, William C.
Olvey, Col. Lee D.
Osborne, Lithgow
Osgood, Robert E.
Owen, Henry

Packard, George B.
Paffrath, Leslie
Palmer, Norman D.
Pantzer, Kurt F.
Park, Richard L.
Parker, Barrett
Parker, Daniel
Parkhurst, George L.
Parsons, John C.
Patterson, Gardner
Patterson, Hugh B. Jr.
Paul, Norman S.
Pearce, William R.
Peardon, Thomas P.
Pedersen, Richard F.
Pell, Caliborne
Pelzer, Karl J.

Penfield, James K.
Perera, Guido R.
Peretz, Don
Perkins, Courtland D.
Petersen, Howard C.
Peterson, Peter G.
Petty, John R.
Phleger, Herman
Pierotti, Roland
Piquet, Howard S.
Plank, John N.
Platig, E. Raymond
Platt, Gen. Jonas M.
Pogue, L. Welch
Poletti, Charles
Polk, William R.
Pool, Ithiel DeSola
Posvar, Wesley W.
Power, Philip H.
Power, Thomas F. Jr.
Praeger, Frederick A.
Price, Don K.
Prizer, John B.
Putzell, Edwin J. Jr.
Pye, Lucian W.

Quester, George H.

Radway, Laurence I.
Ranis, Gustav
Rathjens, George W.
Ravenal, Earl C.
Ravenholt, Albert
Ray, George W. Jr.
Read, Hanjamin H.
Redmon, E. Hayes
Reeves, Jay B.
Rehm, John B.
Reischauer, Edwin O.
Reuss, Henry S.
Revelle, Roger
Reynolds, Lloyd G.
Rich, John H. Jr.
Richardson, David B.
Richardson, Dorsey
Richardson, Elliot L.
Richardson, John Jr.
Ridgeway, Gen. Matthew B.
Ries, Hans A.
Ripley, S. Dillon 2nd
Roberts, Henry L.
Roberts, Walter Orr
Roche, John P.
Rogers, William D.
Roosevelt, Kermit
Rosengarten, Adolph G. Jr.
Ross, Roger

Rostow, Eugene V.
Rostow, Walt W.
Roth, William M. Jr.
Rouse, Robert G.
Rowen, Henry S.
Rubin, Seymour J.
Ruina, J.P.
Rush, Kenneth
Rusk, Dean
Ryan, John T. Jr.

Salomon, Irving
Salzman, Herbert
Samuels, Nathaniel
Satterthwaite, Joseph C.
Sawyer, John E.
Scalapino, Robert A.
Schacht, Henry B.
Schaetzel, J. Robert
Schelling, Thomas C.
Schiff, Frank W.
Schmidt, Adolph W.
Schmoker, J. Benjamin
Schorr, Daniel L.
Schuyler, Gen. C.V.R.
Schwab, William B.
Schwebel, Stephen M.
Scoville, Herbert Jr.
Seaborg, Glenn T.
Seabury, Paul
Sedwitz, Walter J.
Shaplen, Robert
Sharp, Walter R.
Shearer, Warren W.
Shepherd, Mark Jr.
Sherbert, Paul C.
Shields, Murray
Shirer, William L.
Shishkin, Boris
Shuster, George N.
Simons, Howard
Simpson, John L.
Sisco, Joseph J
Skolnikoff, Eugene B.
Slocum, John J.
Smith, Gerard C.
Smith, Horace H.
Smith, Robert W.
Smithies, Arthur
Smyth, Henry DeW.
Solomon, Anthony M.
Sonne, Christian R.
Sonnenfeldt, Helmut
Sontag, Raymond James
Soth, Lauren K.
Southard, Frank A. Jr.

Spaatz, Gen. Carl A.
Spaeth, Carl B.
Spain, James W.
Spang, Kenneth M.
Spencer, John H.
Spencer, William V.
Spiegel, Harold R.
Sprague, Robert C.
Sprout, Harold
Staley, Eugene
Stanley, Timothy W.
Stason, E. Blythe
Stassen, Harold E.
Stein, Eric
Steiner, Daniel
Stephens, Calude O.
Sterling, J.E. Wallace
Sterling, Richard W.
Stevenson, John R.
Stevenson, William E.
Stewart, Robert Burgess
Stilwell, Gen. Richard G.
Stone, Donald C.
Stone, Jeremy J.
Stone, Shepard
Straus, Robert Kenneth
Strausz-Hupe, Robert
Strayer, Joseph R.
Sullivan, William H.
Sulzberger, C.L.
Surrey, Walter Sterling
Swearer, Howard R.
Symington, Stuart

Tanham, George K.
Tannenwald, Theodore Jr.
Taylor, George E.
Taylor, Gen. Maxwell D.
Tennyson, Leonard B.
Thayer, Robert H.
Thompson, James C. Jr.
Thompson, Llewellyn E.

Thorp, Willard L.
Timberlake, Clare H.
Tobin, James S.
Trezise, Philip H.
Triffin, Robert
Truman, David B.
Turkevich, John
Tuthill, John W.
Tyler, William R.

Ullman, Richard H.
Ulmer, Alfred C. Jr.
Upgren, Arthur R.

Vaky, Viron P.
Valentine, Alan
Van Dusen, Rev. Henry P.
Van Slyck, DeForest
Vernon, Raymond
Voicker, Paul A.

Wagley, Charles W.
Wahl, Nicholas
Wait, Richard
Walker, George R.
Walker, Joseph, Jr.
Wallach, Henry C.
Walmsley, Walter N.
Waltz, Kenneth N.
Ward, Adm. Chester
Ward, Robert E.
Warnke, Paul C.
Washburn, Abbott M.
Wasson, R. Gordon
Watkins, Ralph J.
Watson, Arthur K.
Weaver, Georhe L.P.
Wehrle, Leroy S.
Weiner, Myron
Weisskopf, Victor F.
Welch, Leo D.
Wells, Herman B.

West, Robert LeRoy
Westmoreland, Gen. W.C.
Westphal, Albert C.F.
Wharton, Clifton E. Jr.
Wheeler, Oliver P.
Whipple, Gen. William
Whitaker, Arthur P.
Whiting, Allen S.
Wiesner, Jerome B.
Wight, Charles A.
Wilbur, Brayton Jr.
Wilcox, Francis O.
Wilcox, Robert B.
Wilcox, Wayne A.
Wilds, Walter W.
Wilhelm, Harry E.
Williams, Haydn
Williams, John H.
Williams, Langbourne M.
Willits, Joseph H.
Wilmerding, Lucius Jr.
Wilson, Carroll L.
Wimpfheimer, Jacques
Winton, David J.
Wofford, Harris L.
Wohlstetter, Albert
Wohlstetter, Roberta
Wolf, Charles Jr.
Wolfe, Thomas W.
Wood, Harleston R.
Woodbridge, Henry S.
Wright, Adm. Jerauld
Wyzanski, Charles E. Jr.

Yntema, Theodore O.
Young, T. Cuyler
Youngman, William S.
Yudkin, Gen. Richard A.

Zimmerman, Edwin M.

CFR is intended as a "Conglomerate of Leadership" wherein are banded — for purposes of control and direction — the policy-makers and opinion-molders from every facet of American life. The CFR includes representatives of the following International Banking houses: Kuhn, Loeb & Co.; Lazard Freres; Dillon Read; Lehman Brothers; Goldman Schs; Morgan Guaranty Bank; Brown Bros. Harriman; Chase Manhattan Bank; First National City Bank; Chemical Bank & Trust, and Manufacturers Hanover Trust Bank.

Among the major multinational corporations that have men in CFR are Standard Oil, IBM, Xerox, Eastman Kodak, Pan American, Firestone, U.S. Steel, General Electric, I.T.T., etc.

Also in the CFR are representatives of ADA, UFW, such labor leaders as David Dubinsky and Jay Lovestone, religious leaders, educators, etc. CFR is totally interlocked with the major foundations and the so-called "Think Tanks" such as Ford, Carnegie, Rockefeller and similarly oriented Foundations; Rand Corporation, Hudson Institute, Fund for the Republic, Brookings Institute, etc.

Control of mass communications media is one of the chief objectives of CFR. Represented in its membership are NBC, CBS, *Time, Life, Fortune, Newsweek, New York Times, Washington Post, Los Angeles Times, New York Post, Denver Post, Louisville Courier Journal, Minneapolis Tribune,* the Knight Newspapers, McGraw-Hill, Simon & Shuster, Harper Bros., Random House, Little Brown & Co., MacMillan Co., Viking Press, Cowles Publishing, *Saturday Review, Business Week,* the Book of the Month Club, etc.

The following list of CFR members, past and present who have been appointed to positions in the Federal Government by President Nixon, is indicative of the strangle-hold CFR has on our Federal Government:

Anderson, Adm. George W. Jr. Chairman, President's Foreign Intelligence Advisory Board.

Baker, Dr. George P. Advisory Council on Executive Organization.

Ball, George. Consultant to State Department.

Beam, Jacob D. Ambassador to Soviet Union

Bell, David E. National Commission on Population Growth and the American Future.

Bennett, Lt. Gen. Donald V. Director, Defense Intelligence Agency.

Bergsten, National Security Council.

Blake, Robert O. Ambassador to Mali.

Borch, Fred J. Commission on International Trade and Investment Policy.

Brown, Dr. Harold. S.A.L.T. senior delegate.

Buffman, William B. Ambassador to Lebanon.

Bunker, Ellsworth. Ambassador to South Vietnam.

Burkhardt, Frederick. Chairman, National Commission on Libraries and Information Service.

Burns, Dr. Arthur. Federal Reserve Board Chairman.
Byroade, Henry A. Ambassador to the Philippines.
Bloomfield, Lincoln P. President's Commission for
Observance of 25th Anniversary of United Nations.
Brown, Courtney C. Commission on International Trade
and Investment Policy.
Bruce, David K.E. Chief U.S. delegate to Paris Talks.

Cleveland, Harlan. Ambassador to NATO
Cooper, Richard N. National Security Council.
Crowe, Philip E. Ambassador to Norway.
Cowles, Gardner. National Center for Voluntary Action.

Dale, William B. International Monetary Fund.
Davis, Nathaniel. Ambassador to Chile.
Dillon, C. Douglas. U.S. Arms Control and Disarma-
ment Agency.

Finger, Seymour M. Alternate to UN General Assembly.
Firestone, Harvey B. Chairman, U.S.O.
Foster, William C. U.S. Arms Control and Disarmament
Agency.

Gates, Thomas B. Commission on an All-Volunteer
Armed Force.
Gilbert, Carl J. Rep. for Trade Negotiations.
Goodpaster, Gen. Andrew I. Supreme Allied Commander
in Europe.
Gordon, Kermit. U.S. Arms Control & Disarmament
Agency.
Greenwald, Joseph Adolph. Organization for Economic
Cooperation and Development.
Gruenther, Gen. Alfred M. Commission on All-Volunteer
Armed Force.
Gardner, John E. National Center for Voluntary Action.
Gardner, Richard. Commission on International Trade
and Investment Policy.
Glenn, T. Keith. International Atomic Energy Agency.
Gray, Gordon. Civilian Defense Advisory Board.

Halperin, Morton. National Security Council.
Herter, Christian A. Jr. International Joint Commission
—U.S. and Canada
Hesburgh, Rev. Theodore M. U.S. Commission on Civil
Rights.
Huntington, Samuel P. Task Force on International
Development.

Irwin, John N. II. Special Emissary to Peru.

Jamieson, J.K. Industrial Pollution Control Council.

Javits, Sen. Jacob K. Rep. to UN General Assembly.
Johnson, Joseph E. Alternate to UN General Assembly.
Johnson, Howard W. National Commission on Pro-
ductivity.

Killiam, James R. Arms Control & Disarmament Agency.
Kintner, William B. Board of Foreign Scholarships.
Kissinger, Henry A. Chief Foreign Policy Adviser.

Knoppers, Antonie T. Commission on International Trade and Investment Policy.

Lincoln, George A. Office of Emergency Preparedness.
Lodge, Henry Cabot. Chief, Paris Peace Talks.
Lodge, George Cabot. Inter-American Social Development Institute.
Loomis, Henry. U.S.I.A.

MacArthur, Douglas II. Ambassador to Iran.
McClintoc, Robert. Ambassador to Venezuela.
McCloy, John J. Arms Control & Disarmament Agency.
McCracken, Paul W. Council of Economic Advisors.
Mason, Edward S. Task Force on International Development.
Meyer, Charles A. Asst. Secretary of State.
Mills, Bradford. Overseas Private Investment Corp.
Murphy, Franklin D. Foreign Intelligence Advisory Bd.
Murphy, Robert D. Consultant on International Affairs.

Norstad, Gen. Laurie. Arms Control & Disarmament Agency.
Neal, Alfred C. Commission on International Trade and Investment Policy.

O'Connor, Roderic L. Agency for International Development.
Osgood, Robert E. National Security Council.

Pace, Frank Jr. Foreign Intelligence Advisory Board.
Pedersen, Richard F. Counsellor to State Department.
Pell, Sen. Claiborne. Rep. to UN General Assembly.
Petty, John R. Assistant Secretary of the Treasury for International Affairs.
Phillips, Christopher H. Rep. to UN Security Council.
Pifer, Alan. Consultant to the President on Educational Finance.

Rabi, Isidor I. President's Science Advisory Committee.
Resor, Stanley E. Secretary of the Army.
Richardson, Elliot L. Secretary, Dept. of H.E.W.
Richardson, John Jr. Asst. Scty of State for Educational and Cultural Affairs.
Roche, James. National Center for Voluntary Action.
Rockefeller, David. Task Force on International Development.
Rockefeller, John D. III. Commission on Population Growth and the American Future.
Rockefeller, Nelson A. Mission to ascertain views of leaders in the Latin-American Countries.
Rockefeller, Rodman. Advisory Council for Minority Enterprise.
Roosa, Robert V. Task Force on International Development.
Rush, Kenneth. Former Ambassador to West Germany.
Rusk, Dean. Arms Control & Disarmament Agency

Samuels, Nathaniel. Under-Secretary of State.
Schmidt, Adolph William, Ambassador to Canada.
Sisco, Joseph J. Assistant Secretary of State.
Seaborg, Dr. Glenn T. Atomic Energy Commission.
Smith, Gerard. Arms Control & Disarmament Agency.
Smyth, Henry DeW. Rep. to 13th Session of Conference
   of the International Atomic Energy Agency.
Sonnenfeldt, Helmut. National Security Council.
Stanton, John. Advisory Commission on Education.
Stevenson, John R. Legal Advisor to State Department.
Strausz-Hupe, Robert. Ambassador to Ceylon.
Stinebower, Leroy. Commission on International Trade
   and Investment Policy.
Taylor, Maxwell D. Foreign Intelligence Advisory Bd.
Thompson, Llewellyn. S.A.L.T. delegate.
Trezise, Philip H. Assistant Secretary of State.

Vance, Cyrus. Arms Control & Disarmament Agency.

Warner, Rawleigh, Jr. Woodrow Wilson International
   Center for Scholars.
Watson, Arthur K. Ambassador to France.
Whitney, John Hay. Public Broadcasting Corporation.
Wilcox, Francis O. Commission for Observance of 25th
   Anniversary of the United Nations.
Williams, Franklin Hayden. Rep. to Trust Territory of
   the Pacific Islands.
Wriston, Walter. National Commission on Productivity.

Yost, Charles W. Former Ambassador to U.N.

EPILOGUE:

In this Fascistic "New World Order" being fashioned by CFR and allied Elitist Groups, there is a place for an Oligarchy which will own and rule, a place for a Bureaucratic Civil Service which will administer and manage, a place for the Proletarian workers and servers, *but there is no place for the once free and independent Middle Class.* It is to be squeezed out of existence through pressure from the top applied by the CFR Establishment, and through pressure from the bottom applied by radicalized mobs of communists, anarchists, Panthers, Yippies, and other pawns, puppets, and dupes who think they are fighting the Establishment, but who actually are financed, trained and led by the Establishment members! (If the Establishment really wanted the revolutionaries stopped, how long do you think they would be tolerated?)

Words once uttered by Winston Churchill — himself one of the aspiring Oligarchy — might well be spoken of our present predicament:

"If you will not fight for right when you can easily win without bloodshed; if you will not fight when your victory will be sure and not too costly; you may come to the moment when you will have to fight with all the odds against you and only a precarious chance of survival. There may be even a worse fate. You may have to fight when there is no hope of victory, because it is better to perish than live as slaves."

We are, literally, being given the choice of liberty, or death. Are we brave enough to choose as did our forebears?

"Integration Syndrome," an article written by Lt. Col. Archibald E. Roberts for dissemination by the Committee to Restore the Constitution, was subsequently entered in the Congressional Record by the Hon. John R. Rarick, M.C., Congressional Record, November 18, 1969, p. 11057.

Drawing on government documents and the United Nations Charter this work demonstrates how the Constitution of the United States has been superceded by the United Nations Charter as the "Supreme Law of the Land."

CHAPTER SIX

Integration Syndrome

The SPEAKER pro tempore. Under a previous order of the House, the gentleman from Louisiana (Mr. Rarick) is recognized for 15 minutes.

Mr. RARICK. Mr. Speaker, there is an ever-increasing resentment from concerned mothers and dads over the forced integration in public schools by unelected Federal judges and other appointed bureaucrats.

Archibald Edward Roberts, lieutenant colonel, U.S. Army (retired), renowned author and constitutionalist, clearly demonstrates that the source of the instigated racial unrest in the schools lies in the United Nations Organization, and the failure of American elected leaders to act in arresting its usurpation of Government powers by foreign agents. Colonel Roberts' latest article is called "The Integration Syndrome."

In the 90th Congress, I introduced H.R. 6954 to amend

* *Exhibit at end of the article.*

section 242 of title 18 of the United States Code. This bill would protect American citizens from deprivation of their constitutional rights by officials claiming authority under UNO orders, rules, laws, statutes, et cetera.

During the arguments on H.R. 2516, to provide penalties for interference with civil rights, I offered the text of my bill as an amendment to the act, only to have it ruled not germane.

While it has been made a Federal crime for a State official to violate the civil rights of an American citizen, our colleagues lacked the foresight to understand that a State official, or a Federal official, or an individual operating under the orders of an international bureaucracy could likewise deprive an American citizen of rights guaranteed under the Constitution. I have reintroduced this bill as H.R. 1318, on January 3, 1969.

Mr. Speaker, the American people are becoming more and more aroused. They are looking for answers and they are not receiving them. They are not going to like what they find when they come face to face with the truth that their country has been *stolen* from them — their Constitution supplanted by the United Nations organization.

Mr. Speaker, I include Colonel Roberts' article, and pertinent portions of the debate on H.R. 2516:

The Integration Syndrome
(By Archibald Edward Roberts)

The immediate cause for the mounting constitutional crisis over forced integration of State schools is the failure of State governments to take proper legislative action to arrest the *usurpation* of governmental powers by *international* agencies.

In the Mississippi case the contentions of lawyers avoided the real issue involved and merely served to compound the confusion under which usurpation flourishes.

Not one of the States effected by the United States Supreme Court order of 29 October, 1969, which directs "immediate desegregation of thirty-three Mississippi school districts," has organized its legal and legislative forces to meet this challenge to its sovereignty. As a consequence the free public school system in the State, and in America, faces *inevitable collapse* and ultimate assumption by a world government authority.

The real issue before State governments is that: a. Federal "laws" are promulgated by the United Nations Organization, and, b. These ultra vires acts are foisted upon State governments, and the citizens they represent, by federal agencies acting in *violation* of the prohibitions of the United States Constitution.

Clearly, the United States Surpeme Court feels that it is no longer bound by the Constitution for it has assigned to itself the task of implementing United Nations directives. This new extra-national role exceeds the authority granted to the Court by the States under constitutional contract. Being illegal it must be put down.

It is by such deceit that forced integration of the State school systems, and of the American society, became the "Law of the Land."

The origin of this subterfuge is U.N. General Assembly Resolution 1904, "The United Nations Declaration on the Elimination of All Forms of Racial Discrimination." This sweeping decree, humanitarian on the surface but basically subversive, was adopted by the one hundred nineteen nation body on 20 November, 1963. Ambassador Arthur J. Goldberg signed on behalf of the United States on 28 September, 1966. By the end of that year forty-eight U.N. Member States had signed the resolution and five had ratified or acceded to it.

Further in this study it will be shown how such U.N. resolutions are inserted into the U.S. legal code. But, first, it is important to illustrate the implications which Resolution 1904 carries for races and cultures in America.

Resolution 1904 is, or course, couched in the most disarming language.

"The Charter of the United Nations," it begins, "is based on the principle of the dignity and equality of all human beings."

This cruel hoax is rooted in Article 55 of the U.N. Charter, which states in part:

". . . the United Nations shall promote . . . universal respect for . . . human rights and fundamental freedoms for all without distinction as to race, sex, language or religion."

An even earlier source is the cry of the French Revolution (1789), "Liberty, Equality, Fraternity," a slogan which claimed the lives of one and a half million French citizens.

Following a lengthy preamble Resolution 1904 then declares that (because) ". . . the building of a world society free from all forms of racial segregation and discrimination . . . is one of the fundamental objectives of the United Nations . . . All (Member) States shall take effective measures to revise governmental and other public policies and to rescind laws and regulations which have the effect of creating and perpetuating racial discrimination wherever it still exists."

Forced busing, racial balance, and other mandatory directives imposed upon State school systems suggest that the real intent of Resolution 1904 is more than advertised. The "building of a world society free from all forms of racial segregation" may have to be achieved at the cost of eliminating races and cultures. The world of the future would then be populated by the United Nations brown man.

"All effective steps," Resolution 1904 continues, "shall be taken immediately in the fields of teaching, education, and information, with a view to eliminating racial discrimination and prejudice and promoting understanding, tolerance, and friendship . . . among racial groups."

Responding to this astonishing order the vast power of mass media in shaping public opinion began to promote the objectives stipulated by the United Nations. Elemental examination of the current massive attack upon the American public would convince most impartial observers, however, that the true objective of this assault is not the elimination of racial discrimination, but the elimination of social and religious inhibitions against racial assimilation. Hard sell integration, and its predictable consequence, assumes increasing characteristics of *genocide,* planned or otherwise.

In Little Rock, Arkansas, for example, where "tolerance and friendship" was promoted at the point of a bayonet, the graduates of this initial experiment in forced integration are starting their own families. Of the *seven* original negro subjects involved, *five* have married white partners. This miscegenation will result in posterity denied cultural identification with either black or white heritage.

The destructive policy of forced integration has created a nightmare for its victims resulting in the most ominous racial tensions in American history. Our sick society is the product of sick brained men. The cynical program of these madmen will lead, unless reversed, to the eclipse of the American civilization.

The sooner Americans study the skills with which these *mattoids* circumvent the Constitution and impose U.N. edicts upon the States the sooner can such nihilists be neutralized.

U.N. disposition of, "The Question of Southern Rhodesia," offers a convenient case history to illustrate the point. As the following political vignette of 1966-1967 unfolds it will be seen that the hostile contempt displayed by U.N. directors in the sample incident is not necessarily reserved for South Africa.

The pivot factor is U.N. General Assembly Resolution 1904. The central figures are Ambassador Arthur J. Goldberg and President Lyndon B. Johnson.

Two weeks after signing Resolution 1904 on behalf of the United States, Ambassador Goldberg, on 12 October, 1966, announced that South Africa, by the "abhorrent system of racial segregation known as apartheid," had forfeited all right to go on ruling the territory. Goldberg

declared that the United States was committed to take the
territory away from Pretoria and to place South Africa under
U.N. protection. He further indicated that the U.S. must
order immediate sanctions against Rhodesia.

The next move was with the U.N. Security Council.

Allowing a sixty-day propaganda campaign to build world
opinion in support of its forthcoming announcement, the
United Nations Security Council, on 16 December, 1966,
adopted Resolution No. 232, "Question of Southern
Rhodesia." In this order the Council declared that Southern
Rhodesia "constitutes a threat to international peace and
security" and directed Member States to impose an economic
boycott against the government of South Africa. The Council
also reminded U.N. States that failure to implement the
Security Council Resolution "shall constitute a violation of
Article 25 of the Charter."

"The Members of the United Nations agree," states
Article 25, "to accept and carry out the decisions of the
Security Council in accordance with the present Charter."

The ban on Rhodesia was, of course, drawn in conformity with another little-publicized Charter article, No. 39,
which provides that "The Security Council shall determine
the existence of any threat to the peace, breach of the peace,
or act of aggression and shall . . . decide what measures shall
be taken in accordance with Articles 41 and 42 to maintain
or restore international peace and security."

The day following its Security Council decision the
General Assembly, on 17 December, 1966, ordered manda-
tory economic sanctions against Rhodesia and directed
Member States to comply with the decisions of the Security
Council.

Bound by these United Nations directives, President
Lyndon B. Johnson, on 5 January, 1967, issued Executive
Order No. 11322, prohibiting trade and other transactions
with Southern Rhodesia.

The Order stated in part:

"By virtue of my authority under . . . section 5 of the

United Nations Participation Act of 1945 . . . and considering the measures which the Security Council of the United Nations, by Security Council Resolution No. 232 of the Charter of the United Nations . . . has decided upon pursuant to article 41 of the Charter of the United Nations, and which it has called upon all members of the United Nations, including the United States, to apply, it is hereby ordered . . ."

Imprisonment and $10,000.00 fine awaited transgressors.

At the risk of becoming overly technical it is now necessary to identify the U.N. authorities which President Johnson quoted in Executive Order 11322 so that the reader may judge the effect which these agreements have on United States foreign and domestic policy, and on U.S. sovereignty.

First, the *United Nations Participation Act of 1945*, enacted by Senate and House vote on 20 December, amended 19 October, 1949, Section 5:

"Notwithstanding the provisions of any other law, whenever the United States is called upon by the Security Council to apply measures which said Council has decided, pursuant to article 41 of said Charter, are to be employed to give effect to its decisions under said Charter, the President may . . . prohibit, in whole or in part economic relations or rail, sea, air, postal, telegraphic, radio, and other means of communication."

Second, Article 41 of the Charter, which defines the sanctions which Member States are to apply upon call of the Security Council:

"The Security Council may decide what measures not involving the use of armed force are to be employed to give effect to its decision, and it may call upon the Members of the United Nations to apply such measures."

The effect of the foregoing alleged U.N. authorities is to transfer powers of government from the United States to international agencies without the knowledge or consent of the State or its people.

Under color of such illegal and void statutes the executive, legislative, and judicial agents of government now seek to impose the provisions of U.N. Resolution 1904 upon the State and its people to build a *"world society* free from all forms of racial segregation."

This presumption of power is *illegal* and in violation of the authority granted to the executive, legislative, and judicial branches of government by constitutional contract. Only the Sovereign States, as principals to the Constitution, have the authority to change, amend, or modify the Constitution of the United States. This restriction is precisely fixed in the Constitution itself.

Adoption of the so-called *United Nations Treaty*, the equally tainted *United Nations Participation Act,* and the abhorrent *United Nations Declaration on the Elimination of All Forms of Racial Discrimination*, are flagrant abuses of the constitutional contract.

However, when the State fails to repudiate the unauthorized acts of its agents, a presumption arises that the State has approved these actions. The vitality that is thus given to the purported acts of the agent arises from the power of the State in question. The power does not come from the agents who had no power to so act.

The duty of the State government is, therefore, manifest!

The State Legislature, finding that the constitutional contract is being violated, must take action to bring about correction.

To arrest usurpation of governmental powers the State Legislature may convene a fact-finding committee to inquire into the following constitutional questions:

a. Did the United States Senate have authority under the Constitution to ratify the so-called United Nations Treaty?

b. Can any officer or agency of the United States, or of the Sovereign State, accept and carry out the decisions of the Security Council of the United Nations without violating his oath of office, "to support this Constitution," and so render him subject to impeachment?

c. Are the rights, freedoms and privileges guaranteed to the citizens of the State by the Constitution preserved intact by operations of federal agents who accept and carry out decisions and directives from the United Nations Organization, or any agency thereof?

If the State Legislature finds the answer to any of these questions to be "No," then the citizens of the State may demand immediate passage of appropriate laws making it a felony to attempt to enforce within the State any provision, from any source, based upon the United Nations Charter, and providing suitable penalties for infractions thereof.

The citizens of the State are morally and legally obligated to demand of their state legislators an investigation of any threat to the freedoms of person and property guaranteed to the people by the Constitution.

The Integration Syndrome, circulated by sociological drovers posing as humanitarians, constitutes such a threat.

Exhibit A

[From Congressional Record, Aug. 16, 1967]

Amendment Offered by Mr. Rarick

Mr. Rarick. Mr. Chairman, I offer an amendment.

The Clerk read as follows:

"Amendment offered by Mr. Rarick: On page 9, line 19, after (b), strike out lines 19, 20, 21, and 22, and insert:

" '(b) Section 342 of title 18, United States Code is amended to read as follows:

" '242. Deprivation of rights under color of law

" 'Whoever, under color of any law, statute, treaty, ordinance, regulation, or custom (including any order, rule, or regulation issued by the President to apply measures which the Security Council or General Assembly has decided, or may decide, pursuant to chapter 41, or any other chapter, of the Charter of the United Nations, are to be employed to give effect to its decisions or resolutions under such charter, or otherwise), willfully subjects any inhabitant of any State, District, Commonwealth, territory, or possession of the United States to the deprivation of any rights, privileges, immunities secured or protected by the Constitution or laws of the United States, or to different punishments, pains, or penalties, shall be fined not more than $10,000 or imprisoned not more than ten years or both, and if death results shall be subject to imprisonment for any term of years or for life.' "

Mr. Celler. Mr. Chairman, I make a point of order against the amendment on the ground that it is not germane in that in the bill before us all we do with reference to section 242 is to amend the penalties.

But in the amendment as offered by the gentleman from Louisiana the entire section and substance of section 242 of title 18 of the United States Code is added to the bill.

This amendment is purely extraneous matter so far as the bill is concerned and it has no relevancy.

Reference is even made in that section to the United Nations, and of course the United Nations has no relevancy to this act and to the issues that we are debating.

Mr. Chairman, for these reasons I ask that the amendment be declared out of order.

The Chairman. Does the gentleman from Louisiana [Mr. Rarick] desire to be heard on the point of order?

Mr. Rarick. Yes, Mr. Chairman.

The Chairman. The Chair will hear the gentleman.

Mr. Rarick. Mr. Chairman, the bill before us today in subsection (b) does provide for amendment by additional penalties under section 242 of title 18, United States Code.

In substance the amendment that I have offered only provides that in addition to the penalties against States and State officials acting under color of law, an American citizen may also have his constitutional rights denied him by treaties and orders, et cetera, emanating from the United Nations and from other sources.

Therefore, Mr. Chairman, I certainly feel that the amendment is germane and I would ask the Chairman to so rule.

The Chairman (Mr. Bolling). The Chair is prepared to rule. The Chair has had an opportunity to examine the

amendment of the gentleman from Louisiana, and he feels
that it goes well beyond the proposition before the House
and adds additional penalties to title 18, section 242, which
are not germane to the bill. He therefore sustains the point of
order.

The following address by Lt. Col. Archibald E. Roberts before the student body of Frank Phillips College, Borger, Texas, November 6, 1967, was entered in the Congressional Record by the Hon. John R. Rarick, Member of Congress from Louisiana, January 16, 1968, page E27.

Drawing on the evidence of interlocking subversion in government departments Colonel Roberts traces the origin of the American Crisis to the world government philosophy of those who created the United Nations Organization and their spokesmen.

Quoting from authorities contained in his book, "Victory Denied," and from material he presented before a joint session of the Alabama Legislature, Roberts demonstrates that the solution to military, economic, and political chaos will be achieved when the people, acting through their State law-makers, reaffirm the supremacy of the Constitution of the United States as the "Law of the Land."

CHAPTER SEVEN

To Support And Defend This Constitution

Mr. RARICK. Mr. Speaker, Lt. Col. Arch E. Roberts, a true patriotic defender of our U.S. Constitution, on November 6, 1967, addressed the student bodies of Frank Phillips College and Borger, Tex., High School on the topic "To Support and Defend This Constitution."

Because this great voice for constitutional government has so succinctly outlined the case for our people, I include his speech from the Borger,Tex., News-Herald in the Record for all to read, as follows:

To Support and Defend
This Constitution

(Editor's Note.—We had the privilege and pleasure of hearing Lt. Col. Arch E. Roberts when in Borger on the morning of November 6, 1967, he addressed the students of Frank Phillips College and later in the evening spoke to a larger audience in the Borger High School Auditorium. Only recently has Major Roberts been promoted to the rank of Lt. Colonel.

(We find Mr. Roberts to be in every respect a gentleman, a true Christian and certainly a staunch patriotic defender of our self-government within the framework of our republic as founded on the Constitution and its several amendments. The subject of his address was in defense of our Constitution. Lt. Col. Roberts can be reached at P.O. Box 986, Fort Collins, Colorado 80521.

(Because the readers of the News-Herald are firm supporters of our Constitution and form a most effective patriotic community, we are printing for their benefit this latest manuscript by Lt. Col. Roberts in which he even more clearly defines his support of the Constitution and its several amendments.

(We hope you will read it and let the author know what you think about his efforts in defense of this keystone to the liberties we enjoy as American citizens.—J.C.P.)

(Speech by Arch Roberts)

"Let us not make it a blank paper (the Constitution) by construction. I say the same as to the opinion of those who consider the grant of the treaty-making power as boundless. If it is, then we have no Constitution."

——Thomas Jefferson.

Frequent requests and demands have been made upon the Senate of the United States to review the Charter of the United Nations and do what may be necessary to protect the interests of the United States and the people. The Senate has not only failed to comply with these demands, but has delegated more power over our people and over our military establishment to the subversive United Nations.

Therefore, in the light of these failures and because events in Washington disclose that Americans have *lost control* of the Federal Government, I propose that ". . . We, the People" act to force our State Governments to do what may be necessary to ". . . Support and Defend the Constitution of the United States," and to protect the interests of the people.

"Executive failure to conform to the Constitution, principally through abuse of the treaty power," states Warren Jefferson Davis, Constitutional lawyer in his book, *Law of the Land*, is the most dangerous form which subversion within the governmental structure has taken. This has been recognized by the American Bar Association, which, because of its composition of leading lawyers throughout the country, has since 1949 constituted the first line of defense against attempts which have successively been made to subvert the Constitution of the United States."

Needless to say, the American Bar Association has failed to deter the tide of internationalism and subversion.

"The thoroughly corrupt plan to subvert the Constitution from within," Mr. Davis then noted, "has been exposed, but it remains for the people to take back the republic from the alien hands and ideologies into which it has fallen and reconstruct it and confine it within the limits of the Constitution."

Mr. T. David Horton, nationally recognized authority on Constitutional law, explicitly defined the character of the attack upon the Constitution in correspondence to me dated April, 1964.

"Federal Agencies created by the Constitutional Compact are attempting to change and destroy that Constitution by exercising powers that were not delegated to them and which they do not have."

Only the states which won their independence as sovereign nations as a result of the Treaty of Peace that closed the Revolutionary War can be the source of power in the federal agencies which they later created by Constitutional compact.

Mr. Horton then pointed out the action required to correct the usurpation of governmental power and the responsibility of the State Legislatures in defending the Constitutional Compact.

"State Legislators," he said, "are aiding and abetting this subversion of the Constitution by failing to clarify the law and enforce the provisions of the Constitution within their respective states.

"The failure of the state to act," Mr. Horton continued, "creates a presumption which law enforcement officers cannot overturn. This presumption is that the inaction of the states is tacit approval of the unauthorized attempt by the agent to exercise power beyond the authority granted.

"The ordinary citizen also lacks the capacity to overturn the presumption. Failure of the state to clarify the law by statute allows the limits of authority placed upon the federal agencies by the Constitution to become dimmed and in this confusion, usurpation flourishes."

This counsel was subsequently formalized and incorporated in our campaign to arouse meaningful Constitutional action in the respective sovereign State Legislatures; the objective of this effort being to generate legislative investigations of the United Nations Treaty agreement and enactment of statutes which will enforce the limits of the U.S. Constitution.

Grass roots, citizen-generated, Constitutional programs

are currently being implemented in a number of States of this Republic. Among those states in which a public demand for investigation of the U.N. Charter has reached important proportions is the State of Alabama.

"I believe that the Alabama syndrome reveals our sister states in the South comprise the target area for a centrally directed revolution which is intended to eventually engulf the entire United States," I said in the Montgomery speech.

"I believe that we must determine the causes for this revolution.

"And, I believe that 'we, the people,' must do whatever is necessary to '. . . insure domestic tranquillity.'

"The State Legislature," I told the Alabama Legislature, "being the reservoir of all true political power (as the states are the reservoir of all true national wealth) may thus defend the Constitution and protect the freedoms guaranteed to the people by this Constitution."

I then explained the significance of the policy talk by the Secretary of State, John Foster Dulles, before the American Bar Association at Louisville, Kentucky on April 12, 1952.

"Treaties," Mr. Dulles said, "can take powers away from the Congress and give them to the President; they can take powers from the state and give them to the Federal Government or to some international body; and they can cut across the rights given the people by Constitutional Bill of Rights."

This monstrous impertinence is, of course, utterly false, as voiced by the Honorable Henry St. George Tucker, former President, American Bar Association.

"The treaty power can never make Constitutional that which without its sanction is unconstitutional," said Attorney Tucker.

The Record of usurped governmental power which Mr. Dulles presumed to sanction is dramatically demonstrated in the record of hundreds of U.N. enforcing "treaties" which were surreptitiously "ratified" by as few as two or three U.S. Senators convening in secret during the months immediately following passage of the United Nations treaty agreement.

It is now clear that Federal agents, acting under what they assert to be a legal use of the limited powers enumerated in the Constitution, have negotiated with foreign governments in an attempt to coerce these United States into a United Nations Treaty agreement. This U.S. Treaty, if valid, would surrender to these foreign governments the power of government and affect a surrender of the rights and liberties assured to the people under the U.S. Constitution.

The conclusion is inescapable.

Since its ratification by the U.S. Senate on July 28, 1945, the United Nations Charter has been alleged to be the ' Supreme Law of the Land," and our elected and appointed agents in judicial, legislative, and executive office have conducted our affairs in consonance with the provisions of the U.N. Charter.

Americans, of course, have been assured that the Constitutional legality of the United Nations Treaty agreement is found in Article VI of our Constitution. Secretary of State Dulles, remember, stated that "Treaty law can override the Constitution."

A treaty, however, cannot authorize what the Constitution forbids.

No federal agent has the power or the authority to modify or to dissolve the Constitutional Compact.

In Reid vs. Covert, 1957, the United States Supreme Court observed.

It would be manifestly contrary to the objectives of those who created the Constitution as well as those who were responsible for the Bill of Rights — let alone alien to our entire Constitutional history and tradition — to construe Article VI as permitting the United States to exercise power under an international agreement without observing constitutional prohibitions. In effect, such construction would permit amendment of that document in a manner not sanctioned by Article V. The prohibitions of the Constitution were designed to apply to all branches of the national government and they cannot be nullified by the Executive or by the Executive and Senate combined."

Well-concealed Planners in our Federal Government, however, have clearly demonstrated that they would amend the Constitution "in a manner not sanctioned by Article V."

It must be said, too, that the Supreme Court cannot declare a statute of Congress "Unconstitutional." The court can exercise only the judicial power conferred upon it by the Constitution. It can no more "unmake" a legislative act than it can make one.

To strike down a legislative act requires legislative power. No court has such power.

The ordinary citizen also lacks the power to overturn breaches of the Constitution.

Only a state acting in its highest sovereign capacity can repudiate unauthorized acts of its agents.

"Therefore, the proper party to now challenge the validity of the United Nations Treaty agreement is a party to the Constitutional Compact, a sovereign state — the State of Alabama," I stated in the Alabama capitol.

The sovereign power of the state, through its legislative apparatus, can legally clarify this question of attempted usurpation of governmental power.

The action which is proposed for each State Legislature is to clarify the confusion that arises from the attempt by the agencies created by the agreement between the states to exercise a power which was not delegated and which, therefore, these agents do not have.

The Constitution was binding on the thirteen original states when approved and ratified by the people of those states, and the states that have since joined in the contract share in its privileges and obligations.

Each has the same obligation to the others to insure that the provisions of the Contract are enforced within its borders. All state office holders are sworn to achieve this result.

Attempts by federal agents to exceed the limited powers of the Constitution are void and, in law, are no acts at all.

However, when the state fails to repudiate the unauthorized act of its agents, a presumption arises that the state has approved. The vitality that is thus given to the purported act of the agent arises from the power of the state in question. The power does not come from the limited agents who had no power to act.

As the Constitutional authority, Mr. Horton explained to me in his correspondence, "The farmer who sends his hired hand to market to sell part of his potato crop is in the same position when the hired hand sells the team and wagon. Other hired hands can deplore his conduct but they are powerless to correct it. Only the farmer, the principal can correct the excess of his agent. He must do this by an affirmative act of repudiation. If he acquiesces in the unauthorized act of his agent, he will be bound by it. It is not his agent's act, but his own, that makes it binding upon him. If he either does nothing or affirmatively ratifies the agent's act, then he is bound by what the agent did. Only an affirmative repudiation of the agent's act can correct the situation."

In the case of the Cherokee Tobacco (11 Wall 616 1870), Mr. Justice Swayne observed.

"It need hardly be said that a treaty cannot change the Constitution or be held valid if it be in violation of that instrument."

"The so-called United Nations 'Charter,' and other matters arising under the purported authority of the United Nations Organization, are neither executing the laws passed by Congress, as the Chief Executive is obligated to do, nor are they judicial. They are attempts to exercise powers which can be made lawful only by the affirmative action of three-fourths of the states (i.e., by amending the Constitution), because those purported acts seek to have general application within the state; they are legislative in nature; and require legislative power to correct," Mr. Horton told me.

The reason that the people of each state have been burdened with the acts of federal agents in their surrender of the powers of government to the United Nations is because that state has not repudiated the attempts of its agents to act beyond their authority. These acts had the effect of "law" not by reason of any nonexistent authority of the Federal agents, but because of the authority that state gave to those acts by failing to challenge the attempts of its Federal agents to exceed their authority.

The power to correct these excesses by Federal agents is found in the Constitution.

"We, the People of the United States," declares the Preamble to the Constitution, "In Order to form a more perfect Union, establish Justice, insure domestic Tranquility, provide for the common Defense, promote the general Welfare, and secure the Blessings of Liberty to ourselves and our Posterity, do ordain and establish this Constitution for the United States of America."

The Preamble thus clearly defines the sovereignty and the authority of the States as parties to the Constitutional Compact.

The United Nations Treaty agreement is not the first instance in which the sovereign States have found it necessary to reaffirm the restrictions placed upon the Federal Government by the Constitutional Compact. The oppressive Sedition Act of July 14, 1798, by which the U.S. Congress attempted to abridge freedom of the press, elicited the Kentucky Resolution of November 19, 1799, repudiating the unauthorized acts of the Congress.

"Resolved that the several States composing the United States of America," said the Kentucky Legislators, "are not united on the principles of unlimited submission to their general government; but that by Compact under the style and title of a Constitution for the United States and of amendments thereto, they constituted a general government for special purposes, delegated to that government certain definite powers, reserving each State to itself the residuary mass of right to their own self-government; and that whensoever the general government assumes undelegated powers, its acts are unauthoritative, void, and of no force; that to this Compact each State acceded as a State and is an integral party, its co-states forming as to itself the other party, that the government created by this Compact was not made the exclusive or final judge of the extent of the powers delegated to itself since that would have made its discretion, and not the Constitution, the measure of its powers; but that as in all other cases of Compact among parties having no common judge, each party has an equal right to judge for itself, as well of infractions as of the mode and measure of redress."

It is a matter of historical record that the agencies in Washington have fallen into the hands of those who would not only alter the Constitution but would completely abrogate it by means of the so-called United Nations Treaty.

This emasculation of our Constitution most certainly was not authorized by the parties to the Constitutional Compact. Lacking this authority, it is against the law. Being unlawful, it must be put down.

In this respect, State office holders have a positive duty to enforce the provisions of the Constitution. It is a continuing obligation and may not be met merely by an empty oath taken upon accepting public office.

"The language of Article VI, paragraph 3, U.S. Constitution, '. . . shall be bound by Oath or Affirmation to support this Constitution . . .', imposes a continuing duty upon these office holders as long as they continue in office.

"In like manner, I stated in the Alabama address, "the State at the time of its admission into the Union assumes all obligations to the people of that State and to the people of the several States which are parties to the same agreement, to insure that all provisions of the Constitution are respected and enforced within the boundaries of the State.

"Therefore, in conformity with these duties and obligations, I propose that the legislators of the State of Alabama now do what is necessary to defend the Constitution and to protect the rights of the people.

"To this end the limits of authority given by the Constitution must be enforced and violations of those limits must be punished. Events in Washington and in the States disclose a systematic attack upon the liberties and freedoms guaranteed to the people under this Constitution.

"I, therefore, suggest that the legislators of the State of Alabama appoint a special committee comprising members of the House and Senate to investigate the legality of the action of Federal agents with regard to the United Nations and to provide means for the enforcement of the Constitution of the United States in relation thereto.

"I suggest that such committee be authorized and directed to investigate the question of whether the United Nations Treaty agreement, purportedly entered into by Federal agencies acting as representatives of these United States and of the State of Alabama, be within the power and authority granted to said agents under the Constitution of the United States.

"I suggest that this committee be further authorized and directed to investigate the question of whether this purported U.N. Treaty agreement effects the State of Alabama or relates to the relinquishment of any of the laws or rights affecting the State of Alabama or its people.

"This committee must determine whether there is any change proposed to be made under this United Nations Treaty agreement which would deprive the State of Alabama or its people of rights and privileges, or would involve any change in any of the provisions of the Constitution of the United States without the consent of the State of Alabama or of the several states.

"And I suggest that this Committee inquire into what measure may be taken by the State of Alabama to enforce the Constitution of the United States and to punish any infractions thereof that may appear to be endorsed by any unlawful attempt to use authority by any agency not sanctioned by the Constitution of the United States.

"Upon determining that the United Nations Treaty agreement is beyond the authority granted to Federal agents by Constitutional Compact, I propose that the legislators of the State of Alabama introduce 'a bill to provide for the enforcement of the Constitution of the United States with regard to the so-called United Nations Organization.'

"I suggest that this statute declare that the agreements relating to the United Nations Organization are beyond the authority granted to agencies purporting to make these treaties and agreements — and are therefore, null, void, and of no effect within the jurisdiction of the State of Alabama and that any attempt to enforce the provisions of any said treaties or agreements within the State of Alabama is unlawful.

"And lastly, I suggest that any person who shall commit an act in violation of the provisions of this statute shall be guilty of a felony and upon conviction thereof shall be fined not more than $100,000, or be confined in the State penitentiary not more than twenty years, or both."

In providing criminal penalties for attempts to enforce acts that have no authority under the U.S. Constitution, the State Legislature is not asked to declare "unconstitutional" a treaty that is made with regard to the United Nations. The State Legislature is requested to first inquire into the question of whether there was authority to enter into such a treaty. Upon finding that there was not, the State Legislature is asked to provide criminal sanctions for attempts to effectuate in the State that which was never in legal existence.

The Legislature of the State, by adopting this proposed statute, will clarify and make definite the law in the State and will discharge the State's obligation to insure that the limits of the U.S. Constitution are respected within its borders.

Those who occupy executive, legislative, and judicial offices at the federal level of government have demonstrated that they are unwilling or unable to defend the freedom, the proper interest, and the security of the people of the United States.

Effective resistance to United Nations tyranny, therefore, now devolves to the absolute source of all governmental power; the American citizen acting through his State legislature.

"We hold from God the gift which includes all others," said the French economist Frederic Bastiat in *The Law*. This nineteenth century writer then stated:

"Life, faculties, production — in other words, individuality, liberty, property — this is man. And in spite of the cunning of artful political leaders, these three gifts from God precede all human legislation, and are superior to it.

"Life, liberty, and property do not exist because men have made laws. On the contrary," said Bastiat, "it was the fact that life, liberty, and property existed beforehand that causes men to make laws in the first place.

"What, then, is the law? It is the collective organization of the individual right to lawful defense.

"Each of us," the writer said, "has a natural right — from God — to defend his person, his liberty, and his property. These are the three basic requirements of life; the preservation of any one of them is completely dependent upon the preservation of the other two. For what are our faculties but the extension of our individuality? And what is property but an extension of our faculties?"

Mr. Bastiat, a Deputy in the Legislative Assembly, then proclaimed in words which ring with particular urgency today:

"If every person has the right to defend — even by force — his person, his liberty, and his property, then it follows that a group of men have the right to organize and support a common force to protect these rights constantly. Thus the principle of collective right — its reason for existing, its lawfulness — is based on individual right."

"Individual right," so eloquently defended by Frederic Bastiat over one hundred years ago, is embodied in the provisions of the United States Constitution.

The United States Constitution created a new and unique political power in the world: The sovereign individual. To "support and defend the Constitution of the United States," and to preserve those rights of person, liberty, and property which are the foundation of the Constitution, all that is necessary is that Americans assert the authority of their citizenship.

Let each American individually and in concord, assert that authority.

INDEX

Annex I

'The United Nations: Threat to Sovereignty?'

A STUDY AND COMMENTARY

BY

(SECOND PRINTING)

THE ALABAMA LEGISLATIVE COMMISSION

TO

PRESERVE THE PEACE

6

Submitted: August 1967, To Alabama Legislature

COMMISSION MEMBERS

Senator John H. Hawkins, Jr., Chairman

Representative Ira D. Pruitt, Vice-Chairman

Senator James S. Clark

Representative W. M. (Monty) Collins

Representative Robert C. (Bob) Gafford

Edwin Strickland, Staff Director

FOREWORD

The Legislature of Alabama, in its 1966 Regular Session, directed that a study be made by the Alabama Legislative Commission to Preserve the Peace into the possible threat posed by the UNITED NATIONS, its charter and its operation, against the sovereignty of the State Of Alabama and of the United States.

Pursuant to this directive, we have utilized all sources and research material available to us in assessment of this threat.

When the United Nations was organized in San Francisco in 1945, following the close of World War II, the American people, tired of conflict, accepted its promise as an instrument of peace. Few people realized at that time that much of the pre-planning for this meeting was done in Moscow, Russia, or that an American traitor, Alger Hiss, was the chief American architect of this proposed super government.

During the years more and more American citizens, including military leaders, members of congress and persons charged with the security of this nation, have become acutely aware of the threat of the United Nations to the sovereignty and security of this country. J. Edgar Hoover, director of the Federal Bureau of Investigation, has warned repeatedly that we are embracing upon our shores a wellspring of espionage. Repeatedly our government has unearthed spy and espionage rings operating out of the United Nations headquarters in New York. Yet, since these delegates from communist countries enjoy full diplomatic immunity, we can do little except to declare personna non grata those who are apprehended, and to allow them to be replaced by equally well trained communist agents.

Taxpayers of the United States have been placed in the frustrating position of bearing approximately one half the expenses of the U.N. and its various interlocking agencies, while communist countries press for more and more control over American freedoms through exercise of the various charter provisions which supersede our own laws and even constitutional provisions.

We began with the deck stacked against us. As a "have" nation, we stood to lose more, materially, than other U.N. members. As a nation with a proud heritage of freedom, we stood to lose these freedoms while the people of slave nations could not lose what they did not possess.

Today we see most of the members of the U.N. arrayed against the free nations of South Africa and Rhodesia. The

1

United Nations, a "peace" organization, has even planned the invasion of The Republic of South Africa, using American military power and troops. This plan was set forth in detail in what has become known as the "Rand Report" paid for by the Carnegie Foundation.

The influx of "emerging nations" into U.N. membership in recent years has weighed the voting power heavily in favor of communist bloc nations. These unstable nations of Africa look with envy and greed at South Africa and Rhodesia, among the few stable, self-sustaining nations left in that part of the world. The sin of these nations, in the eyes of the U.N., is that they will not submit to takeover by unqualified Negro majorities.

Fresh in the minds of alert Americans is the United Nations fiasco in South Korea, where American troops were under the overall supervision of a Soviet national acting in his United Nations capacity. This was the only war ever fought by American forces in which we were not allowed to bring about military victory, but forced to settle on a communist compromise.

As will be developed in this study, The United States has allowed many of its internal policies, including its racial problems, to be dictated by the United Nations Charter.

The threat to the sovereignty of our nation and to the several states of which it is comprised is becoming widely known. And with this knowledge, freedom loving Americans are mounting a determined counter attack upon the source of this threat—The United Nations.

In the interest of brevity in this study, we have refrained from lengthy documentation on many points raised. Source material is available in the office of this Commission Room 332, State Capitol Building.

We claim no expertise on the subject of the United Nations, but we have used the studies from many sources. Special thanks should be extended to Major Arch E. Roberts, both for his personal help and the valuable background of documentation contained in his authoritative book, VICTORY DENIED.

Edwin Strickland
Staff Director
Alabama Legislative Commissino
To Preserve the Peace

2

UNITED NATIONS — ITS ORIGIN

On April 26, 1945, representatives of most of the civilized nations of the world met in San Francisco to create an organization of nations which would become a pattern for world government and—it was hoped by its sincere supporters—insure lasting peace to a world long weary of war. The conference was completed on June 26, 1945, with the adoption of the UN Charter.

Before the San Francisco convention, however, much groundwork had been done by various groups in the United States and elsewhere, designed to make the world organization acceptable to the United States, which had, after World War I, rejected membership in the League of Nations.

For a period of approximately three years before the actual formation of the United Nations, there was conducted in the United States a full-blown, expensive campaign to overcome the natural objections of a free and powerful nation to giving up its national sovereignty.

In 1941, there was organized a group called the INTERNATIONAL FREE WORLD ASSOCIATION, and this group began publishing a magazine called *Free World*. The secretary of this group was Louis Dolivert, who was later identified in testimony before the Senate Internal Securities Subcommittee by Louis Bundez as a member of the Communist Party. (see IPR Hearings, 1951-51, P. 526.) Bundez was a high Communist Party functionary who defected and gave valuable testimony to the U.S. Government concerning communist spy networks in America.

The fact that the United Nations was envisioned by its planners as a world government, superseding the sovereignty of nations, was not hidden. On Aug. 6, 1946, the Chicago Tribune published an article concerning the one-world plans of the UN, and headed it "Radicals, Rich Unite To Push World State; Fight Defenders of U.S. Sovereignty."

The Council on Foreign Relations, in conjunction with the U.S. State Department, played an important role in the "conditioning" of the U.S. Congress and public to accept the UN Charter and its restrictions on national sovereignty. This is set out in State Department Publication 3580 (1950) an P. 108. This SUBCOMMITTEE ON INTERNATIONAL ORGANIZATION was headed by Summer Wells, of the State Department. Proving the direct link between the old League of Nations and the United Nations, was the fact that two members of this subcommittee had also served on the staff of Col. E. M. House

3

at the Paris Peace Conference in 1918, at the time of the founding of the League of Nations. They were Dr. James T. Shotwell and Isaiah Bowman.

Before the San Francisco Conference, preliminary meetings were held in Moscow, Russia, in October, 1943, to lay groundwork for the United Nations. The Moscow Conference was attended by the top diplomats of the United States, Russia, Great Britain and by the Chinese Ambassador to Russia. This meeting was held under the cold, calculating eye of Joseph Stalin, and received his blessing.

Later, at Dumbarton Oaks, final plans for the United Nations organization were hammered out. The chief planner at this conference, and later a top aide at the United Nations Convention, was Alger Hiss, who was later to be exposed as a Soviet spy working inside the U.S. Government.

To fully understand the planning behind the United Nations prior to 1945, we should look more closely at the FREE WORLD ASSOCIATION, which had such close ties to our own State Department. The organization, through its publication, *Free World*, made no effort to hide the fact that they were planning a world organization, with powers to enforce international decrees, and that the sovereignty of nations could no longer be allowed to stand in the way of this lofty goal.

One of those most active in the FREE WORLD ASSOCIATION was Carlo Emmanuel a Prato, who was a member of the International Editorial Board of *Free World*.

For background on Mr. Prato, we quote from the Congressional Record, July 11, 1950, P. A5016:

"Associated in the OWI Division under the control of Alan Cranston was an alleged Italian Communist, Carlo Emanuel a Prato, who had been expelled from Switzerland as a Soviet agent, entered the United States on a Czech passport issued to Milan Janota."

An ad in *Free World*, August, 1945, made the following statement:

"This month marks the *Free World's* fourth anniversary. Its first objective—a character for world organization—is realized. Now we move on toward broader world democracy."

The objectives of the FREE WORLD ORGANIZATION was set out as early as October, 1942, in its publication:

"The creation of the machinery for a world government in which the United Nations will serve as a nucleus is a necessary task of the present in order to prepare in time the foundations for a future world order."

4

Following the formation of the United Nations, and continuing right up until today, numerous ultra liberal and "left" organizations have been organized around the promotion and defense of the United Nations. One of the earliest of these was UNITED WORLD FEDERATISTS, formed on Feb. 22, 1947, by merger of several other organizations interested in world government. These merged groups were AMERICANS UNITED FOR WORLD GOVERNMENT; WORLD FEDERALISTS; MASSACHUSETTS COMMITTEE FOR WORLD FEDERATION; STUDENT FEDERALISTS; WORLD CITIZENS OF GEORGIA, and WORLD REPUBLIC. (N.Y. Times, Feb. 23, 1947, P. 25)

Their statement quoted at that time included the following:

". . . World peace can be created and maintained only under world law, universal and strong enough to prevent armed conflict between nations . . . Therefore, while endorsing the efforts of the United Nations to bring about a world community favorable to peace, we will work primarily to strengthen the United Nations into a world government of limited powers adequate to prevent a war and *having direct jurisdiction over the individual.*" (italics added).

The frankness with which the proponents of one-world government discussed their plans, alarmed many Americans who objected to surrendering our sovereignty, and even the basic right to defend ourselves.

In 1953 the move was made by the UN forces when the WORLD FEDERAL GOVERNMENT CONFERENCE met in Copenhagen, and recommended a revision of the UN Charter to provide for the following:

1. That the United Nations be made into a World Federal Government.

2. That there must be universal membership.

3. No right of secession.

4. Complete and simultaneous disarmament, enforced by UN inspection and UN police powers.

5. International courts, world legislature, world executive Council be established.

6. World citizenship through UN Membership, with world law applicable to individuals.

These proposals, if adopted, would have removed all traces of national sovereignty and, by definition, the sovereignty of member states. Implicit with this proposal was the power of

5

taxation of the individual by a world legislature dominated by have-not nations envious of the great wealth and industry of the United States, where resides only six percent of the world population, but which controls half the world wealth and production capacity.

In 1954 another similar conference was held in London by a group known as WORLD MOVEMENT FOR WORLD FEDERATION. Similar proposals were made. The membership and makeup of these two conferences indicated that they were being given considerable weight in official U.S. circles.

It was these blatant movements to end national sovereignty that caused Senator John Bricker to propose his "Bricker Amendment, which would have written into the U.S. Constitution the safeguards against our making of treaties which would bring about world government through treaty law.

The Bricker Amendment, after a long battle, fell just one vote short of receiving the necessary two-thirds majority in the Senate.

Frank Holman, former president of the American ar Association, wrote of the Bricker Amendment:

"The Amendment is designed to write clearly into the Constitution the simple proposition that treaties and executive agreements shall not make domestic law for the people of this country except by congressional legislation within the constitutional power of the Congress. Then no State Department, now or in the future, would be able, by an international agreement, to authorize or permit the representatives of other nations to have a voice in our domestic affairs and initiate changes in our basic rights as protected by our own Constitution and Bill of Rights."

Holman warned of the dangers inherent in the defeat of the Bricker Amendment in the following terms:

"We must never forget that the issue involved in the Bricker Amendment is the greatest issue which faces America today . . . The Bricker Amendment is a Bill of Rights against uncontrolled "treaty power." The issue is the basic issue of whether we and our children are to have a government of men or a government of adequate constitutional safeguards . . . ."

Of course the Bricker Amendment was fought by all the "one-world" organizations and the internationalists" in and out of government. Among those high in our federal government who led the fight were U.S. Supreme Court Justice William O. Douglas. Sen. Ralph Flanders, (R. Vt.), Sen. Hubert

Humphrey, (D. Minn.), ohn J. McCloy, former assistant Secretary of War and former High Commissioner to Germany; Paul G. Hoffman, of the State Department, Thomas K. Finletter, and many others.

Prior to the introduction of the Bricker Amendment, a joint resolution was introduced in the House of Representatives, and passed, having the following wording:

"Resolved by the House of Representatives (the Senate Concurring) that it is the sense of the Congress that it should be a fundamental objective of the foreign policy of the United States to support and strengthen the United Nations and to seek its development into a world federation, open to all nations, with defined and limited powers adequate to preserve peace and prevent aggression *through the enactment, interpretation and enforcement of world law.*" (italics added) (Cong. Record June 7, 1949, p. 7356-7)

It is significant that this resolution, which was sponsored by many of the House liberals, called for acceptance of the United Nations as a proper body to *make* international law, interpret international law, and *enforce*, international law.

By February, 1950, the stampede was on by congressmen who had endorsed the world government resolution, to revoke such endorsement. They had heard from an irate public back home.

Rep. Bernard W. Kearney (R. N.Y.) called a meeting of the sponsors of HCR 64, and made the following statement:

"We signed the resolution believing we were sponsoring a movement to set up a stronger power within the United Nations for world peace.

Then we learned that various organizations were working on state legislatures and on peace movements for world government action under which the entire U.S. Government would be submerged in a super world government.

Perhaps we should have read the fine print in the first place. We do not intend to continue in the role of sponsors of any movement which undermine U.S. sovereignty. Many other congressmen feel as I do. We will make our position thoroughly clear."

Rep. Kearney had reference to the fact that the world government advocates had gone to the various state legislatures and induced many of them to follow the Congressional resolution, endorsing the UN as a vehicle for world government. A total of 23 states had responded.

Within two years, 18 of the states which had passed the resolution, had rescinded it.

By this time we had gone through the Korean War, in which Russia, a member of the United Nations, had directed a war of aggression against South Korea, and against American and United Nations forces defending South Korea. This was a bizarre and sobering experience for many Americans. They saw the United Nations (largely represented by U.S. forces) engaged in fighting communist aggressors, while the United Nations machinery having direct involvement in the war was under control of a Russian national, and Russia was aiding the communist aggressor forces.

On May 15, 1954, the U.S. Defense Department released an official statement of Russian involvement in Korea. This statement was summarized by U. S. News & World Report (5-28-54) and follows:

"It is the evidence of direct Russian participation in the Korean War . . . It shows, in detail, how Russians planned the Korean attack, built up the forces required, ordered the assault, then directed the communist forces in action . . . you get the evidence, too, of more than 10,000 soldiers and vast stocks of Russian arms used in that "non-Russian" war."

We have examined in some degree how the communist influence exerted by such persons as Hiss, Dolivert an Carlo a Prato, was dominant in the thinking and planning of the United Nations. Other State Department planners with established communist links, such as Phillip Jessup and Dean Achison, were of nearly equal importance. (Phillip Jessup now sits on the UN World Court as the American representative.)

It is important at this point to show that the American people really had no choice in accepting or rejecting our role in the United Nations.

Dr. James T. Shotwell, another left-leaner, admitted in his book, AN AUTOBIOGRAPHY (Bobbs-Merrill Co., 1961), that it was he who in 1939 set up a group called a COMMISSION TO STUDY THE ORGANIZATION OF PEACE. He said there were 100 members of the group who met in small committees to study the question.

"This work was, naturally, well known to the State Department. When it set up a small committee with Summer Wells, the Under-Secretary of State, as chairman to draft a post-war policy, both Clark Eichelberger, of the League of Nations Association, and I were invited to serve on it."

The result of this committee's work, with few revisions, became the Charter of the United Nations, Shotwell said.

8

But to show how closely it was coordinated with communist world leaders, we again quote:

"The work of the planning committee of the State Department was kept secret until finally, at a conference of foreign ministers in *Moscow* in November, 1943, Secretary Hull *secured the consent of Stalin* to establish a general organization . . . for the maintenance of international peace and security."

This agreement with Stalin resulted in the San Francisco meeting in April, 1945, to draft the UN Charter. That, supposedly, was the beginning of the United Nations. But in a State Department publication. No. 3580, released February, 1950, we find the following references to the United Nations, which supposedly was yet to be born. The report was from the first meeting of an ADVISORY COMMITTEE ON POST-WAR FOREIGN POLICY, held February 12, 1942, in the office of Sumner Wells.

"Thought was given to the possibility of informing the public immediately of the establishment and work of the committee. It was felt that the circumstances at the moment, when the United States was being driven back in the Pacific and the *United Nations* cause was suffering on every front, rendered secrecy imperative until a favorable turn in the war . . ."

The work of the subcommittee referred to, the report revealed, established that an international organization should be set up during the war to be ready when needed to create a world political organization.

The political subcommittee which worked out these details was discussed in the report:

"Its discussions throughout were founded upon belief in unqualified victory by the *United Nations*. (Italics ours) It predicted, as an absolute prerequisite for world peace, the continuing strength of the United Nations through unbroken cooperation after the war."

The United Nations was created with a Security Council consisting of 11 members, which has veto power. The five permanent members are the United States, Russia, France, United Kingdom and China. The membership in the other six places is rotated.

A General Assembly of the UN constitutes the other main organ of the organization itself. It is comprised of all the members of the United Nations in good standing, and has no enforcement powers.

The UN, however, quickly set up many specialized agencies to work under U. N. banners in all member countries and in almost every field of human endeavor. Some of the major subsidiary organizations are:

The World Health Organization; The United Nations Educational, Scientific and Cultural Organization; The World Court cational, Scientific and Cultural Organization; The World Court of Justice; The United Nations International Childrens Emergency Fund; The Economic and Social Council; The Commission on Human Rights; International Labor Organization; Commission on the Status of Women, and many, many others. Subcommittees of these committees are formed in great proliferation. It gives the UN the machinery to interfere or interject its influence into the affairs of any member nation.

One of the most important departments of the United Nations itself is the Department of Political and Security Affairs, a part of the UN Secretariat, and the head of this is appointed by the Secretary-General.

In a letter dated June 24, 1966, the United Nations described the duties of this department thusly:

"This Department provides such services as are required by the Security Council and its subsidiary organs, the Political Committee of the general assembly, the Disarmament Commission, and other bodies set up to deal with matters relating to the maintenance of international peace and security. This includes issuing documentation required, providing secretariat services during meetings, and drafting the annual report. The Department may also prepare memoranda to assist the Secretary-General or in pursuance of resolutions of the United Nations organs.

"The post of the Under-Secretary for political and Security Council Affairs has been held by the following people:

1946-49   Arkady Sobolev (USSR)
1949-53   Constantine Zinchenko (USSR)
1953-54   Ilya Tcherychev (USSR)
1954-57   Dragoslav Protich (Yugoslavia)
1957-60   Anatoly Dobrynin (USSR)
1960-62   George Arkadev (USSR)
1962-63   E. D. Kiselev (USSR)
1963-65   V. P. Suslov (USSR)
1965-67   A. E. Nesterenko (USSR).

Thus, during the Korean War, when the United States was fighting under UN banners in Korea against Russia aggression, the United Nations official in command of military affairs was Constantine Zinchenko, of Russia.

10

This same department, under Suslov, a Russian, and currently under Nesterenko, a Russian, has been and is in control of present UN plans to overthrow the established government of Rhodesia. This department served as "advisor" to plans set forth in the Rand Report, financed by the tax-exempt Carnegie Foundation. The Rand Report, which will be further discussed, is a plan for UN action, using American and Russian forces as a requisite, to militarily invade South Africa to overthrow the constituted government of this member nation.

It should be noted that the under-secretary in charge of the Department of Political and Security Council Affairs has, in all cases except one, been a Russian national. In that single exemption, he was a communist national of Yugoslavia. This is not by accident. Secretary-General Dag Hammerskjold revealed that his hands were tied by an agreement between Russia and the American planners, granting Russia the permanent right to name the person who should hold this important post.

With this agreement in effect, and with the precedent set in an unbroken line, Russia would, in effect, have complete control over any military planning and military operation of forces put under UN Command.

Article 25, of the UN Charter carries the authority to force members to obey decisions of the Security Council. It reads:

"The Members of the United Nations agree to accept and carry out the decisions of the Security Council in accordance with the present Charter."

Article 26 reads:

"In order to promote the establishment and maintenance of international peace and security with the least diversion for armaments of the world's human and economic resources, the Security Council shall be responsibile for formulating, with the assistant of the Military Staff Committee referred to in Article 47, plans to be submitted to the Members of the United Nations for the establishment of a system for the regulation of armaments."

Here, again, we see the strategic position occupied by Russia under its agreement to permanently name the chief of the UN Staff for military operations.

Articles 41 through 51, reproduced below, deal with action that the UN may take against any nation, whether member or not, to enforce its decrees and policies. This may consist of measures short of war, such as withdrawal of diplomatic relations, economic relations, even postal, radio, air service, sea, rail or telegraphic contact by UN Members with such a quaranteened nation. (This has currently been applied, with some modifications, to Rhodesia).

The next step authorized is the use of military demonstrations, blockade, etc., of the target nation.

Articles 43 through 45, requires member nations to furnish military forces to be used against such nation, under UN command.

Article 48, gives the UN the power to select *which* nations may be ordered to furnish armed might, and how much.

Article 41

The Security Council may decide what measures not involving the use of armed force are to be employed to give effect to its decisions, and it may call upon the Members of the United Nations to apply such measures. These may include complete or partial interruption of economic relations and of rail, sea, air, postal, telegraphic, radio, and other means of communication, and the severance of diplomatic relations.

Article 42

Should the Security Council consider that measures provided for in Article 41 would be inadequate or have proved to be inadequate, it may take such action by air, sea, or land forces as may be necessary to maintain or restore international peace and security. Such action may include demonstrations, blockade, and other operations by air, sea, or land forces of Members of the United Nations.

Article 43

1. All Members of the United Nations, in order to contribute to the maintenance of international peace and security, undertake to make available to the Security Council, on its call and in accordance with a special agreement or agreements, armed forces, assistance, and facilities, including rights of passage, necessary for the purpose of maintaining international peace and security.

2. Such agreement or agreements shall govern the numbers and types of forces, their degree of readiness and general location, and the nature of the facilities and assistance to be provided.

3. The agreement or agreements shall be negotiated as soon as possible on the initiative of the Security Council. They shall be concluded between the Security Council and Members or between the Security Council and groups of Members and shall be subject to ratification by the signatory states in accordance with their respective constitutional process.

Article 44

When the Security Council has decided to use force it shall, before calling upon a Member not represented on it to provide armed forces in fulfillment of the obligations assumed under Article 43, invite that Member, if the Member so desires, to participate in the decisions of the Security Council concerning the employment of contingents of that Member's armed forces.

Article 45

In order to enable the United Nations to take urgent military measures, Members shall hold immediately available national air-force contingents for combined international enforcement action. The strength and degree of readiness of these contingents and plans for their combined action shall be determined, within the limits laid down in the special agreement or agreements referred to in Article 43, by the Security Council with the assistance of the Military Staff Committee.

Article 46

Plans for the application of armed force shall be made by the Security Council with the assistance of the Military Staff Committee.

Article 47

1. There shall be established a Military Staff Committee to advise and assist the Security Council on all questions relating to the Security Council's military requirements for the maintenance of international peace and security, the employment and command of forces planned at its disposal, the regulation of armaments, and possible disarmament.

2. The Military Staff Committee shall consist of the Chiefs of Staff of the permanent members of the Security Council or their representatives. Any Member of the United Nations not permanently represented on the Committee shall be invited by the Committee to be associated with it when the efficient discharge of the Committee's responsibilities requires the participation of that Member in its work.

3. The Military Staff Committee shall be responsible under the Security Council for the strategic direction of any armed forces placed at the disposal of the Security Council. Questions relating to the command of such forces be worked out subsequently.

4. The Military Staff Committee. with the authorization of the Security Council and after consultation with appropriate regional agencies, may establish regional subcommittees.

Article 48

1. The action required to carry out the decisions of the Security Council for the maintenance of international peace and security shall be taken by all the Members of the United Nations or by some of them, as the Security Council may determine.

Article 49

The Members of the United Nations shall join in affording mutual assistance in carrying out the measures decided upon by the Security Council.

Article 50

If preventive or enforcement measures against any state are taken by the Security Council, any other state, whether a Member of the United Nations or not, which finds itself confronted with special economic problems arising from the carrying out of those measures shall have the right to consult the Security Council with regard to a solution of those problems.

Article 51

Nothing in the present Charter shall impair the inherent right of individual or collective self-defense if an armed attack occurs against a Member of the United Nations, until the Security Council has taken the measures necessary to maintain international peace and security. Measures taken by Members in the exercise of this right of self-defense shall be immediately reported to the Security Council and shall not in any way affect the authority and responsibility of the Security Council under the present Charter to take at any time such action as it deems necessary in order to maintain or restore international peace and security.

Articles 52 through 54 deals with regional agreements, such as NATO, SEATO and Organization of American States, and places them under UN authority, and makes them available, at UN command, to be used in enforcing UN policy.

14

Our operation in Vietnam is under our SEATO commitment, therefore, under UN Charter control.

CHAPTER VIII—REGIONAL ARRANGEMENTS

Article 52

1. Nothing in the present Charter precludes the existence of regional arrangements or agencies for dealing with such matters relating to the maintenance of international peace and security as are appropriate for regional action, provided that such arrangements or agencies and their activities are consistent with the purposes and principles of the United Nations.

2. The Members of the United Nations entering into such arrangements or constituting such agencies shall make every effort to achieve pacific settlement of local disputes through such regional arrangements or by such regional agencies before referring them to the Security Council.

3. The Security Council shall encourage the development of pacific settlement of local disputes through such regional arrangements or by such regional agencies either on the initiative o fthe states concerned or by reference from the Security Council.

4. This Article in no way impairs the application of Articles 34 and 35.

Article 53

1. The Security Council shall, where appropriate, utilize such regional arrangements or agencies for enforcement action under its authority. But no enforcement agencies shall be taken under regional arrangements or by regional agencies without the authorization of the Security Council, with the exception of measures against any enemy state, as defined in paragraph 2 of this Article, provided for pursuant to Article 107 or in regional arrangements directed against renewal of aggressive policy on the part of any such state, until such time as the Organization may, on request of the Governments concerned, be charged with the responsibility for preventing further aggression by such a state.

2. The term enemy state as used in paragraph 1 of this Article applies to any state which during the Second World War has been an enemy of any signatory of the present Charter.

Article 54

The Security Council shall at all times be kept fully informed of activities undertaken or in contemplation under regional arrangements or by regional agencies for the maintenance of international peace and security.

Chapter IX and Chapter X of the Charter deal with internal affairs of member nations, and their provisions may be invoked by a majority of the members of the General Assembly present and voting. (There is no veto provision in the General Assembly, which is presently dominated by the have-not, emerging nations and weighted heavily against the United States.)

Under these sections, the UN is given authority to enforce domestic policy dealing with equal employment, human rights, economic development, cultural matters and matters relating to health. It is under these sections that many specialized agencies have been set up, and their policies dealing with many domestic matters have been enacted into law in the United States after first having been pronounced by the agencies of the United Nations.

CHAPTER IX—INTERNATIONAL ECONOMIC AND SOCIAL COOPERATION

Article 55

With a view to the creation of conditions of stability and well-being which are necessary for peaceful and friendly relations among nations based on respect for the principle of equal rights and self-determination of peoples, the United Nations shall promote:

a. higher standards of living, full employment, and conditions of economic and social progress and development;

b. solutions of international economic, social, health, and related problems; and international cultural and educational cooperation; and

c. universal respect for, and observance of, human rights and fundamental freedoms for all without distinction as to race, sex, lnaguage, or religion.

Article 56

All Members pledge themselves to take joint and separate action in cooperation with the Organization for the achievement of the purposes set forth in Article 55.

Article 57

1. The various specialized agencies, established by intergovernmental agreement and having wide international responsibilities, as defined in their basic instruments, in economic, social, cultural, educational, health, and related fields, shall be brought into relationship with the United Nations in accordance with the provisions of Article 63.

16

2. Such agencies thus brought into relationship with the United Nations are hereinafter referred to as specialized agencies.

Article 58

The Organization shall make recommendations for the co-ordination of the policies and activities of the specialized agencies.

Article 59

The Organization shall, where appropriate, initiate negotiations among the states concerned for the creation of any new specialized agencies required for the accomplishment of the purposes set forth in Article 55.

Article 60

Responsibility for the discharge of the functions of the Organization set forth in this Chapter shall be vested in the General Assembly and, under the authority of the General Assembly, in the Economic and Social Council, which shall have for this purpose the powers set forth in Chapter X.

CHAPTER X—THE ECONOMIC AND SOCIAL COUNCIL
COMPOSITION

Article 61

1. The Economic and Social Council shall consist of eighteen Members of the United Nations elected by the General Assembly.

2. Subject to the provisions of paragraph 3, six members of the Economic and Social Council shall be elected each year for a term of three years. A retiring member shall be eligible for immediate re-election.

3. At the first election, eighteen members of the Economic and Social Council shall be chosen. The term of office of six members so chosen shall expire at the end of one year, and of six other members at the end of two years in accordance with arrangements made by the General Assembly.

4. Each member of the Economic and Social Council shall have one representative.

FUNCTIONS AND POWERS
Article 62

1. The Economic and Social Council may make or initiate studies and reports with respect to international economic,

social, cultural, educational, health, and related matters and may make recommendations with respect to any such matters to the General Assembly, to the Members of the United Nations, and to the specialized agencies concerned.

2. It may make recommendations for the purpose of promoting respect for, and observance of, human rights and fundamental freedoms for all.

3. It may prepare draft conventions for submission to the General Assembly, with respect to matters falling within its cmopetence.

4. It may call, in accordance with the rules prescribed by the United Nations, international conferences on matters falling within its competence.

Article 63

1. The Economic and Social Council may enter into agreements with any of the agencies referred to in Article 57, defining the terms on which the agency concerned shall be brought into relationship with the United Nations. Such agreements shall be subject to approval by the General Assembly.

2. It may coordinate the activities of the specialized agencies through consultation with and recommendations to such agencies and through recommendations to the General Assembly and to the Members of the United Nations.

Article 64

1. The Economic and Social Council may take appropriate steps to obtain regular reports from the specialized agencies. It may make arrangements with the Members of the United Nations and with the specialized agencies to obtain reports on the steps taken to give effect to its own recommendations and to recommendations on matters falling within its competence made by the General Assembly.

2. It may communicate its observations on these reports to the General Assembly.

Article 65

The Economic and Social Council may furnish information to the Security Council and shall assist the Security Council upon its request.

Article 66

1. The Economic and Social Council shall perform such functions as fall within its competence in connection with carrying out of the recommendations of the General Assembly.

18

2. It may, with the approval of the General Assembly, perform services at the request of Members of the United Nations and at the request of specialized agencies.

3. It shall perform such other functions as are specified elsewhere in the present Charter or as may be assigned to it by the General Assembly.

In this connection we point out that the fact that the year 1968 has been designated by UN resolution, as the INTERNATIONAL YEAR FOR HUMAN RIGHTS.

Under this noble sounding purpose, the resolution proposes to:

1. Abolish all racial discrimination.

2. Abolish right to work laws (in effect) under resolutions adopted by the International Labor Organization.

3. Deal with the Status of women.

4. Urge all governments to review their own laws and policies and bring them into conformity with the UNIVERSAL DECLARATION OF HUMAN RIGHTS, adopted by the UN.

5. Elimination of apartheid, and all forms of discrimination in education.

6. Use the medium of press, radio, movies and the performing arts in a mass propaganda assault upon any practices not in line with UN pronouncement.

This was set forth in detail by Hon. John R. Rarick, (D. La) on March 20, 1967. (Cong. Record, March 20, 1967, p A1386-89)

In his opening remarks, Rep. Rarick titled his speech "Target Date for Subjugation: 1968."

"Mr. Speaker, many taxpayers, constituents puzzled businessmen and concerned parents are writing inquiries as to why all the emphasis is being placed on 1968 as a must year for forceful compliance with every guideline, edict, and program to regulate our lives, our businesses, our unions, and our children's futures, our manner of worship in this country.

"So that all may know and remember the sources of the pressure and the cause, I am asking that the international blueprint, that is, the UN resolution—'International Year For Human Rights', designating the year 1968 as the International Year—be printed en toto in the Record, with this question: Must the Governments of South Rhodesia and South Africa be overthrown before the end of 1968?"

19

To indicate, further, to what degree the United States has imperiled its own sovereignty and emasculated its own power, we have but to look at the hearings, conducted by the Senate Internal Security Sub-Committee in March, 1954, on the *Activities of United States Citizens Employed by the United Nations.*

These United States citizens referred to in this report virtually thumbed their noses at their own government, even after the communist party affiliations of many of them were disclosed. The U.S. demanded that they be fired by the United Nations. The Secretary General did fire many of them the complaint and evidnece furnished by the United States, but a judicial body of the U.N. overturned every one of the dismissals that was based upon communist affiliations, and held that the U.S. had no power to inquire into the political beliefs of employes of the United Nations even though they were United States citizens.

This action was taken despite the fact that almost half of the financial support of the United Nations if furnished by the United States, and in spite of the further fact that the United Nations headquarters is located on United States soil.

Through he medium of the United Nations, Russia has benefitted to a greater degree than any nation. This is evident by the fact that the United States government, following an unbroken line of appeasement, has continued to give economic aid to the Soviets, and her satellites, even while we are engaged in serious confrontation in Berlin, in Cuba, in Vietnam and in scores of other places in South America, Asia and Africa. We have bolstered the Russian economy by furnishing wheat to Russia, while that country was aiding Cuba with shipping food and machinery; we continue our foreign aid programs to Russian dominated nations in Europe, thereby alleviating pressure which would be exerted on the struggling Russian economy.

The United States challenged Russia and France in the UN Security Council, for failing to pay "peace-keeping" assessments in the Congo. All during the 1964-65 session the U.S. stood firm under article 19, against allowing Russia to vote. Then came ambassador Goldberg and capitulation. After admitting defeat, and wallowing in humility, the United States again gave in to Russia. It is reliably reported out of Washington that the United States is merely waiting for an opportune time to make up the UN deficit by a large "voluntary contribution."

All this degradation of the United States is "official policy" in Washington despite the fact that J. Edgar Hoover, Director of the FBI, and several congressmen, have continued to warn that we harbour in this country a well-spring of subversion in the hundreds of Communists and pro-Communist delegates at the UN.

With unbecoming audacity—and in light of the still unpaid "peace-keeping" bills incurred while trying to overthrow .Tshombia, of the Congo, (one of the few pro-Western African leaders) the UN is now putting out unofficial feelers aimed toward the military subjugation of anti-Communist South Africa. This feeler was in the form of a study prepared under the auspices of The Carnegie Endowment for International Peace. (It might be noted that while this tax exempt foundation is not an official appendage of the United Nations, it is headquartered at the United Nations Plaza, 46 St. New York, N.Y.

The study, edited and largely written by Amelia C. Leiss, is called APARTHEID AND UNITED NATIONS COLLECTIVE MEASURES, published in March, 1965.

In the foreword to this amazing tome, the editor professes a long history of interest in the United Nations on the part of the Carnegie Foundation.

In the concluding chapter, though professing to recommend no course of action, the author discusses in great detail the naval, air and ground forces estimated to be necessary for the military subjugation of The Republic of South Africa, a stable nation and, incidentally, a dues-paying member of the United Nations. Adding another ironic touch the editor credited Major Sam C. Sarkesian, Department of Social Science, U.S. military Academy, with assisting on the chapter dealing with military measures.

This brings up a delicate point of order; Should an officer of the United States military forces engage in plans for a military invasion of a friendly nation on behest of an "unofficial" study group?

The United Nations has not limited its activities to international issues but has insinuated itself even into the internal affairs of sovereign states of the United States. One such incidence was on the occasion of the Selma- to- Montgomery Civil Rights march in the Spring of 1965. An official of the United Nations, Ralph Bunche, participated in the march and the banner of the United Nations was carried at the head of this rag-tag parade which featured many known communists and fellow travelers. Bunche also launched a verbal attack on Alabama and on the governor of Alabama in addressing the mob in front of the Alabama State capitol.

The head of the United Nations was much in evidence in the shaping of the 1964 Civil Rights law. This was purely internal legislative matter, but this did not deter this international group of social architects from intervening.

This thinking is reflected in the Carnegie Endowment study previously referred to. On page 159 of this study the author: observes;

"Nevertheless the question must be asked: what will be the impact on the capacity of the United Nations to grow and to enhance its authority if it demonstrates that it can not only discuss and pass judgement upon a member's social system but also change it by force?"

The mere voicing of this philosophy is sinister in meaning. But when it is coupled with the avowed aim of the United Nations (i.e. to exercise a sovereignty above that of member states) it becomes more sinister. The early pronouncements and actions of Ambassador Goldberg seem to indicate that he will be more favorable to relinquishing U.S. sovereignty in specific instances, than have been any of his predecessors

Chapter XVI, including Articles 102 through 105 of the UN Charter, are called "Miscellaneous Provisions."

In these articles the right of the UN to physically come onto or occupy the land territory of a member state, for fulfillment of its purposes" is further spelled out.

This, taken together with the rights to intrude into domestic affairs, as grante dunder Chapter IX and X, and the proposals for the year 1968, will demonstrate to what extent the sovereignty of any local territory, or subdivision, of a member state, may be abridged by UN authority.

CHAPTER XVI —MISCELLANEOUS PROVISIONS

Chapter 102

1. Every treaty and every international agreement entered into by any Member of the United Nations after the present Charter comes into force shall as soon as possible be registered with the Secretariat and published by it.

2. No party to any such treaty or international agreement which has not been registered in accordance with the provisions of paragraph 1 of this Article may invoke that treaty or agreement before any organ of the United Nations.

Article 103

In the event of a conflict between the obligations of the Members of the United Nations under the present Charter and their obligations under any other international agreement, their obligations under the present Charter shall prevail.

Article 104

The Organization shall enjoy in the territory of each of its Members such legal capacity as may be necessary for the exercise of its functions and the fulfillment of its purposes.

Article 105

1. The Organization shall enjoy in the territory of each of its Members such priviledges and immunities as are necessary for the fulfillment of its purposes.

2. Representatives of the Members of the United Nations and officials of the Organization shall similarly enjoy such priviledges and immunities as are necessary for the independent exercise of their functions in connection with the Organization.

3. The General Assembly may make recommendations with a view to determining the details of the application of paragraphs 1 and 2 of this Article or may propose conventions to the Members of the United Nations for this purpose.

By ratification of the UN Charter and by subsequent ratification by the United States of various declarations and documents of the United Nations, our government is bound under treaty law to its provisions. This includes, incidentally, the declarations on the INTERNATIONAL YEAR OF HUMAN RIGHTS for 1968, which received an affirmative vote by Ambassador Goldberg.

Under this treaty law, the provisions of the United Nations Charter, and the declarations of its various specialized agencies, have application in all states and territories of the United States. State and federal courts have ruled in many cases that the UN treaty law was superior to the laws of states or of the federal government. A number of such rulings have been made in California.

We do not here treat with the authority of this legislature, or of the legislature of any state, to rescind or nullify such treaty law as ultra vires or against public policy.

We herein respectfully submit our findings in accordance with the request of the Alabama Legislature, as heretofore set out.

Annex II

The Campaign to Restore the Constitution

"The reason that the people of each State have been burdened with the acts of Federal agents in their surrender of the powers of government to the United Nations is because that State has not repudiated the attempts of its agents to act beyond their authority. These acts had the effect of 'law,' not by reason of any non-existent authority of the Federal agent, but because of the authority that State gave to these acts by failing to challenge the attempts of its Federal agents to exceed their authority.

"The power to correct these excesses by Federal agents is found in the Constitution."

VICTORY DENIED by Arch E. Roberts, Major, AUS, ret.

The Committee to Restore the Constitution, a national organization headed by a star-studded council of congressmen, religious leaders, generals, and conservative opinion molders, wants the respective State legislatures to enforce the provisions of the U.S. Constitution and restore control of government to the people "where it properly belongs," according to spokesman, Archibald E. Roberts, retired army lieutenant colonel.

A prime target is the United Nations which its directors allege has usurped constitutional authority in violation of the prohibitions of the Constitution.

"Freedom of person and property held in trust for the American people by the Congress have been illegally transferred to the Security Council and other offices of the United Nations under coloration of 'treaty law'," Roberts declared.

The non-partisan, Colorado corporation, claimed by its directors to be operational in twenty-two States, seeks the participation of conscientious citizens in its demand for investigation by State legislatures of the relationships of federal agencies with the United Nations Organization. The States, they believe, must learn if there has been any change in the Constitution resulting from these relationships.

If it is found that the Constitution has been modified in any way by adoption of the United Nations Charter, then the Committee asks that the State determine whether or not there is any provision in the Constitution which authorizes the U.S. Senate to enter into an agreement which transfers powers of government to international agencies. If there is not, they say, then the State is duty bound, by oath of elected officials "to defend and preserve the Constitution," to declare Senate ratification of the U.N. Charter ultra vires and of no effect within the borders of the State.

"The State may then enact statutes which will enforce the articles of the Constitution and provide criminal sanctions for violators," the Committee director stated.

In carrying this message to the people and to the elected officials who represent them, Roberts, author of the award-winning book, "Victory Denied," has addressed joint sessions of the Alabama and Mississippi legislatures, has testified before state committees in Wisconsin, Oregon, Florida, Massachusetts, Kansas, and Minnesota, and has conferred with officeholders across the nation on the issue of U.S. Sovereignty vs. world government and the United Nations.

Rejecting a suggestion that state governments have no jurisdiction in United Nations affairs, or have no right to question congressional actions which bind the States to articles of the U.N. Charter, Roberts quoted the late John Janney, constitutional authority who inspired the founding of the Committee to Restore the Constitution.

"The one law involved," said Mr. Janney in 1965, "is the fundamental law of agency. This law was clarified by a masterpiece analysis by Blackstone in his Blackstone commentary just at the time the Constitution was being drafted. Some of his Oxford students were in the Constitutional Convention. One of them was Mr. Colthsworth Pinkney of South Carolina.

"This refers," Janney noted, "to the simple law that the acts of an agent are not binding upon his employer of master, if not previously authorized. The exception is where the master subsequently ratifies the act and accepts and approves it which he has the right to do in any ordinary contract. There is a question whether a state can subsequently ratify the acts of an agent under the constitutional contract because the state owes a duty to the other states also parties."

Great grandson of an Attorney General under Presidents Washington and Adams, Mr. Janney then observed:

"The law that; (1) the Federal Agents created by the Constitution is strictly limited in what he can lawfully do by the authority granted in the Constitution and (2) that what he does beyond that authority is void, is the point of law that has to be dealt with in handling the usurpation of unauthorized power by Federal Agents.

"There are eighty decisions of the Supreme Court," Janney continued, "which declare that such an act is void and yet (we have trouble finding members of the State legislatures) who could grasp, comprehend, and apply these decisions, to acts of Congress or illegal acts of the Supreme Court where their definite limits of authority have been exceeded.

"Do you think the matters have been developed far enough now to form voters organizations where the leading citizens, who are free from political entanglements and controls, will take an active part in such a plan to prevent the destruction of our nation, if not of our christian civilization," he queried Roberts in the formative days of the Committee to Restore the Constitution.

"I believe you have started such a movement in Colorado," Mr. Janney concluded, "and hope you have been able to assemble the manpower hours to form a deep-rooted and solid movement concentrating on the one point to enforce the Constitution by using the States' powers to curb the usurpation of authority by Federal agents. This our retiring President George Washington warned us was our greatest danger. The neglect of this advice, we are find out, is not just an accident."

In further amplification Mr. T. David Horton, District Attorney and Committee Counsel, subsequently stated:

"The Constitution was . . . built upon the established law of agency. Its ninth and tenth amendments are surplusage, but the statement in these amendments of what already was the law hurt nothing.

"These amendmants," Mr. Horton pointed out, "serve only to make doubly clear that the Court has no power, to either set or change the limits of its own authority or to fix the authority of any other agency of the States' creation. Nowhere in the Constitution is the Supreme Court given the power to 'decide all questions arising under the Constitution.' The Court is expressly limited to judicial power. Such power is further limited to certain cases. Questions arising under the Constitution," he said, "can be decided only by the parties to the agreement who created it.

"This limitation of power to specific grants," Horton noted, "applies alike to each of the three agencies created under the Agreement. The President cannot lawfully act beyond powers granted.

"The Congress has power only to enact statutes that are in conformity with the Constitution. Only such statutes are or can be the 'supreme law of the land.' They are made supreme by the authority granted by the States," said attorney Horton.

"Unauthorized actions of Congress can be enforced as genuine," he declared, "only because the State has not acted. Only the State as principal under the Constitutional Compact has authority to repudiate the unauthorized act. Such ultra vires acts do not pass as genuine in a State because they are valid, but because of the implied approval that results from inaction by the State. When the only authority having power to do so fails to repudiate the unauthorized act of the agent, this leaves the counterfeit 'act' of the agent to pass as genuine.

"In summary," said Committee counsel, "the situation we face today can be explained by analogy:

"A farmer sends his hired hand to market on a horse to sell the sheep. The hired hand sells the horse. If the farmer fails to repudiate this act, who else has authority to do so? Remonstrances from another agent, or from another farmer are ineffectual.

"It is the law that only the principal can repudiate the unauthorized act of its agent," said the Nevada attorney.

The Committee to Restore the Constitution declares that it is pursuing the "established law of agency" by prevailing upon State legislatures to expose and neutralize interlocking subversion in government departments.

"In a shocking display of contempt for constitutional prohibitions," Colonel Roberts reported, "the United States Senate, in Senate Document No. 87, 'Review of the United Nations Charter,' dated January 7, 1954, declared:

'The (U.N.) Charter has become the supreme Law of the Land; and the Judges in every State shall be bound thereby, any Thing in the Constitution or Laws of any State to the Contrary notwithstanding'."

The Committee further charges that the three Federal agencies of government created by the Constitutional Compact have repeatedly demonstrated that they conduct the affairs of this nation in conformity with the articles of the United Nations Charter and not by virtue of their authority under the United States Constitution. They are prepared to testify before State Committees to prove their case.

The Committee to Restore the Constitution says that, by employing logic and persuasion, it hopes to motivate fellow Americans to act within the authority of the Constitution in defense of their lives, their property, and their freedom and thus restore the Constitution as the "supreme law of the land."

To accomplish this task the Committee, and its affiliates in the respective States, are organizing networks of survival-oriented voters and young citizens; promoting the active support of religious, youth, labor, veteran's, and women's groups, and establishing liaison with members of the State legislatures.

The objective, they say, is to submit to State lawmakers resolutions to form special joint committees to study the constitutionality of the relations of Federal Agencies with the United Nations Organization, and with other international organizations such as the Council on Foreign Relations and the Federal Reserve System.

Annex III

A PHOTOGRAPHIC EXTRACT REPRINT   25¢

83D CONGRESS *2d Session*	SENATE	DOCUMENT No. 87

REVIEW OF THE UNITED NATIONS CHARTER

A COLLECTION OF DOCUMENTS

SUBCOMMITTEE ON THE UNITED NATIONS CHARTER

Pursuant to S. Res. 126

83d Congress, 1st Session

PRESENTED BY MR. WILEY

JANUARY 7, 1954.—Ordered to be printed with illustrations

UNITED STATES
GOVERNMENT PRINTING OFFICE
WASHINGTON : 1954

41403

COMMITTEE ON FOREIGN RELATIONS

ALEXANDER WILEY, Wisconsin, *Chairman*

H. ALEXANDER SMITH, New Jersey	WALTER F. GEORGE, Georgia
BOURKE B. HICKENLOOPER, Iowa	THEODORE FRANCIS GREEN, Rhode Island
WILLIAM LANGER, North Dakota	J. WILLIAM FULBRIGHT, Arkansas
HOMER FERGUSON, Michigan	JOHN J. SPARKMAN, Alabama
WILLIAM F. KNOWLAND, California	GUY M. GILLETTE, Iowa
———— ————	HUBERT H. HUMPHREY, Minnesota
———— ————	MIKE MANSFIELD, Montana

FRANCIS O. WILCOX, *Chief of Staff*
CARL MARCY, *Consultant*
JULIUS N. CAHN, *Counsel*
PAT HOLT, *Consultant*
ALWYN V. FREEMAN, *Consultant*
C. C. O'DAY, *Clerk*
MORELLA HANSEN, *Research Assistant*

SUBCOMMITTEE CREATED PURSUANT TO SENATE RESOLUTION 126 ON THE UNITED NATIONS CHARTER

ALEXANDER WILEY, Wisconsin, *Chairman*

HOMER FERGUSON, Michigan	JOHN J. SPARKMAN, Alabama
WILLIAM F. KNOWLAND, California	GUY M. GILLETTE, Iowa
JOHN S. COOPER,[1] Kentucky	MIKE MANSFIELD, Montana
	SPESSARD L. HOLLAND,[1] Florida

FRANCIS O. WILCOX, *Chief of Staff*
CARL MARCY, *Consultant*
FRANCIS R. VALEO, *Staff Associate*
(*on loan from the Legislative Reference Service, Library of Congress*)

[1] Appointed by the Vice President to serve with the subcommittee.

II

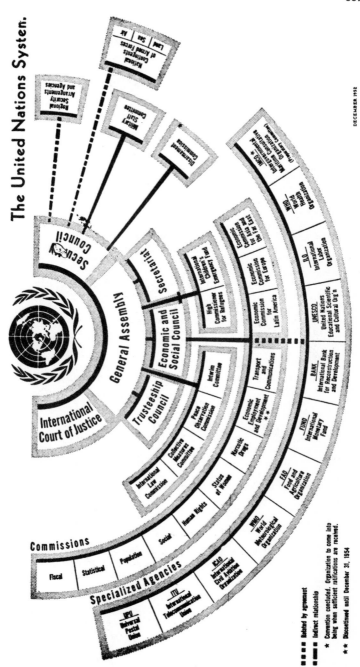

The United Nations System.

DECEMBER 1952

■■■■ Related by agreement
■■ Indirect relationship
* Convention concluded. Organization to come into being when sufficient ratifications are reached.
** Discontinued until December 31, 1954

XIII

REVIEW OF THE UNITED NATIONS CHARTER

1. CHARTER OF THE UNITED NATIONS AND STATUTE OF THE INTERNATIONAL COURT OF JUSTICE, SIGNED JUNE 26, 1945 [1]

CHARTER OF THE UNITED NATIONS

We the peoples of the United Nations determined

to save succeeding generations from the scourge of war, which twice in our lifetime has brought untold sorrow to mankind, and

to reaffirm faith in fundamental human rights, in the dignity and worth of the human person, in the equal rights of men and women and of nations large and small, and

to establish conditions under which justice and respect for the obligations arising from treaties and other sources of international law can be maintained, and

to promote social progress and better standards of life in larger freedom,

and for these ends

to practice tolerance and live together in peace with one another as good neighbors, and

to unite our strength to maintain international peace and security, and

to ensure, by the acceptance of principles and the institution of methods, that armed force shall not be used, save in the common interest, and

to employ international machinery for the promotion of the economic and social advancement of all peoples,

have resolved to combine our efforts to accomplish these aims.

Accordingly, our respective Governments, through representatives assembled in the city of San Francisco, who have exhibited their full powers found to be in good and due form, have agreed to the present Charter of the United Nations and do hereby establish an international organization to be known as the United Nations.

CHAPTER I—PURPOSES AND PRINCIPLES

Article 1

The Purposes of the United Nations are:

1. To maintain international peace and security, and to that end: to take effective collective measures for the prevention and removal of threats to the peace, and for the suppression of acts of aggression or other breaches of the peace, and to bring about by peaceful means, and in conformity with the principles of justice and international law, adjustment or settlement of interna-

---

[1] Department of State Publication 2353.

tional disputes or situations which might lead to a breach of the peace;

2. To develop friendly relations among nations based on respect for the principle of equal rights and self-determination of peoples, and to take other appropriate measures to strengthen universal peace;

3. To achieve international cooperation in solving international problems of an economic, social, cultural, or humanitarian character, and in promoting and encouraging respect for human rights and for fundamental freedoms for all without distinction as to race, sex, language, or religion; and

4. To be a center for harmonizing the actions of nations in the attainment of these common ends.

Article 2

The Organization and its Members, in pursuit of the Purposes stated in Article 1, shall act in accordance with the following Principles.

1. The Organization is based on the principle of the sovereign equality of all its Members.

2. All Members, in order to ensure to all of them the rights and benefits resulting from membership, shall fulfil in good faith the obligations assumed by them in accordance with the present Charter.

3. All Members shall settle their international disputes by peaceful means in such a manner that international peace and security, and justice, are not endangered.

4. All Members shall refrain in their international relations from the threat or use of force against the territorial integrity or political independence of any state, or in any other manner inconsistent with the Purposes of the United Nations.

5. All Members shall give the United Nations every assistance in any action it takes in accordance with the present Charter, and shall refrain from giving assistance to any state against which the United Nations is taking preventive or enforcement action.

6. The Organization shall ensure that states which are not Members of the United Nations act in accordance with these Principles so far as may be necessary for the maintenance of international peace and security.

7. Nothing contained in the present Charter shall authorize the United Nations to intervene in matters which are essentially within the domestic jurisdiction of any state or shall require the Members to submit such matters to settlement under the present Charter; but this principle shall not prejudice the application of enforcement measures under Chapter VII.

CHAPTER II—MEMBERSHIP

Article 3

The original Members of the United Nations shall be the states which, having participated in the United Nations Conference on International Organization at San Francisco, or having previously signed the Declaration by United Nations of January 1, 1942, sign the present Charter and ratify it in accordance with Article 110.

Article 4

1. Membership in the United Nations is open to all other peace-loving states which accept the obligations contained in the present Charter and, in the judgment of the Organization, are able and willing to carry out these obligations.

2. The admission of any such state to membership in the United Nations will be effected by a decision of the General Assembly upon the recommendation of the Security Council.

Article 5

A Member of the United Nations against which preventive or enforcement action has been taken by the Security Council may be suspended from the exercise of the rights and privileges of membership by the General Assembly upon the recommendation of the Security Council. The exercise of these rights and privileges may be restored by the Security Council.

Article 6

A Member of the United Nations which has persistently violated the Principles contained in the present Charter may be expelled from the Organization by the General Assembly upon the recommendation of the Security Council.

CHAPTER III—ORGANS

Article 7

1. There are established as the principal organs of the United Nations: a General Assembly, a Security Council, an Economic and Social Council, a Trusteeship Council, an International Court of Justice, and a Secretariat.

2. Such subsidiary organs as may be found necessary may be established in accordance with the present Charter.

Article 8

The United Nations shall place no restrictions on the eligibility of men and women to participate in any capacity and under conditions of equality in its principal and subsidiary organs.

CHAPTER IV—THE GENERAL ASSEMBLY

COMPOSITION

Article 9

1. The General Assembly shall consist of all the Members of the United Nations.

2. Each Member shall have not more than five representatives in the General Assembly.

FUNCTIONS AND POWERS

Article 10

The General Assembly may discuss any questions or any matters within the scope of the present Charter or relating to the powers and functions of any organs provided for in the present Charter, and except as provided in Article 12, may make recommendations to the Members of the United Nations or to the Security Council or to both on any such questions or matters.

Article 11

1. The General Assembly may consider the general principles of cooperation in the maintenance of international peace and security, including the principles governing disarmament and the regulation of armaments, and may make recommendations with regard to such principles to the Members or to the Security Council or to both.

2. The General Assembly may discuss any questions relating to the maintenance of international peace and security brought before it by any Member of the United Nations, or by the Security Council, or by a state which is not a Member of the United Nations in accordance with Article 35, paragraph 2, and, except as provided in Article 12, may make recommendations with regard to any such questions to the state or states concerned or to the Security Council or to both. Any such question on which action is necessary shall be referred to the Security Council by the General Assembly either before or after discussion.

3. The General Assembly may call the attention of the Security Council to situations which are likely to endanger international peace and security.

4. The powers of the General Assembly set forth in this Article shall not limit the general scope of Article 10.

Article 12

1. While the Security Council is exercising in respect of any dispute or situation the functions assigned to it in the present Charter, the General Assembly shall not make any recommendation with regard to that dispute or situation unless the Security Council so requests.

2. The Secretary-General, with the consent of the Security Council, shall notify the General Assembly at each session of any matters relative to the maintenance of international peace and security which are being dealt with by the Security Council and shall similarly notify the General Assembly, or the Members of the United Nations if the General Assembly is not in session, immediately the Security Council ceases to deal with such matters.

Article 13

1. The General Assembly shall initiate studies and make recommendations for the purpose of:

    a. promoting international cooperation in the political field and encouraging the progressive development of international law and its codification;

    b. promoting international cooperation in the economic, social, cultural, educational, and health fields, and assisting in the realization of human rights and fundamental freedoms for all without distinction as to race, sex, language, or religion.

2. The further responsibilities, functions, and powers of the General Assembly with respect to matters mentioned in paragraph 1 (b) above are set forth in Chapters IX and X.

Article 14

Subject to the provisions of Article 12, the General Assembly may recommend measures for the peaceful adjustment of any situation, regardless of origin, which it deems likely to impair the general welfare or friendly relations among nations, including situations resulting from a violation of the provisions of the present Charter setting forth the Purposes and Principles of the United Nations.

Article 15

1. The General Assembly shall receive and consider annual and special reports from the Security Council ; these reports shall include an account of the measures that the Security Council has decided upon or taken to maintain international peace and security.
2. The General Assembly shall receive and consider reports from the other organs of the United Nations.

Article 16

The General Assembly shall perform such functions with respect to the international trusteeship system as are assigned to it under Chapters XII and XIII, including the approval of the trusteeship agreements for areas not designated as strategic.

Article 17

1. The General Assembly shall consider and approve the budget of the Organization.
2. The expenses of the Organization shall be borne by the Members as apportioned by the General Assembly.
3. The General Assembly shall consider and approve any financial and budgetary arrangements with specialized agencies referred to in Article 57 and shall examine the administrative budgets of such specialized agencies with a view to making recommendations to the agencies concerned.

VOTING

Article 18

1. Each member of the General Assembly shall have one vote.
2. Decisions of the General Assembly on important questions shall be made by a two-thirds majority of the members present and voting. These questions shall include: recommendations with respect to the maintenance of international peace and security, the election of the non-permanent members of the Security Council, the election of the members of the Economic and Social Council, the election of members of the Trusteeship Council in accordance with paragraph 1 (c) of Article 86, the admission of new Members to the United Nations, the suspension of the rights and privileges of membership, the expulsion of Members, questions relating to the operation of the trusteeship system, and budgetary questions.
3. Decisions on other questions, including the determination of additional categories of questions to be decided by a two-thirds majority, shall be made by a majority of the members present and voting.

Article 19

A member of the United Nations which is in arrears in the payment of its financial contributions to the Organization shall have no vote in the General Assembly if the amount of its arrears equals or exceeds the amount of the contributions due from it for the preceding two full years. The General Assembly may, nevertheless, permit such a Member to vote if it is satisfied that the failure to pay is due to conditions beyond the control of the Member.

PROCEDURE

Article 20

The General Assembly shall meet in regular annual sessions and in such special sessions as occasion may require. Special sessions shall be convoked by the Secretary-General at the request of the Security Council or of a majority of the Members of the United Nations.

Article 21

The General Assembly shall adopt its own rules of procedure. It shall elect its President for each session.

Article 22

The General Assembly may establish such subsidiary organs as it deems necessary for the performance of its functions.

CHAPTER V—THE SECURITY COUNCIL

COMPOSITION

Article 23

1. The Security Council shall consist of eleven Members of the United Nations. The Republic of China, France, and the Union of Soviet Socialist Republics, the United Kingdom of Great Britain and Northern Ireland, and the United States of America shall be permanent members of the Security Council. The General Assembly shall elect six other Members of the United Nations to be non-permanent members of the Security Council, due regard being specially paid, in the first instance to the contribution of Members of the United Nations to the maintenance of international peace and security and to the other purposes of the Organization, and also to equitable geographical distribution.

· 2. The non-permanent members of the Security Council shall be elected for a term of two years. In the first election of the non-permanent members, however, three shall be chosen for a term of one year. A retiring member shall not be eligible for immediate re-election.

3. Each member of the Security Council shall have one representative.

FUNCTIONS AND POWERS

Article 24

1. In order to ensure prompt and effective action by the United Nations, its Members confer on the Security Council primary responsibility for the maintenance of international peace and security, and agree that in carrying out its duties under this responsibility the Security Council acts on their behalf.

2. In discharging these duties the Security Council shall act in accordance with the Purposes and Principles of the United Nations. The specific powers granted to the Security Council for the discharge of these duties are laid down in Chapters VI, VII, VIII, and XII.

3. The Security Council shall submit annual and, when necessary, special reports to the General Assembly for its consideration.

Article 25

The Members of the United Nations agree to accept and carry out the decisions of the Security Council in accordance with the present Charter.

Article 26

In order to promote the establishment and maintenance of international peace and security with the least diversion for armaments of the world's human and economic resources, the Security Council shall be responsible for formulating, with the assistance of the Military Staff Committee referred to in Article 47, plans to be submitted to the Members of the United Nations for the establishment of a system for the regulation of armaments.

VOTING

Article 27

1. Each member of the Security Council shall have one vote.

2. Decisions of the Security Council on procedural matters shall be made by an affirmative vote of seven members.

3. Decisions of the Security Council on all other matters shall be made by an affirmative vote of seven members including the concurring votes of the permanent members; provided that, in decisions under Chapter VI, and under paragraph 3 of Article 52, a party to a dispute shall abstain from voting.

PROCEDURE

Article 28

1. The Security Council shall be so organized as to be able to function continuously. Each member of the Security Council shall for this purpose be represented at all times at the seat of the Organization.

2. The Security Council shall hold periodic meetings at which each of its members may, if it so desires, be represented by a member of the government or by some other specially designated representative.

3. The Security Council may hold meetings at such places other than the seat of the Organization as in its judgment will best facilitate its work.

Article 29

The Security Council may establish such subsidiary organs as it deems necessary for the performance of its functions.

Article 30

The Security Council shall adopt its own rules of procedure, including the method of selecting its President.

Article 31

Any Member of the United Nations which is not a member of the Security Council may participate, without vote, in the discussion of any question brought before the Security Council whenever the latter considers that the interests of that Member are specially affected.

Article 32

Any Member of the United Nations which is not a member of the Security Council or any state which is not a Member of the United Nations, if it is a party to a dispute under consideration by the Security Council, shall be invited to participate, without vote, in the discussion relating to the dispute. The Security Council shall lay down such conditions as it deems just for the participation of a state which is not a Member of the United Nations.

CHAPTER VI—PACIFIC SETTLEMENT OF DISPUTES

Article 33

1. The parties to any dispute, the continuance of which is likely to endanger the maintenance of international peace and security, shall, first of all, seek a solution by negotiation, enquiry, mediation, conciliation, arbitration, judicial settlement, resort to regional agencies or arrangements, or other peaceful means of their own choice.
2. The Security Council shall, when it deems necessary, call upon the parties to settle their dispute by such means.

Article 34

The Security Council may investigate any dispute, or any situation which might lead to international friction or give rise to a dispute, in order to determine whether the continuance of the dispute or situation is likely to endanger the maintenance of international peace and security.

Article 35

1. Any Member of the United Nations may bring any dispute, or any situation of the nature referred to in Article 34, to the attention of the Security Council or of the General Assembly.
2. A state which is not a Member of the United Nations may bring to the attention of the Security Council or of the General Assembly

any dispute to which it is a party if it accepts in advance, for the purposes of the dispute, the obligations of pacific settlement provided in the present Charter.

3. The proceedings of the General Assembly in respect of matters brought to its attention under this Article will be subject to the provisions of Articles 11 and 12.

Article 36

1. The Security Council may, at any stage of a dispute of the nature referred to in Article 33 or of a situation of like nature, recommend appropriate procedures or methods of adjustment.

2. The Security Council should take into consideration any procedures for the settlement of the dispute which have already been adopted by the parties.

3. In making recommendations under this Article the Security Council should also take into consideration that legal disputes should as a general rule be referred by the parties to the International Court of Justice in accordance with the provisions of the Statute of the Court.

Article 37

1. Should the parties to a dispute of the nature referred to in Article 33 fail to settle it by the means indicated in that Article, they shall refer it to the Security Council.

2. If the Security Council deems that the continuance of the dispute is in fact likely to endanger the maintenance of international peace and security, it shall decide whether to take action under Article 36 or to recommend such terms of settlement as it may consider appropriate.

Article 38

Without prejudice to the provisions of Articles 33 to 37, the Security Council may, if all the parties to any dispute so request, make recommendations to the parties with a view to a pacific settlement of the dispute.

CHAPTER VII—ACTION WITH RESPECT TO THREATS TO THE PEACE, BREACHES OF THE PEACE, AND ACTS OF AGGRESSION

Article 39

The Security Council shall determine the existence of any threat to the peace, breach of the peace, or act of aggression and shall make recommendations, or decide what measures shall be taken in accordance with Articles 41 and 42, to maintain or restore international peace and security.

Article 40

In order to prevent an aggravation of the situation, the Security Council may, before making the recommendations or deciding upon the measures provided for in Article 39, call upon the parties concerned to comply with such provisional measures as it deems necessary or desirable. Such provisional measures shall be without prejudice to the rights, claims, or position of the parties concerned. The

Security Council shall duly take account of failure to comply with such provisional measures.

Article 41

The Security Council may decide what measures not involving the use of armed force are to be employed to give effect to its decisions, and it may call upon the Members of the United Nations to apply such measures. These may include complete or partial interruption of economic relations and of rail, sea, air, postal, telegraphic, radio, and other means of communication, and the severance of diplomatic relations.

Article 42

Should the Security Council consider that measures provided for in Article 41 would be inadequate or have proved to be inadequate, it may take such action by air, sea, or land forces as may be necessary to maintain or restore international peace and security. Such action may include demonstrations, blockade, and other operations by air, sea, or land forces of Members of the United Nations.

Article 43

1. All Members of the United Nations, in order to contribute to the maintenance of international peace and security, undertake to make available to the Security Council, on its call and in accordance with a special agreement or agreements, armed forces, assistance, and facilities, including rights of passage, necessary for the purpose of maintaining international peace and security.

2. Such agreement or agreements shall govern the numbers and types of forces, their degree of readiness and general location, and the nature of the facilities and assistance to be provided.

3. The agreement or agreements shall be negotiated as soon as possible on the initiative of the Security Council. They shall be concluded between the Security Council and Members or between the Security Council and groups of Members and shall be subject to ratification by the signatory states in accordance with their respective constitutional processes.

Article 44

When the Security Council has decided to use force it shall, before calling upon a Member not represented on it to provide armed forces in fulfillment of the obligations assumed under Article 43, invite that Member, if the Member so desires, to participate in the decisions of the Security Council concerning the employment of contingents of that Member's armed forces.

Article 45

In order to enable the United Nations to take urgent military measures, Members shall hold immediately available national air-force contingents for combined international enforcement action. The strength and degree of readiness of these contingents and plans for their combined action shall be determined, within the limits laid down in the special agreement or agreements referred to in Article 43, by the Security Council with the assistance of the Military Staff Committee.

Article 46

Plans for the application of armed force shall be made by the Security Council with the assistance of the Military Staff Committee.

Article 47

1. There shall be established a Military Staff Committee to advise and assist the Security Council on all questions relating to the Security Council's military requirements for the maintenance of international peace and security, the employment and command of forces placed at its disposal, the regulation of armaments, and possible disarmament.

2. The Military Staff Committee shall consist of the Chiefs of Staff of the permanent members of the Security Council or their representatives. Any Member of the United Nations not permanently represented on the Committee shall be invited by the Committee to be associated with it when the efficient discharge of the Committee's responsibilities requires the participation of that Member in its work.

3. The Military Staff Committee shall be responsible under the Security Council for the strategic direction of any armed forces placed at the disposal of the Security Council. Questions relating to the command of such forces shall be worked out subsequently.

4. The Military Staff Committee, with the authorization of the Security Council and after consultation with appropriate regional agencies, may establish regional subcommittees.

Article 48

1. The action required to carry out the decisions of the Security Council for the maintenance of international peace and security shall be taken by all the Members of the United Nations or by some of them, as the Security Council may determine.

2. Such decisions shall be carried out by the Members of the United Nations directly and through their action in the appropriate international agencies of which they are members.

Article 49

The Members of the United Nations shall join in affording mutual assistance in carrying out the measures decided upon by the Security Council.

Article 50

If preventive or enforcement measures against any state are taken by the Security Council, any other state, whether a Member of the United Nations or not, which finds itself confronted with special economic problems arising from the carrying out of those measures shall have the right to consult the Security Council with regard to a solution of those problems.

Article 51

Nothing in the present Charter shall impair the inherent right of individual or collective self-defense if an armed attack occurs against a Member of the United Nations, until the Security Council has taken the measures necessary to maintain international peace and security. Measures taken by Members in the exercise of this right of self-defense shall be immediately reported to the Security Council and shall not in any way affect the authority and responsibility of the Security Council under the present Charter to take at any time such action as it deems necessary in order to maintain or restore international peace and security.

CHAPTER VIII—REGIONAL ARRANGEMENTS

Article 52

1. Nothing in the present Charter precludes the existence of regional arrangements or agencies for dealing with such matters relating to the maintenance of international peace and security as are appropriate for regional action, provided that such arrangements or agencies and their activities are consistent with the Purposes and Principles of the United Nations.

2. The Members of the United Nations entering into such arrangements or constituting such agencies shall make every effort to achieve pacific settlement of local disputes through such regional arrangements or by such regional agencies before referring them to the Security Council.

3. The Security Council shall encourage the development of pacific settlement of local disputes through such regional arrangements or by such regional agencies either on the initiative of the states concerned or by reference from the Security Council.

4. This Article in no way impairs the application of Articles 34 and 35.

Article 53

1. The Security Council shall, where appropriate, utilize such regional arrangements or agencies for enforcement action under its authority. But no enforcement action shall be taken under regional arrangements or by regional agencies without the authorization of the Security Council, with the exception of measures against any enemy state, as defined in paragraph 2 of this Article, provided for pursuant to Article 107 or in regional arrangements directed against renewal of aggresive policy on the part of any such state, until such time as the Organization may, on request of the Governments concerned, be charged with the responsibility for preventing further aggression by such a state.

2. The term enemy state as used in paragraph 1 of this Article applies to any state which during the Second World War has been an enemy of any signatory of the present Charter.

Article 54

The Security Council shall at all times be kept fully informed of activities undertaken or in contemplation under regional arrangements or by regional agencies for the maintenance of international peace and security.

CHAPTER IX—INTERNATIONAL ECONOMIC AND SOCIAL COOPERATION

Article 55

With a view to the creation of conditions of stability and well-being which are necessary for peaceful and friendly relations among nations based on respect for the principle of equal rights and self-determination of peoples, the United Nations shall promote:

a. higher standards of living, full employment, and conditions of economic and social progress and development;

b. solutions of international economic, social, health, and related problems; and international cultural and educational cooperation; and

c. universal respect for, and observance of, human rights and fundamental freedoms for all without distinction as to race, sex, language, or religion.

Article 56

All Members pledge themselves to take joint and separate action in cooperation with the Organization for the achievement of the purposes set forth in Article 55.

Article 57

1. The various specialized agencies, established by intergovernmental agreement and having wide international responsibilities, as defined in their basic instruments, in economic, social, cultural, educational, health, and related fields, shall be brought into relationship with the United Nations ir accordance with the provisions of Article 63.

2. Such agencies thus brought into relationship with the United Nations are hereinafter referred to as specialized agencies.

Article 58

The Organization shall make recommendations for the coordination of the policies and activities of the specialized agencies.

Article 59

The Organization shall, where appropriate, initiate negotiations among the states concerned for the creation of any new specialized agencies required for the accomplishment of the purposes set forth in Article 55.

Article 60

Responsibility for the discharge of the functions of the Organization set forth in this Chapter shall be vested in the General Assembly and, under the authority of the General Assembly, in the Economic and Social Council, which shall have for this purpose the powers set forth in Chapter X.

CHAPTER X—THE ECONOMIC AND SOCIAL COUNCIL

COMPOSITION

Article 61

1. The Economic and Social Council shall consist of eighteen Members of the United Nations elected by the General Assembly.

2. Subject to the provisions of paragraph 3, six members of the Economic and Social Council shall be elected each year for a term of three years. A retiring member shall be eligible for immediate re-election.

3. At the first election, eighteen members of the Economic and Social Council shall be chosen. The term of office of six members so chosen shall expire at the end of one year, and of six other members at the end of two years in accordance with arrangements made by the General Assembly.

4. Each member of the Economic and Social Council shall have one representative.

FUNCTIONS AND POWERS

Article 62

1. The Economic and Social Council may make or initiate studies and reports with respect to international economic, social, cultural, educational, health, and related matters and may make recommendations with respect to any such matters to the General Assembly, to the Members of the United Nations, and to the specialized agencies concerned.

2. It may make recommendations for the purpose of promoting respect for, and observance of, human rights and fundamental freedoms for all.

3. It may prepare draft conventions for submission to the General Assembly, with respect to matters falling within its competence.

4. It may call, in accordance with the rules prescribed by the United Nations, international conferences on matters falling within its competence.

Article 63

1. The Economic and Social Council may enter into agreements with any of the agencies referred to in Article 57, defining the terms on which the agency concerned shall be brought into relationship with the United Nations. Such agreements shall be subject to approval by the General Assembly.

2. It may coordinate the activities of the specialized agencies through consultation with and recommendations to such agencies and through recommendations to the General Assembly and to the Members of the United Nations.

Article 64

1. The Economic and Social Council may take appropriate steps to obtain regular reports from the specialized agencies. It may make arrangements with the Members of the United Nations and with the specialized agencies to obtain reports on the steps taken to give effect

to its own recommendations and to recommendations on matters falling within its competence made by the General Assembly.

2. It may communicate its observations on these reports to the General Assembly.

Article 65

The Economic and Social Council may furnish information to the Security Council and shall assist the Security Council upon its request.

Article 66

1. The Economic and Social Council shall perform such functions as fall within its competence in connection with the carrying out of the recommendations of the General Assembly.

2. It may, with the approval of the General Assembly, perform services at the request of Members of the United Nations and at the request of specialized agencies.

3. It shall perform such other functions as are specified elsewhere in the present Charter or as may be assigned to it by the General Assembly.

VOTING

Article 67

1. Each member of the Economic and Social Council shall have one vote.

2. Decisions of the Economic and Social Council shall be made by a majority of the members present and voting.

PROCEDURE

Article 68

The Economic and Social Council shall set up commissions in economic and social fields and for the promotion of human rights, and such other commissions as may be required for the performance of its functions.

Article 69

The Economic and Social Council shall invite any Member of the United Nations to participate, without vote, in its deliberations on any matter of particular concern to that Member.

Article 70

The Economic and Social Council may make arrangements for representatives of the specialized agencies to participate, without vote, in its deliberations and in those of the commissions established by it, and for its representatives to participate in the deliberations of the specialized agencies.

Article 71

The Economic and Social Council may make suitable arrangements for consultation with non-governmental organizations which are concerned with matters within its competence. Such arrangements may be made with international organizations and, where appropriate, with national organizations after consultation with the Member of the United Nations concerned.

Article 72

1. The Economic and Social Council shall adopt its own rules of procedure, including the method of selecting its President.
2. The Economic and Social Council shall meet as required in accordance with its rules, which shall include provision for the convening of meetings on the request of a majority of its members.

CHAPTER XI—DECLARATION REGARDING NON-SELF-GOVERNING TERRITORIES

Article 73

Members of the United Nations which have or assume responsibilities for the administration of territories whose peoples have not yet attained a full measure of self-government recognize the principle that the interests of the inhabitants of these territories are paramount, and accept as a sacred trust the obligation to promote to the utmost, within the system of international peace and security established by the present Charter, the well-being of the inhabitants of these territories, and, to this end:

   a. to ensure, with due respect for the culture of the peoples concerned, their political, economic, social, and educational advancement, their just treatment, and their protection against abuses;

   b. to develop self-government, to take due account of the political aspirations of the peoples, and to assist them in the progressive development of their free political institutions, according to the particular circumstances of each territory and its peoples and their varying stages of advancement;

   c. to further international peace and security;

   d. to promote constructive measures of development, to encourage research, and to cooperate with one another and, when and where appropriate, with specialized international bodies with a view to the practical achievement of the social, economic, and scientific purposes set forth in this Article; and

   e. to transmit regularly to the Secretary-General for information purposes, subject to such limitation as security and constitutional considerations may require, statistical and other information of a technical nature relating to economic, social, and educational conditions in the territories for which they are respectively responsible other than those territories to which Chapters XII and XIII apply.

Article 74

Members of the United Nations also agree that their policy in respect of the territories to which this Chapter applies, no less than in respect of their metropolitan areas, must be based on the general principle of good-neighborliness, due account being taken of the interests and well-being of the rest of the world, in social, economic, and commercial matters.

Chapter XII—International Trusteeship System

Article 75

The United Nations shall establish under its authority an international trusteeship system for the administration and supervision of such territories as may be placed thereunder by subsequent individual agreements. These territories are hereinafter referred to as trust territories.

Article 76

The basic objectives of the trusteeship system, in accordance with the Purposes of the United Nations laid down in Article 1 of the present Charter, shall be:

a. to further international peace and security;

b. to promote the political, economic, social, and educational advancement of the inhabitants of the trust territories, and their progressive development towards self-government or independence as may be appropriate to the particular circumstances of each territory and its peoples and the freely expressed wishes of the peoples concerned, and as may be provided by the terms of each trusteeship agreement;

c. to encourage respect for human rights and for fundamental freedoms for all without distinction as to race, sex, language, or religion, and to encourage recognition of the interdependence of the peoples of the world; and

d. to ensure equal treatment in social, economic, and commercial matters for all Members of the United Nations and their nationals, and also equal treatment for the latter in the administration of justice, without prejudice to the attainment of the foregoing objectives and subject to the provisions of Article 80.

Article 77

1. The trusteeship system shall apply to such territories in the following categories as may be placed thereunder by means of trusteeship agreements:

a. territories now held under mandate;

b. territories which may be detached from enemy states as a result of the Second World War; and

c. territories voluntarily placed under the system by states responsible for their administration.

2. It will be a matter for subsequent agreement as to which territories in the foregoing categories will be brought under the trusteeship system and upon what terms.

Article 78

The trusteeship system shall not apply to territories which have become Members of the United Nations, relationship among which shall be based on respect for the principle of sovereign equality.

Article 79

The terms of trusteeship for each territory to be placed under the trusteeship system, including any alteration or amendment, shall be

agreed upon by the states directly concerned, including the mandatory power in the case of territories held under mandate by a Member
of the United Nations, and shall be approved as provided for in Articles 83 and 85.

Article 80

1. Except as may be agreed upon in individual trusteeship agreements, made under Articles 77, 79, and 81, placing each territory
under the trusteeship system, and until such agreements have been
concluded, nothing in this Chapter shall be construed in or of itself
to alter in any manner the rights whatsoever of any states or any
peoples or the terms of existing international instruments to which
Members of the United Nations may respectively be parties.

2. Paragraph 1 of this Article shall not be interpreted as giving
grounds for delay or postponement of the negotiation and conclusion
of agreements for placing mandated and other territories under the
trusteeship system as provided for in Article 77.

Article 81

The trusteeship agreement shall in each case include the terms
under which the trust territory will be administered and designate
the authority which will exercise the administration of the trust
territory. Such authority, hereinafter called the administering authority, may be one or more states or the Organization itself.

Article 82

There may be designated, in any trusteeship agreement, a strategic
area or areas which may include part or all of the trust territory to
which the agreement applies, without prejudice to any special agreement or agreements made under Article 43.

Article 83

1. All functions of the United Nations relating to strategic areas,
including the approval of the terms of the trusteeship agreements
and of their alteration or amendment, shall be exercised by the Security Council.

2. The basic objectives set forth in Article 76 shall be applicable
to the people of each strategic area.

3. The Security Council shall, subject to the provisions of the trusteeship agreements and without prejudice to security considerations,
avail itself of the assistance of the Trusteeship Council to perform
those functions of the United Nations under the trusteeship system
relating to political, economic, social, and educational matters in the
strategic areas.

Article 84

It shall be the duty of the administering authority to ensure that
the trust territory shall play its part in the maintenance of international peace and security. To this end the administering authority
may make use of volunteer forces, facilities, and assistance from the
trust territory in carrying out the obligations towards the Security
Council undertaken in this regard by the administering authority, as

well as for local defense and the maintenance of law and order within the trust territory.

Article 85

1. The functions of the United Nations with regard to trusteeship agreements for all areas not designated as strategic, including the approval of the terms of the trusteeship agreements and of their alteration or amendment, shall be exercised by the General Assembly.

2. The Trusteeship Council, operating under the authority of the General Assembly, shall assist the General Assembly in carrying out these functions.

CHAPTER XIII—THE TRUSTEESHIP COUNCIL

COMPOSITION

Article 86

1. The Trusteeship Council shall consist of the following Members of the United Nations:

a. those Members administering trust territories;

b. such of those Members mentioned by name in Article 23 as are not administering trust territories; and

c. as many other Members elected for three-year terms by the General Assembly as may be necessary to ensure that the total number of members of the Trusteeship Council is equally divided between those Members of the United Nations which administer trust territories and those which do not.

2. Each member of the Trusteeship Council shall designate one specially qualified person to represent it therein.

FUNCTIONS AND POWERS

Article 87

The General Assembly and, under its authority, the Trusteeship Council, in carrying out their functions, may:

a. consider reports submitted by the administering authority;

b. accept petitions and examine them in consultation with the administering authority;

c. provide for periodic visits to the respective trust territories at times agreed upon with the administering authority; and

d. take these and other actions in conformity with the terms of the trusteeship agreements.

Article 88

The Trusteeship Council shall formulate a questionnaire on the political, economic, social, and educational advancement of the inhabitants of each trust territory, and the administering authority for each trust territory within the competence of the General Assembly shall make an annual report to the General Assembly upon the basis of such questionnaire.

41403—54——3

Article 89

1. Each member of the Trusteeship Council shall have one vote.
2. Decisions of the Trusteeship Council shall be made by a majority of the members present and voting.

PROCEDURE

Article 90

1. The Trusteeship Council shall adopt its own rules of procedure, including the method of selecting its President.
2. The Trusteeship Council shall meet as required in accordance with its rules, which shall include provision for the convening of meetings on the request of a majority of its members.

Article 91

The Trusteeship Council shall, when appropriate, avail itself of the assistance of the Economic and Social Council and of the specialized agencies in regard to matters with which they are respectively concerned.

CHAPTER XIV—THE INTERNATIONAL COURT OF JUSTICE

Article 92

The International Court of Justice shall be the principal judicial organ of the United Nations. It shall function in accordance with the annexed Statute, which is based upon the Statute of the Permanent Court of International Justice and forms an integral part of the present Charter.

Article 93

1. All Members of the United Nations are *ipso facto* parties to the Statute of the International Court of Justice.
2. A state which is not a Member of the United Nations may become a party to the Statute of the International Court of Justice on conditions to be determined in each case by the General Assembly upon the recommendation of the Security Council.

Article 94

1. Each Member of the United Nations undertakes to comply with the decision of the International Court of Justice in any case to which it is a party.
2. If any party to a case fails to perform the obligations incumbent upon it under a judgment rendered by the Court, the other party may have recourse to the Security Council, which may, if it deems necessary, make recommendations or decide upon measures to be taken to give effect to the judgment.

Article 95

Nothing in the present Charter shall prevent Members of the United Nations from entrusting the solution of their differences to other tribunals by virtue of agreements already in existence or which may be concluded in the future.

Article 96

1. The General Assembly or the Security Council may request the International Court of Justice to give an advisory opinion on any legal question.

2. Other organs of the United Nations and specialized agencies, which may at any time be so authorized by the General Assembly, may also request advisory opinions of the Court on legal questions arising within the scope of their activities.

CHAPTER XV—THE SECRETARIAT

Article 97

The Secretariat shall comprise a Secretary-General and such staff as the Organization may require. The Secretary-General shall be appointed by the General Assembly upon the recommendation of the Security Council. He shall be the chief administrative officer of the Organization.

Article 98

The Secretary-General shall act in that capacity in all meetings of the General Assembly, of the Security Council, of the Economic and Social Council, and of the Trusteeship Council, and shall perform such other functions as are entrusted to him by these organs. The Secretary-General shall make an annual report to the General Assembly on the work of the Organization.

Article 99

The Secretary-General may bring to the attention of the Security Council any matter which in his opinion may threaten the maintenance of international peace and security.

Article 100

1. In the performance of their duties the Secretary-General and the staff shall not seek or receive instructions from any government or from any other authority external to the Organization. They shall refrain from any action which might reflect on their position as international officials responsible only to the Organization.

2. Each Member of the United Nations undertakes to respect the exclusively international character of the responsibilities of the Secretary-General and the staff and not to seek to influence them in the discharge of their responsibilities.

Article 101

1. The staff shall be appointed by the Secretary-General under regulations established by the General Assembly.

2. Appropriate staffs shall be permanently assigned to the Economic and Social Council, the Trusteeship Council, and, as required, to other organs of the United Nations. These staffs shall form a part of the Secretariat.

3. The paramount consideration in the employment of the staff and in the determination of the conditions of service shall be the necessity of securing the highest standards of efficiency, competence, and integrity. Due regard shall be paid to the importance of recruiting the staff on as wide a geographical basis as possible.

CHAPTER XVI—MISCELLANEOUS PROVISIONS

Article 102

1. Every treaty and every international agreement entered into by any Member of the United Nations after the present Charter comes into force shall as soon as possible be registered with the Secretariat and published by it.

2. No party to any such treaty or international agreement which has not been registered in accordance with the provisions of paragraph 1 of this Article may invoke that treaty or agreement before any organ of the United Nations.

Article 103

In the event of a conflict between the obligations of the Members of the United Nations under the present Charter and their obligations under any other international agreement, their obligations under the present Charter shall prevail.

Article 104

The Organization shall enjoy in the territory of each of its Members such legal capacity as may be necessary for the exercise of its functions and the fulfillment of its purposes.

Article 105

1. The Organization shall enjoy in the territory of each of its Members such privileges and immunities as are necessary for the fulfillment of its purposes.

2. Representatives of the Members of the United Nations and officials of the Organization shall similarly enjoy such privileges and immunities as are necessary for the independent exercise of their functions in connection with the Organization.

3. The General Assembly may make recommendations with a view to determining the details of the application of paragraphs 1 and 2 of this Article or may propose conventions to the Members of the United Nations for this purpose.

CHAPTER XVII—TRANSITIONAL SECURITY ARRANGEMENTS

Article 106

Pending the coming into force of such special agreements referred to in Article 43 as in the opinion of the Security Council enable it to begin the exercise of its responsibilities under Article 42, the parties to the Four-Nation Declaration, signed at Moscow, October 30, 1943, and France, shall, in accordance with the provisions of paragraph 5 of that Declaration, consult with one another and as occasion requires with other Members of the United Nations with a view to such joint action on behalf of the Organization as may be necessary for the purpose of maintaining international peace and security.

Article 107

Nothing in the present Charter shall invalidate or preclude action, in relation to any state which during the Second World War has been an enemy of any signatory to the present Charter, taken or authorized as a result of that war by the Governments having responsibility for such action.

CHAPTER XVIII—AMENDMENTS

Article 108

Amendments to the present Charter shall come into force for all Members of the United Nations when they have been adopted by a vote of two thirds of the members of the General Assembly and ratified in accordance with their respective constitutional processes by two thirds of the Members of the United Nations, including all the permanent members of the Security Council.

Article 109

1. A General Conference of the Members of the United Nations for the purpose of reviewing the present Charter may be held at a date and place to be fixed by a two-thirds vote of the members of the General Assembly and by a vote of any seven members of the Security Council. Each Member of the United Nations shall have one vote in the conference.

2. Any alteration of the present Charter recommended by a two-thirds vote of the conference shall take effect when ratified in accordance with their respective constitutional processes by two-thirds of the Members of the United Nations including all the permanent members of the Security Council.

3. If such a conference has not been held before the tenth annual session of the General Assembly following the coming into force of the present Charter, the proposal to call such a conference shall be placed on the agenda of that session of the General Assembly, and the conference shall be held if so decided by a majority vote of the members of the General Assembly and by a vote of any seven members of the Security Council.

CHAPTER XIX—RATIFICATION AND SIGNATURE

Article 110

1. The present Charter shall be ratified by the signatory states in accordance with their respective constitutional processes.

2. The ratifications shall be deposited with the Government of the United States of America, which shall notify all the signatory states of each deposit as well as the Secretary-General of the Organization when he has been appointed.

3. The present Charter shall come into force upon the deposit of ratifications by the Republic of China, France, the Union of Soviet Socialist Republics, the United Kingdom of Great Britain and Northern Ireland, and the United States of America, and by a majority of other signatory states. A protocol of the ratifications deposited shall thereupon be drawn up by the Government of the United States of America which shall communicate copies thereof to all the signatory states.

4. The states signatory to the present Charter which ratify it after it has come into force will become original Members of the United Nations on the date of the deposit of their respective ratifications.

Article 111

The present Charter, of which the Chinese, French, Russian, English, and Spanish texts are equally authentic, shall remain deposited in the archives of the Government of the United States of America. Duly certified copies thereof shall be transmitted by that Government to the Governments of the other signatory states.

IN FAITH WHEREOF the representatives of the Governments of the United Nations have signed the present Charter.

DONE at the city of San Francisco the twenty-sixth day of June, one thousand nine hundred and forty-five.

STATUTE OF THE INTERNATIONAL COURT OF JUSTICE

Article 1

The International Court of Justice established by the Charter of the United Nations as the principal judicial organ of the United Nations shall be constituted and shall function in accordance with the provisions of the present Statute.

CHAPTER I—ORGANIZATION OF THE COURT

Article 2

The Court shall be composed of a body of independent judges, elected regardless of their nationality from among persons of high moral character, who possess the qualifications required in their respective countries for appointment to the highest judicial offices, or are juris-consults of recognized competence in international law.

Article 3

1. The Court shall consist of fifteen members, no two of whom may be nationals of the same state.

2. A person who for the purposes of membership in the Court could be regarded as a national of more than one state shall be deemed to be a national of the one in which he ordinarily exercises civil and political rights.

Article 4

1. The members of the Court shall be elected by the General Assembly and by the Security Council from a list of persons nominated by the national groups in the Permanent Court of Arbitration, in accordance with the following provisions.

2. In the case of Members of the United Nations not represented in the Permanent Court of Arbitration, candidates shall be nominated by national groups appointed for this purpose by their governments under the same conditions as those prescribed for members of the Permanent Court of Arbitration by Article 44 of the Convention of The Hague of 1907 for the pacific settlement of international disputes.

3. The conditions under which a state which is a party to the present Statute but is not a Member of the United Nations may participate in electing the members of the Court shall, in the absence of a special agreement, be laid down by the General Assembly upon recommendation of the Security Council.

Article 5

1. At least three months before the date of the election, the Secretary-General of the United Nations shall address a written request to the members of the Permanent Court of Arbitration belonging to the states which are parties to the present Statute, and to the members of the national groups appointed under Article 4, paragraph 2, inviting them to undertake, within a given time, by national groups, the nomination of persons in a position to accept the duties of a member of the Court.

2. No group may nominate more than four persons, not more than two of whom shall be of their own nationality. In no case may the number of candidates nominated by a group be more than double the number of seats to be filled.

Article 6

Before making these nominations, each national group is recommended to consult its highest court of justice, its legal faculties and schools of law, and its national academies and national sections of international academies devoted to the study of law.

Article 7

1. The Secretary-General shall prepare a list in alphabetical order of all the persons thus nominated. Save as provided in Article 12, paragraph 2, these shall be the only persons eligible.

2. The Secretary-General shall submit this list to the General Assembly and to the Security Council.

Article 8

The General Assembly and the Security Council shall proceed independently of one another to elect the members of the Court.

Article 9

At every election, the electors shall bear in mind not only that the persons to be elected should individually possess the qualifications required, but also that in the body as a whole the representation of the main forms of civilization and of the principal legal systems of the world should be assured.

Article 10

1. Those candidates who obtain an absolute majority of votes in the General Assembly and in the Security Council shall be considered as elected.

2. Any vote of the Security Council, whether for the election of judges or for the appointment of members of the conference envisaged in Article 12, shall be taken without any distinction between permanent and non-permanent members of the Security Council.

3. In the event of more than one national of the same state obtaining an absolute majority of the votes both of the General Assembly and of the Security Council, the eldest of these only shall be considered as elected.

Article 11

If, after the first meeting held for the purpose of the election, one or more seats remain to be filled, a second and, if necessary, a third meeting shall take place.

Article 12

1. If, after the third meeting, one or more seats still remain unfilled, a joint conference consisting of six members, three appointed by the General Assembly and three by the Security Council, may be formed at any time at the request of either the General Assembly or the Security Council, for the purpose of choosing by the vote of an absolute majority one name for each seat still vacant, to submit to the General Assembly and the Security Council for their respective acceptance.

2. If the joint conference is unanimously agreed upon any person who fulfils the required conditions, he may be included in its list, even though he was not included in the list of nominations referred to in Article 7.

3. If the joint conference is satisfied that it will not be successful in procuring an election, those members of the Court who have already been elected shall, within a period to be fixed by the Security Council, proceed to fill the vacant seats by selection from among those candidates who have obtained votes either in the General Assembly or in the Security Council.

4. In the event of an equality of votes among the judges, the eldest judge shall have a casting vote.

Article 13

1. The members of the Court shall be elected for nine years and may be re-elected; provided, however, that of the judges elected at the first election, the terms of five judges shall expire at the end of three years and the terms of five more judges shall expire at the end of six years.

2. The judges whose terms are to expire at the end of the above-mentioned initial periods of three and six years shall be chosen by lot to be drawn by the Secretary-General immediately after the first election has been completed.

3. The members of the Court shall continue to discharge their duties until their places have been filled. Though replaced, they shall finish any cases which they may have begun.

4. In the case of the resignation of a member of the Court, the resignation shall be addressed to the President of the Court for transmission to the Secretary-General. This last notification makes the place vacant.

Article 14

Vacancies shall be filled by the same method as that laid down for the first election, subject to the following provision: the Secretary-General shall, within one month of the occurrence of the vacancy, proceed to issue the inviations provided for in Article 5 and the date of the election shall be fixed by the Security Council.

Article 15

A member of the Court elected to replace a member whose term of office has not expired shall hold office for the remainder of his predecessor's term.

Article 16

1. No member of the Court may exercise any political or administrative function, or engage in any other occupation of a professional nature.

2. Any doubt on this point shall be settled by the decision of the Court.

Article 17

1. No member of the Court may act as agent, counsel, or advocate in any case.

2. No member may participate in the decision of any case in which he has previously taken part as agent, counsel, or advocate for one of the parties, or as a member of a national or international court, or of a commission of enquiry, or in any other capacity.

3. Any doubt on this point shall be settled by the decision of the Court.

Article 18

1. No member of the Court can be dismissed unless, in the unanimous opinion of the other members, he has ceased to fulfil the required conditions.

2. Formal notification thereof shall be made to the Secretary-General by the Registrar.

3. This notification makes the place vacant.

Article 19

The members of the Court, when engaged on the business of the Court, shall enjoy diplomatic privileges and immunities.

Article 20

Every member of the Court shall, before taking up his duties, make a solemn declaration in open court that he will exercise his powers impartially and conscientiously

Article 21

1. The Court shall elect its President and Vice-President for three years; they may be re-elected.

2. The Court shall appoint its Registrar and may provide for the appointment of such other officers as may be necessary.

Article 22

1. The seat of the Court shall be established at The Hague. This, however, shall not prevent the Court from sitting and exercising its functions elsewhere whenever the Court considers it desirable.

2. The President and the Registrar shall reside at the seat of the Court.

Article 23

1. The Court shall remain permanently in session, except during the judicial vacations, the dates and duration of which shall be fixed by the Court.

2. Members of the Court are entitled to periodic leave, the dates and duration of which shall be fixed by the Court, having in mind the distance between The Hague and the home of each judge.

3. Members of the Court shall be bound, unless they are on leave or prevented from attending by illness or other serious reasons duly explained to the President, to hold themselves permanently at the disposal of the Court.

Article 24

1. If, for some special reason, a member of the Court considers that he should not take part in the decision of a particular case, he shall so inform the President.

2. If the President considers that for some special reason one of the members of the Court should not sit in a particular case, he shall give him notice accordingly.

3. If in any such case the member of the Court and the President disagree, the matter shall be settled by the decision of the Court.

Article 25

1. The full Court shall sit except when it is expressly provided otherwise in the present Statute.

2. Subject to the condition that the number of judges available to constitute the Court is not thereby reduced below eleven, the Rules of the Court may provide for allowing one or more judges, according to circumstances and in rotation, to be dispensed from sitting.

3. A quorum of nine judges shall suffice to constitute the Court.

Article 26

1. The Court may from time to time form one or more chambers, composed of three or more judges as the Court may determine, for dealing with particular categories of cases; for example, labor cases and cases relating to transit and communications.

2. The Court may at any time form a chamber for dealing with a particular case. The number of judges to constitute such a chamber shall be determined by the Court with the approval of the parties.

3. Cases shall be heard and determined by the chambers provided for in this Article if the parties so request.

Article 27

A judgment given by any of the chambers provided for in Articles 26 and 29 shall be considered as rendered by the Court.

Article 28

The chambers provided for in Articles 26 and 29 may, with the consent of the parties, sit and exercise their functions elsewhere than at The Hague.

Article 29

With a view to the speedy despatch of business, the Court shall form annually a chamber composed of five judges which, at the request of the parties, may hear and determine cases by summary procedure. In addition, two judges shall be selected for the purpose of replacing judges who find it impossible to sit.

Article 30

1. The Court shall frame rules for carrying out its functions. In particular, it shall lay down rules of procedure.

2. The Rules of the Court may provide for assessors to sit with the Court or with any of its chambers, without the right to vote.

Article 31

1. Judges of the nationality of each of the parties shall retain their right to sit in the case before the Court.

2. If the Court includes upon the Bench a judge of the nationality of one of the parties, any other party may choose a person to sit as judge. Such person shall be chosen preferably from among those persons who have been nominated as candidates as provided in Articles 4 and 5.

3. If the Court includes upon the Bench no judge of the nationality of the parties, each of these parties may proceed to choose a judge as provided in paragraph 2 of this Article.

4. The provisions of this Article shall apply to the case of Articles 26 and 29. In such cases, the President shall request one or, if necessary, two of the members of the Court forming the chamber to give place to the members of the Court of the nationality of the parties concerned, and, failing such, or if they are unable to be present, to the judges specially chosen by the parties.

5. Should there be several parties in the same interest, they shall, for the purpose of the preceding provisions, be reckoned as one party only. Any doubt upon this point shall be settled by the decision of the Court.

6. Judges chosen as laid down in paragraphs 2, 3, and 4 of this Article shall fulfil the conditions required by Articles 2, 17 (paragraph 2), 20, and 24 of the present Statute. They shall take part in the decision on terms of complete equality with their colleagues.

Article 32

1. Each member of the Court shall receive an annual salary.

2. The President shall receive a special annual allowance.

3. The Vice-President shall receive a special allowance for every day on which he acts as President.

4. The judges chosen under Article 31, other than members of the Court, shall receive compensation for each day on which they exercise their functions.

5. These salaries, allowances, and compensation shall be fixed by the General Assembly. They may not be decreased during the term of office.

6. The salary of the Registrar shall be fixed by the General Assembly on the proposal of the Court.

7. Regulations made by the General Assembly shall fix the conditions under which retirement pensions may be given to members of the Court and to the Registrar, and the conditions under which members of the Court and the Registrar shall have their traveling expenses refunded.

8. The above salaries, allowances, and compensation shall be free of all taxation.

Article 33

The expenses of the Court shall be borne by the United Nations in such a manner as shall be decided by the General Assembly.

CHAPTER II—COMPETENCE OF THE COURT

Article 34

1. Only states may be parties in cases before the Court.

2. The Court, subject to and in conformity with its Rules, may request of public international organizations information relevant to cases before it, and shall receive such information presented by such organizations on their own initiative.

3. Whenever the construction of the constituent instrument of a public international organization or of an international convention adopted thereunder is in question in a case before the Court, the Registrar shall so notify the public international organization concerned and shall communicate to it copies of all the written proceedings.

Article 35

1. The Court shall be open to the states parties to the present Statute.

2. The conditions under which the Court shall be open to other states shall, subject to the special provisions contained in treaties in force, be laid down by the Security Council, but in no case shall such conditions place the parties in a position of inequality before the Court.

3. When a state which is not a Member of the United Nations is a party to a case, the Court shall fix the amount which that party is to contribute towards the expenses of the Court. This provision shall not apply if such state is bearing a share of the expenses of the Court.

Article 36

1. The jurisdiction of the Court comprises all cases which the parties refer to it and all matters specially provided for in the Charter of the United Nations or in treaties and conventions in force.

2. The states parties to the present Statute may at any time declare that they recognize as compulsory *ipso facto* and without special agreement, in relation to any other state accepting the same obligation, the jurisdiction of the Court in all legal disputes concerning:

    a. the interpretation of a treaty;

    b. any question of international law;

    c. the existence of any fact which, if established, would constitute a breach of an international obligation;

    d. the nature or extent of the reparation to be made for the breach of an international obligation.

3. The declarations referred to above may be made unconditionally or on condition of reciprocity on the part of several or certain states, or for a certain time.

4. Such declarations shall be deposited with the Secretary-General of the United Nations, who shall transmit copies thereof to the parties to the Statute and to the Registrar of the Court.

5. Declarations made under Article 36 of the Statute of the Permanent Court of International Justice and which are still in force shall be deemed, as between the parties to the present Statute, to be acceptances of the compulsory jurisdiction of the International Court of Justice for the period which they still have to run and in accordance with their terms.

6. In the event of a dispute as to whether the Court has jurisdiction, the matter shall be settled by the decision of the Court.

Article 37

Whenever a treaty or convention in force provides for reference of a matter to a tribunal to have been instituted by the League of Nations, or to the Permanent Court of International Justice, the matter shall, as between the parties to the present Statute, be referred to the International Court of Justice.

Article 38

1. The Court, whose function is to decide in accordance with international law such disputes as are submitted to it, shall apply:

    a. international conventions, whether general or particular, establishing rules expressly recognized by the contesting states;

    b. international custom, as evidence of a general practice accepted as law;

    c. the general principles of law recognized by civilized nations;

    d. subject to the provisions of Article 59, judicial decisions and the teachings of the most highly qualified publicists of the various nations, as subsidiary means for the determination of rules of law.

2. This provision shall not prejudice the power of the Court to decide a case *ex aequo et bono*, if the parties agree thereto.

Chapter III—Procedure

Article 39

1. The official languages of the Court shall be French and English. If the parties agree that the case shall be conducted in French, the judgment shall be delivered in French. If the parties agree that the case shall be conducted in English, the judgment shall be delivered in English.

2. In the absence of an agreement as to which language shall be employed, each party may, in the pleadings, use the language which it prefers; the decision of the Court shall be given in French and English. In this case the Court shall at the same time determine which of the two texts shall be considered as authoritative.

3. The Court shall, at the request of any party, authorize a language other than French or English to be used by that party.

Article 40

1. Cases are brought before the Court, as the case may be, either by the notification of the special agreement or by a written application addressed to the Registrar. In either case the subject of the dispute and the parties shall be indicated.

2. The Registrar shall forthwith communicate the application to all concerned.

3. He shall also notify the Members of the United Nations through the Secretary-General, and also any other states entitled to appear before the Court.

Article 41

1. The Court shall have the power to indicate, if it considers that circumstances so require, any provisional measures which ought to be taken to preserve the respective rights of either party.

2. Pending the final decision, notice of the measures suggested shall forthwith be given to the parties and to the Security Council.

Article 42

1. The parties shall be represented by agents.

2. They may have the assistance of counsel or advocates before the Court.

3. The agents, counsel, and advocates of parties before the Court shall enjoy the privileges and immunities necessary to the independent exercise of their duties.

Article 43

1. The procedure shall consist of two parts: written and oral.

2. The written proceedings shall consist of the communication to the Court and to the parties of memorials, counter-memorials and, if necessary, replies; also all papers and documents in support.

3. These communications shall be made through the Registrar, in the order and within the time fixed by the Court.

4. A certified copy of every document produced by one party shall be communicated to the other party.

5. The oral proceedings shall consist of the hearing by the Court of witnesses, experts, agents, counsel, and advocates.

Article 44

1. For the service of all notices upon persons other than the agents, counsel, and advocates, the Court shall apply direct to the government of the state upon whose territory the notice has to be served.
2. The same provision shall apply whenever steps are to be taken to procure evidence on the spot.

Article 45

The hearing shall be under the control of the President or, if he is unable to preside, of the Vice-President; if neither is able to preside, the senior judge present shall preside.

Article 46

The hearing in Court shall be public, unless the Court shall decide otherwise, or unless the parties demand that the public be not admitted.

Article 47

1. Minutes shall be made at each hearing and signed by the Registrar and the President.
2. These minutes alone shall be authentic.

Article 48

The Court shall make orders for the conduct of the case, shall decide the form and time in which each party must conclude its arguments, and make all arrangements connected with the taking of evidence.

Article 49

The Court may, even before the hearing begins, call upon the agents to produce any document or to supply any explanations. Formal note shall be taken of any refusal.

Article 50

The Court may, at any time, entrust any individual, body, bureau, commission, or other organization that it may select, with the task of carrying out an enquiry or giving an expert opinion.

Article 51

During the hearing any relevant questions are to be put to the witnesses and experts under the conditions laid down by the Court in the rules of procedure referred to in Article 30.

Article 52

After the Court has received the proofs and evidence within the time specified for the purpose, it may refuse to accept any further oral or written evidence that one party may desire to present unless the other side consents.

Article 53

1. Whenever one of the parties does not appear before the Court, or fails to defend its case, the other party may call upon the Court to decide in favor of its claim.
2. The Court must, before doing so, satisfy itself, not only that it has jurisdiction in accordance with Articles 36 and 37, but also that the claim is well founded in fact and law.

Article 54

1. When, subject to the control of the Court, the agents, counsel, and advocates have completed their presentation of the case, the President shall declare the hearing closed.
2. The Court shall withdraw to consider the judgment.
3. The deliberations of the Court shall take place in private and remain secret.

Article 55

1. All questions shall be decided by a majority of the judges present.
2. In the event of an equality of votes, the President or the judge who acts in his place shall have a casting vote.

Article 56

1. The judgment shall state the reasons on which it is based.
2. It shall contain the names of the judges who have taken part in the decision.

Article 57

If the judgment does not represent in whole or in part the unanimous opinion of the judges, any judge shall be entitled to deliver a separate opinion.

Article 58

The judgment shall be signed by the President and by the Registrar. It shall be read in open court, due notice having been given to the agents.

Article 59

The decision of the Court has no binding force except between the parties and in respect of that particular case.

Article 60

The judgment is final and without appeal. In the event of dispute as to the meaning or scope of the judgment, the Court shall construe it upon the request of any party.

Article 61

1. An application for revision of a judgment may be made only when it is based upon the discovery of some fact of such a nature as to be a decisive factor, which fact was, when the judgment was given, unknown to the Court and also to the party claiming revision, always provided that such ignorance was not due to negligence.

2. The proceedings for revision shall be opened by a judgment of the Court expressly recording the existence of the new fact, recognizing that it has such a character as to lay the case open to revision, and declaring the application admissible on this ground.

3. The Court may require previous compliance with the terms of the judgment before it admits proceedings in revision.

4. The application for revision must be made at latest within six months of the discovery of the new fact.

5. No application for revision may be made after the lapse of ten years from the date of the judgment.

Article 62

1. Should a state consider that it has an interest of a legal nature which may be affected by the decision in the case, it may submit a request to the Court to be permitted to intervene.

2. It shall be for the Court to decide upon this request.

Article 63

1. Whenever the construction of a convention to which states other than those concerned in the case are parties is in question, the Registrar shall notify all such states forthwith.

2. Every state so notified has the right to intervene in the proceedings; but if it uses this right, the construction given by the judgment will be equally binding upon it.

Article 64

Unless otherwise decided by the Court, each party shall bear its own costs.

CHAPTER IV—ADVISORY OPINIONS

Article 65

1. The Court may give an advisory opinion on any legal question at the request of whatever body may be authorized by or in accordance with the Charter of the United Nations to make such a request.

2. Questions upon which the advisory opinion of the Court is asked shall be laid before the Court by means of a written request containing an exact statement of the question upon which an opinion is required, and accompanied by all documents likely to throw light upon the question.

Article 66

1. The Registrar shall forthwith give notice of the request for an advisory opinion to all states entitled to appear before the Court.

2. The Registrar shall also, by means of a special and direct communication, notify any state entitled to appear before the Court or international organization considered by the Court, or, should it not be sitting, by the President, as likely to be able to furnish information on the question, that the Court will be prepared to receive, within a time limit to be fixed by the President, written statements, or to hear, at a public sitting to be held for the purpose, oral statements relating to the question.

3. Should any such state entitled to appear before the Court have failed to receive the special communication referred to in paragraph 2 of this Article, such state may express a desire to submit a written statement or to be heard; and the Court will decide.

4. States and organizations having presented written or oral statements or both shall be permitted to comment on the statements made by other states or organizations in the form, to the extent, and within the time limits which the Court, or should it not be sitting, the President, shall decide in each particular case. Accordingly, the Registrar shall in due time communicate any such written statements to states and organizations having submitted similar statements.

Article 67

The Court shall deliver its advisory opinions in open court, notice having been given to the Secretary-General and to the representatives of Members of the United Nations, of other states and of international organizations immediately concerned.

Article 68

In the exercise of its advisory functions the Court shall further be guided by the provisions of the present Statute which apply in contentious cases to the extent to which it recognizes them to be applicable.

CHAPTER V—AMENDMENT

Article 69

Amendments to the present Statute shall be effected by the same procedure as is provided by the Charter of the United Nations for amendments to that Charter, subject however to any provisions which the General Assembly upon recommendation of the Security Council may adopt concerning the participation of states which are parties to the present Statute but are not Members of the United Nations.

Article 70

The Court shall have power to propose such amendments to the present Statute as it may deem necessary, through written communications to the Secretary-General, for consideration in conformity with the provisions of Article 69.

2. MEMBERS OF THE UNITED NATIONS [2]

The United Nations has sixty members.

The original Members of the United Nations are those fifty-one which took part in the San Francisco Conference or had previously signed the United Nations Declaration of 1 January 1942, and which signed and ratified the Charter.

---

[2] *Everyman's United Nations*, 1952, pp. 7–8.

Argentine Republic	Iraq
Australia	Lebanon
Belgium	Liberia
Bolivia	Luxembourg
Brazil	Mexico
Byelorussian S. S. R.	Netherlands
Canada	New Zealand
Chile	Nicaragua
China	Norway
Colombia	Panama
Costa Rica	Paraguay
Cuba	Peru
Czechoslovakia	Philippine Republic
Denmark	Poland
Dominican Republic	Saudi Arabia
Ecuador	Syria
Egypt	Turkey
El Salvador	Ukrainian S. S. R.
Ethiopia	Union of South Africa
France	U. S. S. R.
Greece	United Kingdom
Guatemala	United States
Haiti	Uruguay
Honduras	Venezuela
India	Yugoslavia
Iran	

New Members are admitted by a two-thirds vote of the General Assembly upon the recommendation of at least seven members of the Security Council, including its permanent members.

The following nine new Members have been admitted:

Afghanistan became a Member on 19 November 1946.
Iceland became a Member on 19 November 1946.
Sweden became a Member on 19 November 1946.
Siam became a Member on 16 December 1946.
Pakistan became a Member on 30 September 1947.
Yemen became a Member on 30 September 1947.
Union of Burma became a Member on 19 April 1948.
Israel became a Member on 11 May 1949.
Indonesia became a Member on 28 September 1950.

A. BACKGROUND DOCUMENTS

3. THE ATLANTIC CHARTER, AUGUST 14, 1941 [3]

Joint declaration of the President of the United States of America and the Prime Minister, Mr. Churchill, representing His Majesty's Government in the United Kingdom, being met together, deem it right to make known certain common principles in the national policies of their respective countries on which they base their hopes for a better future for the world.

First, their countries seek no aggrandizement, territorial or other;

Second, they desire to see no territorial changes that do not accord with the freely expressed wishes of the peoples concerned;

---

[3] Department of State Publication 1732, p. 4.

Third, they respect the right of all people to choose the form of government under which they will live; and they wish to see sovereign rights and self-government restored to those who have been forcibly deprived of them;

Fourth, they will endeavor, with due respect for their existing obligations, to further the enjoyment by all States, great or small, victor or vanquished, of access, on equal terms, to the trade and to the raw materials of the world which are needed for their economic prosperity;

Fifth, they desire to bring about the fullest collaboration between all nations in the economic field with the object of securing, for all, improved labor standards, economic advancement and social security;

Sixth, after the final destruction of the Nazi tyranny, they hope to see established a peace which will afford to all nations the means of dwelling in safety within their own boundaries, and which will afford assurance that all the men in all the lands may live out their lives in freedom from fear and want;

Seventh, such a peace should enable all men to traverse the high seas and oceans without hindrance;

Eighth, they believe that all of the nations of the world, for realistic as well as spiritual reasons, must come to the abandonment of the use of force. Since no future peace can be maintained if land, sea or air armaments continue to be employed by nations which threaten, or may threaten, aggression outside of their frontiers, they believe, pending the establishment of a wider and permanent system of general security, that the disarmament of such nations is essential. They will likewise aid and encourage all other practicable measures which will lighten for peace-loving peoples the crushing burden of armaments.

4. DECLARATION BY UNITED NATIONS, JANUARY 1, 1942 [4]

The Governments signatory hereto,

Having subscribed to a common program of purposes and principles embodied in the Joint Declaration of the President of the United States of America and the Prime Minister of the United Kingdom of Great Britain and Northern Ireland dated August 14, 1941, known as the Atlantic Charter.

Being convinced that complete victory over their enemies is essential to defend life, liberty, independence and religious freedom, and to preserve human rights and justice in their own lands as well as in other lands, and that they are now engaged in a common struggle against savage and brutal forces seeking to subjugate the world,

declare:

(1) Each Government pledges itself to employ its full resources, military or economic, against those members of the Tripartite Pact, and its adherents with which such government is at war.

(2) Each Government pledges itself to cooperate with the Governments signatory hereto and not to make a separate armistice or peace with the enemies.

---

[4] Department of State Publication 1732, p. 1.

The foregoing declaration may be adhered to by other nations which are, or which may be, rendering material assistance and contributions in the struggle for victory over Hitlerism.

DONE at Washington January First, 1942

Original Signatories:

Australia, Belgium, Canada, China, Costa Rica, Cuba, Czecho-Slovakia, Dominican Republic, El Salvador, Greece, Guatemala, Haiti, Honduras, India, Luxembourg, Netherlands, New Zealand, Nicaragua, Norway, Panama, Poland, Union of South Africa, Union of Soviet Socialist Republics, United Kingdom of Great Britain and Northern Ireland, United States of America, Yugoslavia.

Later Adherents:

Bolivia, Brazil, Chile, Colombia, Ecuador, Ethiopia, Egypt, France, Iran, Iraq, Lebanon, Liberia, Mexico, Paraguay, Peru, The Philippines, Saudi Arabia, Syria, Turkey, Uruguay, Venezuela.

Publisher: James Townsend
Editor: John Steinbacher
Book Design: Joseph Sutton
Composition: KISHI Graphics
Typographer: Jeri Lynn Hayes
Cover Design: Joseph Sutton

Quality Educational Tools from Educator Publications

THE CHILD SEDUCERS

by John Steinbacher. A massive book. The biggest selling book on Education in history. Now in 2,000 libraries. A textbook in scores of colleges. Scores of thousands sold. $3.95 (paper) and $5 (hardcover, while they last.).

BITTER HARVEST

by John Steinbacher. The ONLY major work on Cesar Chavez. The book that exposed the true facts about the farm labor war. $1.00 pp.

THE CONSPIRATORS:

MEN AGAINST GOD by John Steinbacher. 250 years of conspiratorial operations in the West. Critically acclaimed as "book of the century." $6.50 (hardcover).

REVOLUTION AND COUNTER-REVOLUTION

By Prof. Pinio Correa de Oliveira. 3 million sold in Europe and Latin America. English translation. The publishing event of the decade.

THE HATE FACTORY

by Erica Carle; foreword by John Steinbacher. The ONLY book dealing with influence of sociologists over the American school system. Written for parents and teachers in a readable, easy to understand style. $1 (paperback).

WAR LORDS OF WASHINGTON

an Interview with COL. CURTIS DALL by Anthony J. Hilder. Here are the never-before-told secrets of Pearl Harbor from the former son-in-law of President Franklin Roosevelt. $1 (paperback).

PUBLIC EDUCATION:

River of Pollution and THE SOURCE OF THE RIVER OF POLLUTION by Joseph Bean, M.D. with appendixes on Secular Humanism and PPBS by research psychologist Mary Royer and Cavell Bean. Only 50 cents each, while they last.

LONG PLAY RECORD ALBUMS:

$4 each. THE CHILD SEDUCERS, narrated by John Carradine; BITTER HARVEST; THEY DIED FOR NOTHING. These three albums are in LIMITED supply.

NOTE: Add 25 cents postage & handling per item.

Order from

EDUCATOR Publications

BOX 333, FULLERTON, CALIF. 92630